Prayers from the Pit

What the Ten Prayers of Jesus Teach About Praying in Times of Pain

He always hears - even in the pit.

Chris

Chris Altrock

21st Century Christian Publishing

ISBN: 978-0-89098-541-0

eISBN: 978-0-89098-951-7

Cover design by Jonathan Edelhuber

Acknowledgments

I am indebted to Laura Bontrager and Leslie Jerkins for your inspiring and practical advice on each chapter. The long but fulfilling journey of this book has been much more enjoyable and fruitful because of your company.

I am thankful for my spiritual family at the Highland Church of Christ and their positive reception of early versions of this material. Your enthusiastic response gave me the courage to continue my study of these prayers and to tackle the project you now hold in your hands.

I am grateful for my wife Kendra and my children Jordan and Jacob who graciously granted me time on weekends and weekdays to learn from Jesus about prayer and turn those lessons into this book.

I am blessed to be working with the godly and talented team of 21st Century Christian. I pray this project will contribute to your already significant kingdom impact.

Finally, I am inspired by the lives and teachings of Randy Harris, Gary Holloway, and Earl Lavender. You are the modern monks and mystics who've made me hungry to know the prayers of Jesus. I hope this book will bear as much fruit in the lives of its readers as you have born in mine.

Table of Contents

Resource 1

The Ten Prayers of Jesus

1. At that time Jesus declared, "I thank you, Father, Lord of heaven and earth, that you have hidden these things from the wise and understanding and revealed them to little children; yes, Father, for such was your gracious will" (Matthew 11:25-26).

2. And Jesus lifted up his eyes and said, "Father, I thank you that you have heard me. I knew that you always hear me, but I said this on account of the people standing around, that they may believe that you sent me." When he had said these things, he cried out with a loud voice, "Lazarus, come out" (John 11:41-43).

3. And Jesus answered them, "The hour has come for the Son of Man to be glorified. Truly, truly, I say to you, unless a grain of wheat falls into the earth and dies, it remains alone; but if it dies, it bears much fruit. Whoever loves his life loses it, and whoever hates his life in this world will keep it for eternal life. If anyone serves me, he must follow me; and where I am, there will my servant be also. If anyone serves me, the Father will honor him. Now is my soul troubled. And what shall I say? 'Father, save me from this hour'? But for this purpose I have come to this hour. Father, glorify your name." Then a voice came from heaven: "I have glorified it, and I will glorify it again." The crowd that stood there and heard it said that it had thundered. Others said, "An angel has spoken to him" (John 12:23-29).

4. When Jesus had spoken these words, he lifted up his eyes to heaven, and said, "Father, the hour has come; glorify your Son that the Son may glorify you, since you have given him authority over all flesh, to give eternal life to all whom you have given him. And this is eternal life, that they know you the only true God, and Jesus Christ whom you have sent. I glorified you on earth, having accomplished the work that

you gave me to do. And now, Father, glorify me in your own presence with the glory that I had with you before the world existed. I have manifested your name to the people whom you gave me out of the world. Yours they were, and you gave them to me, and they have kept your word. Now they know that everything that you have given me is from you. For I have given them the words that you gave me, and they have received them and have come to know in truth that I came from you; and they have believed that you sent me. I am praying for them. I am not praying for the world but for those whom you have given me, for they are yours. All mine are yours, and yours are mine, and I am glorified in them. And I am no longer in the world, but they are in the world, and I am coming to you. Holy Father, keep them in your name, which you have given me, that they may be one, even as we are one. While I was with them, I kept them in your name, which you have given me. I have guarded them, and not one of them has been lost except the son of destruction, that the Scripture might be fulfilled. But now I am coming to you, and these things I speak in the world, that they may have my joy fulfilled in themselves. I have given them your word, and the world has hated them because they are not of the world, just as I am not of the world. I do not ask that you take them out of the world, but that you keep them from the evil one. They are not of the world, just as I am not of the world. Sanctify them in the truth; your word is truth. As you sent me into the world, so I have sent them into the world. And for their sake I consecrate myself, that they also may be sanctified in truth. I do not ask for these only, but also for those who will believe in me through their word, that they may all be one, just as you, Father, are in me, and I in you, that they also may be in us, so that the world may believe that you have sent me. The glory that you have given me I have given to them, that they may be one even as we are one, I in them and you in me, that they may become perfectly one, so that the world may know that you sent me and loved them even as you loved me. Father, I desire that they also, whom you have given me, may be with me where I am, to see my glory that you have given me because you loved me before the foundation of the world. O righteous Father, even though the world does not know you, I know you, and these know that you have sent me. I made known to them your name, and I will continue to make it known, that the love with which you have loved me may be in them, and I in them" (John 17:1-26).

5. Then Jesus went with them to a place called Gethsemane, and he said to his disciples, "Sit here, while I go over there and pray." And taking with him Peter and the two sons of Zebedee, he began to be sorrowful and troubled. Then he said to them, "My soul is very sorrowful, even to death; remain here, and watch with me." And going a little farther he fell on his face and prayed, saying, "My Father, if it be possible, let this cup pass from me; nevertheless, not as I will, but as you will." And he came to the disciples and found them sleeping. And he said to Peter, "So, could you not watch with me one hour? Watch and pray that you may not enter into temptation. The spirit indeed is willing, but the flesh is weak." Again, for the second time, he went away and prayed, "My Father, if this cannot pass unless I drink it, your will be done." And again he came and found them sleeping, for their eyes were heavy. So, leaving them again, he went away and prayed for the third time, saying the same words again. Then he came to the disciples and said to them, "Sleep and take your rest later on. See, the hour is at hand, and the Son of Man is betrayed into the hands of sinners. Rise, let us be going; see, my betrayer is at hand" (Matthew 26:36-46).

6. Two others, who were criminals, were led away to be put to death with him. And when they came to the place that is called The Skull, there they crucified him, and the criminals, one on his right and one on his left. And Jesus said, "Father, forgive them, for they know not what they do" (Luke 23:32-34).

7. And when the sixth hour had come, there was darkness over the whole land until the ninth hour. And at the ninth hour Jesus cried with a loud voice, "Eloi, Eloi, lema sabachthani?" which means, "My God, my God, why have you forsaken me?" And some of the bystanders hearing it said, "Behold, he is calling Elijah." And someone ran and filled a sponge with sour wine, put it on a reed and gave it to him to drink, saying, "Wait, let us see whether Elijah will come to take him down." And Jesus uttered a loud cry and breathed his last (Mark 15:33-37).

8. After this, Jesus, knowing that all was now finished, said (to fulfill the Scripture), "I thirst." A jar full of sour wine stood there, so they put a sponge full of the sour wine on a hyssop branch and held it to his mouth (John 19:28-29).

9. It was now about the sixth hour, and there was darkness over the whole land until the ninth hour, while the sun's light failed. And the curtain of the temple was torn in two. Then Jesus, calling out with a loud voice, said, "Father, into your hands I commit my spirit!" And having said this he breathed his last (Luke 23:44-46).

10. When Jesus had received the sour wine, he said, "It is finished," and he bowed his head and gave up his spirit (John 19:30).

Chapter 1

Prayers from the Pit:

Discovering the Importance of the Prayers of Jesus

Days of Darkness and Despair

Darkness and despair. This painful pair greeted me over the course of twenty-five days—days which concluded one year and began another. Their cold chill arrived from three countries and four states.

One early morning in the first days of 2010 during a period of quiet reflection, I began to sense a pattern to the previous days and weeks. A disturbing pattern. I jotted down dates and details to try to put words to my intuition. Gradually, I realized just how much over the past twenty-five days I had witnessed loss and sorrow. For almost one month I had occupied a seat far too close to the ringside of disease and death.

This time period spanned two years: 2009's final breath and 2010's first cries. The former year ended in me sitting with a family at their home as we witnessed their middle-aged father and husband slip from this life to the next. His death occurred the day after Christmas. The latter year began with news that doctors had found a tumor in the brain of the gentle woman who had babysat our daughter for years.

And the bad news just continued. It reached out to me from four states during these twenty-five days. In Kentucky a longtime friend from graduate school lost his job. From Arizona came the phone call stating that my wife's mother had been found unconscious and unresponsive. In Tennessee the mother of a former youth intern from our congregation was placed in hospice for her dying days. From New Jersey arrived the report that the younger sister of my stepfather had succumbed to breast, liver, and bone cancer.

I literally left the country and still the suffering followed me. While in the Philippines to visit missionaries, the vehicle I sat in was rushed at stop signs and stoplights by young poverty-stricken children begging for spare change. Four blocks from the middle-class neighborhood where I stayed in Bacolod, Philippines, I saw families living in tin shacks with neither water nor electricity. Days later, while walking the streets of Bangkok,

Thailand where my mission team was on layover, I saw disfigured men and women begging on the streets—forgotten and forlorn. And while I was in Bangkok, I watched on television the unearthly images from the devastation caused by the Haitian earthquake. Hundreds of thousands crushed. Millions displaced. And this, in a country where already fifty percent live on less than one dollar per day and eighty percent live below the poverty line.

Darkness and despair.

Providentially, during this same twenty-five-day period, I had entered into a personal study of the prayer-life and prayer-words of Jesus. Seeking to grow deeper in my own experience of prayer, I sought to be mentored by Jesus. And on January 19, 2010, these two streams converged: the pain of the past twenty-five days and the prayers of a two-thousand-year-old Messiah. I began to wonder: How do you pray in the midst of pain? How do you talk to God when God seems absent? What kind of supplication fits these times of suffering? I began searching for answers in the prayer-life and prayer-words of Jesus.

Thankfully, I found more than I could have expected and more than I could have hoped for. I eventually learned that Jesus was the master of praying from the pits.

Days of Prayer and Petition

Luke reveals more about the prayer-life of Jesus than any other biographer. In fact, Jesus' prayers are the bookends between which Luke's story rests.

♦ Luke opens his Gospel with Jesus praying: "Now when all the people were baptized, and when Jesus also had been baptized and was *praying*..." (Luke 3:21, emphasis added).

♦ Luke closes his Gospel with Jesus praying: "Then he led them out as far as Bethany, and lifting up his hands he *blessed* them. While he *blessed* them, he parted from them and was carried up into heaven" (Luke 24:50-51, emphasis added).

Luke seems to be saying that to understand the life of Jesus we must understand the prayers of Jesus. Jesus' story makes the most sense when seen through the lens of prayer, which begins and ends Luke's Gospel.

Not only is the prayer-life of Jesus critical to understanding Jesus. It is critical to understanding those who followed him. In his comprehensive study of New Testament prayer Richard Longenecker writes, "One cannot claim to understand the New Testament without grasping the importance and function of prayer in the life and ministry of Jesus...."[1] Jesus and prayer are so intertwined that one cannot be understood without the other. Both become the key to unlocking the significance of the rest of the New Testament.

Yet there is so much to learn from Jesus about prayer, it can be overwhelming. Authors much wiser than I am have pointed me to about thirty references in the Gospels to the prayers and prayer-life of Jesus. The closer you examine the life of Jesus, the more you realize there was hardly a time when he wasn't praying. Which lessons from Jesus' prayer-life matter most? More importantly, what does his example teach about praying in times of darkness and despair?

The Prayers of Jesus

The answers to these questions materialize when we travel in chronological fashion over the prayer-life of Jesus. Of the thirty or so references in the Gospels to the prayer-life and prayer-words of Jesus, approximately twenty of these are general in nature. They simply tell us *that* Jesus prayed. They do not describe in detail *what* Jesus prayed.

Yet there are at least ten occasions on which the Gospel authors record the words Jesus actually spoke in prayer. We aren't just told in general that Christ conversed with the Father. We overhear the specific content of the conversation. Without a doubt these must be the most important prayers in Scripture. If the Bible teaches anything about prayer, its greatest insight will come from the ten prayers containing the actual words used by Christ.

It is difficult to discern any particular grouping, scheme, or emphasis when scanning the entire list of the approximately thirty references to Jesus' prayers and prayer-life. But when we focus only on the ten actual prayers of Jesus, a pattern quickly emerges. This pattern becomes crystal clear when one verse, Luke 9:51, is used as a filter: "When the days drew near for him to be taken up, he set his face to go to Jerusalem." This is the literal and metaphorical turning point in Luke's portrait of Jesus' life. It falls on the heels of the Transfiguration and the twofold prediction of Jesus' death which surrounds the Transfiguration (Luke 9:22, 44). From this point forward, every syllable Jesus speaks and every deed Jesus does is colored by Jerusalem and its cross. The pain, suffering, and humiliation of the crucifixion become the interpretive filter for everything in Luke's Gospel starting here.

Prayer and Pain in Jesus' Life

What does Luke 9:51 have to do with the ten prayers of Jesus? Just this: the

Gospels do not give us the words of a single prayer of Jesus until *after* Luke 9:51.[2] We read at least eleven general references to Jesus' praying prior to this marker. But we cannot find a specific prayer from Jesus' lips in any of those references. Every one of the ten prayers of Jesus for which we have the actual words occurs after Jesus sets his face toward Jerusalem. While Jesus obviously prayed many prayers, the Gospel authors intentionally chose to include only the prayers which Jesus prayed in the shadow of Jerusalem and its cross. It was only after Jesus set his face toward Jerusalem that the Gospel authors felt liberated to start lining their pages with the words of Jesus' prayers. What most interested them was *how* Jesus would pray and *what* Jesus would pray as the pain of the cross grew nearer and stronger.

Of the ten prayers of Jesus for which we have his spoken words, two take place during the final journey toward Jerusalem (Matthew 11:25-26; John 11:41-43). The other eight take place within Jerusalem during Passion Week (John 12:23-29; John 17; Matthew 26:36-46; Luke 23:32-34; Mark 15:33-37; John 19:28-29; Luke 23:44-46; John 19:30). Thus, the Gospel authors primarily wanted to preserve the petitions which would demonstrate how Jesus would pray and what Jesus would pray in times of stress.

Of the eight prayers which take place within Jerusalem during Passion Week, five are spoken on the cross itself (Luke 23:32-34; Mark 15:33-37; John 19:28-29; Luke 23:44-46; John 19:30). Jesus must have prayed countless prayers during his life. Yet the Gospel authors give us only ten of those prayers. And half of these are words Jesus prayed from the cross. Clearly, what Jesus' biographers believed to be most important about the actual prayers of Jesus was the way in which they would model for us how to pray in times of pain.

Prayer and Pain in the Old Testament

But why was this connection between pain and prayer so important to the Gospel authors? Its importance becomes clear when we realize that supplication and suffering are also intimately linked in the Old Testament. Jesus' prayers are, to use a word from Old Testament scholar Walter Brueggemann, prayers of "*disorientation.*"[3] The word "disorientation" comes from Brueggemann's study of the Psalms, the prayer-book of the Old Testament. Brueggemann theorized that most of the Psalms were of three types: prayers of orientation, prayers of reorientation, and prayers of disorientation.

 ◆ In psalms of *orientation* God is viewed as trustworthy and reliable. Life is happy and the one praying is grateful for the stability and predictability of life. Orientation psalms provide opportunities to pray about some of the most basic things of life which are responsible for the pleasantness of life. Examples include Psalms 19, 104, and 119.

- Like psalms of orientation, psalms of *reorientation* are also prayers of praise and thanksgiving. But rather than focus on the stability and dependability of the life which God has created, reorientation prayers rejoice for some recent way in which God has delivered the author from despair and danger. They offer praise at its highest and loudest. Examples include Psalms 16, 23, 100, and 150.

- Psalms of *disorientation* stand in stark contrast to the other two. These are prayers gasped and groaned when life is at its worst. In them, God seems neither dependable nor desirable. Those who are praying lament their situation in life and beg God for a change in their circumstances. These are the most disturbing prayers in the Old Testament. They include Psalms 13, 51, and 69. Interestingly, of the ten prayers of Jesus, two are direct quotes from disorientation psalms (Mark 15:33-37 = Psalm 22; Luke 23:46 = Psalm 31).

I've found it helpful to reclassify these Old Testament prayers as prayers of the *plain* (orientation), prayers of the *peak* (reorientation), and prayers of the *pit* (disorientation).

- Prayers of the *plain* are those psalms in which life is ordinary and routine and we thank God for the basic things of life that make life so good.

- Prayers of the *peak* are those psalms in which life is unusually good and we thank God for a specific way in which he has been active in our lives.

- Prayers of the *pit* are those psalms in which life is hard and horrible and we give voice to our harshest feelings. They are the prayers colored primarily by challenge and suffering in life.

What the prayers from the pit in the Psalms are to the Old Testament, the prayers of Jesus in the Gospels are to the New Testament. Appearing as they do after Luke 9:51, every detailed prayer of Jesus which is preserved for us is influenced by the challenge and suffering brought by the cross in Jerusalem. These are prayers from the deepest and darkest pit of any moment in Scripture. And just as the prayers from the pit in the Psalms are intended to guide us in praying through our pain, so Jesus' prayers from the pit in the Gospels are similarly intended. There is no greater assistance in knowing how to pray and what to pray in darkness and despair than that found in the ten prayers of Jesus from the pit.

Three Types of Pit Prayers

Jesus' prayers offer this assistance in many remarkable ways. These ten prayers are surprisingly diverse. We get some of what we might expect: pain, frustration, and agony. But we also get much of what we don't expect: joy, thanksgiving, and concern for others—all in the shadow of Jerusalem's cross! In fact, Jesus' "prayers from the pit" cover the whole of the spiritual life: inward, upward, and outward.

Henri Nouwen suggested these three areas—inward, upward, and outward—are the most critical in our spiritual lives and that they are the three areas which Jesus' spiritual life points us toward. Nouwen was a Dutch-born Catholic priest and author. He taught at the University of Notre Dame, Yale University, and Harvard University. He spent his life's final season serving the mentally handicapped at the L'Arche community of Daybreak in Toronto, Canada until his death in 1986. Nouwen believed the example of Jesus, including the prayer-life of Jesus, pointed toward the importance of dealing with the *inward* matters of the heart, the *upward* matters of faith in God, and the *outward* matters of how we respond to people. He noted that Jesus was the master of the spiritual life because Jesus had mastered all three of these components of life.[4]

And these tend to be the three areas most deeply affected when we face times of pain. A few days ago my friend Jon stopped me in the hallway in the school building where our congregation worships. "Hey," he said, "this thing with Jenny has put me into a spiritual crisis." Jenny was a thirty-one-year-old mother who had died days earlier from unexpected complications from pneumonia. "Thousands of people were praying for her," Jon said. "But she still died." With tears in his eyes Jon said, "I just don't know what the point is anymore. Why pray if this is what's going to happen?"

It was clear that *inwardly* Jon was struggling with matters of the heart. Emotionally he was deeply affected. This, in turn, resulted in serious *upward* questions about God, God's sovereignty, and God's work on this earth. Finally, Jon was questioning the efficacy of his attempts to minister *outwardly* to others through prayer. This one tragedy created crisis in all three areas of Jon's life: inward, upward, and outward. If we wish to navigate the churning waters of pain in our lives, we need assistance with all three.

Richard Foster affirms the importance of this trio. In fact, he argues that the ideal prayer-life includes prayers devoted to all three of these areas. Foster is a Quaker, author, and founder of Renovaré—an organization devoted to classic forms of Christian spiritual formation. Just as Nouwen's study of the spiritual life of Jesus led him to propose the importance of inward attention, upward attention, and outward attention, so Foster's study of the spiritual life of Jesus' followers led him to similar conclusions. Surveying thousands of years of Christian prayer, Foster found that Christians have tended to rely upon three basic prayers:[5]

- First, Christians have relied heavily upon *inward* prayers. These are the prayers that are focused on the self—our own sin, our own despair, our own transformation and spiritual growth. Matters of the heart.

- Second, Christians have depended upon *upward* prayers. These are the prayers that are focused on God—who God is and what God has done. These are prayers of thanksgiving, gratitude, joy, and praise. Matters of faith.

- Finally, Christians have long counted on *outward* prayers. These are the prayers focused on the needs of others—prayers of intercession in which we bring people and their pain or praise before God. Matters of compassion.

Foster believes that the healthiest spiritual life requires all three: inward, upward, and outward prayers. These are the very areas covered by Jesus' prayers. Jesus' ten prayers from the pit include inward prayers of complaint, upward prayers of confidence, and outward prayers of compassion.

Inward Prayers of Complaint

In the shadow of his cross, we find Jesus praying inward prayers of complaint:

- "...let this cup pass from me..." (Matthew 26:39). Jesus seems to be lamenting, "I am despondent. My circumstances seem hopeless and I wish you would change them."

- "...why have you forsaken me?" (Mark 15:34). Jesus is crying out, "I am deserted. Everyone has abandoned me. I have no friends. Even you, Father, are gone."

- "I thirst" (John 19:28). Jesus is groaning, "I am deprived. I do not even have the basic necessities of life. Not even a drop of water."

Here, Jesus gives voice to his deepest feelings of disappointment and discouragement. His inward prayers of complaint model for us how to say to God what we may think shouldn't be said. They mentor us in how to say to the Father, "I am despondent," "I am deserted," or "I am deprived."

Upward Prayers of Confidence

In the shadow of the cross, we also find Jesus praying upward prayers of confidence:

- "I thank you, Father, Lord of heaven and earth, that you have hidden these things from the wise and understanding and revealed them to little children; yes, Father, for such was your gracious will" (Matthew 11:25-26). Jesus is confidently stating, "You still rule. In spite of the chaos and the craziness of life, I believe you are still in charge and you are still at work."

- "Father, I thank you that you have heard me. I knew that you always hear me…" (John 11:41-42). Jesus is boldly proclaiming, "You still listen. Though I stand here in the face of death, in a shadow where you seem to be absent, I know you are present. I know your ears are open."

- "Father, glorify your name" (John 12:28); "Father, the hour has come; glorify your Son that the Son may glorify you….. And now, Father, glorify me in your own presence with the glory that I had with you before the world existed" (John 17:1, 5). Jesus is shouting, "You still reveal. Though I am in the dark, I believe you will bring the light. I believe you can glorify yourself through these events. I trust that you will reveal yourself through this difficult time."

- "…nevertheless, not as I will, but as you will…your will be done" (Matthew 26:39-42). Jesus is prayerfully reporting, "You still matter. As much as I want my hopeless circumstance to change, what I want more is this: your will. Your dreams and your plans and your purposes still matter to me more than anything—even my own life."

- "Father, into your hands I commit my spirit!" (Luke 23:46). Jesus is courageously saying, "You still hold. In the midst of the despair, I know your hands are still strong enough to hold me. Though everything around me tempts me to believe otherwise, I know you still hold me in your hands."

- "It is finished" (John 19:30). Jesus is thankfully praying, "You still stop. You still bring sorrow to an end. You do not permit it to linger forever. You do what must be done and then you put an end to it. You have accomplished all you needed to through my suffering and now you have ended it."

Despite the darkness and the despair, Jesus is able in prayer to express his confidence that God still rules, listens, reveals, matters to him, holds him, and stops his pain. Through these prayers Jesus shows his trust that God's plan—though it involves darkness—is still best.

Outward Prayers of Compassion

Finally, in the shadow of the cross, we find Jesus praying outward prayers of compassion:

- "Holy Father, keep them in your name, which you have given me, that they may be one, even as we are one....I do not ask that you take them out of the world, but that you keep them from the evil one.....Sanctify them in the truth" (John 17:11, 15, 17). On behalf of his disciples, Jesus is asking, "Mind their mission. As you send them out to serve, protect them, guide them, and watch over them."

- "I do not ask for these only, but also for those who will believe in me through their word, that they may all be one, just as you, Father, are in me, and I in you, that they also may be in us, so that the world may believe that you have sent me.....Father, I desire that they also, whom you have given me, may be with me where I am, to see my glory that you have given me...." (John 17:20-21, 24). On behalf of all who would believe in him, Jesus is praying, "Concentrate their community. May those who follow me experience authentic and lasting intimacy with each other and with us."

- "Father, forgive them, for they know not what they do" (Luke 23:34). For those who caused his death, Jesus is praying, "Forgive their faults. Heal their hostility. Do not hold this sin against them."

Through these prayers, Jesus is able to look beyond his own circumstance and express compassion for others. He intercedes for those around him, even for those who have contributed to his despair.

Perhaps knowing our greatest needs, the biographers of Jesus have only recorded one type of prayer from the lips of Jesus. No prayers from the plain. No prayers from the peak. Only prayers from the pit. The sole prayer-words we have from Jesus are those spoken when his life was tough and trying. And through these words, we learn God's greatest lessons for conversing with him in days of darkness and despair.

In the remaining pages of this book, allow Jesus' *inward prayers of complaint* to coach you in expressing discouragement and disappointment to God. Permit Jesus' *upward prayers of confidence* to equip you to trust and believe even when you want to doubt and deny. And, invite Jesus' *outward prayers of compassion* to gently turn your focus from your own hurt to the hurts of others, compelling you to intercede even for those who may be the source of your suffering.

At the end of each chapter you'll find a "Practicing This Prayer" section which provides some basic guidance in how the prayer focused on in that chapter can be implemented in your life. Ideally, you'll want to read one chapter each week, taking six or seven days to put that chapter's prayer at work in your own prayer-life before moving on. Because we often need the encouragement of others as we make changes in our prayer-lives, we've included some study guides designed to walk your Bible class or small group through these prayers (Resource 3). Using them, you can investigate Jesus' prayers within community.

If you want to explore more about Jesus and prayer, you'll find a section at the end of this book designed to help you survey almost everything the Gospels tell us about Jesus' prayer-life. During a forty-day period, this section will lead you through this material (Resource 2). Finally, for quick reference, the ten specific prayers which serve as the foundation of this book are written out in full near the book's beginning (Resource 1).

Your True Possession

The book *A Thousand Splendid Suns* focuses on two women named Mariam and Laila.[6] The women lived in Kabul, Afghanistan in the late twentieth and early twenty-first centuries. During the Soviet occupation of Afghanistan, women enjoyed new freedoms such as attending school and working. But after the overthrow of the Soviets, conditions in the country, and especially in Kabul, became unbearable. Warlords of local tribes fought for power. Kabul and its residents suffered daily bombs and sniper fire.

When the Taliban took control, the violence lessened but conditions worsened. Women could not work, could not be educated, and could not even be on the street without a male relative or laugh in public. Only one hospital in Kabul remained open to women and it had few doctors and fewer supplies.

On top of it all, Laila and Mariam had both been forced to marry a cruel man named Rasheed who beat them and abused them. Laila gave birth to a little girl, Aziza. Rasheed, who wanted a boy, despised baby Aziza. But Laila and Mariam loved her.

As Aziza grew, Mariam began to teach her to pray. The prayers were from Mariam's childhood. They were the only prayers Mariam knew. But she wanted to pass something on to Aziza. So she prayed the prayers with

Aziza. At one point Mariam confessed: *"These are all I have. They are my only true possession."*

These prayers had carried Mariam through extreme times including her mother's death and her arranged marriage to Rasheed. These prayers had comforted her through seven miscarriages and her husband's abuse. These prayers had strengthened her when Kabul was riddled with violence. They were her only possession. And Mariam knew that they would be all young Aziza would need as she grew.

Similarly, the authors of the Gospels knew that we need prayer to uphold us during difficult times. These ten prayers from Jesus are the only prayers we know of that sustained him in the most difficult times of life. These are the only prayers we know of that strengthened and encouraged the Messiah. They are our prize possession.

Practicing This Prayer

This chapter has covered all ten of Jesus' prayers. Thus the practice will focus on all ten prayers as well. This week pray through all ten of Jesus' prayers each day. Become familiar with their language. Get used to their content. Strive to feel what Jesus felt as he prayed them. As much as possible, use Jesus' own words. Where necessary, paraphrase using your own words. Resource 1 will provide you easy access to all ten prayers for this practice.

---

1. Richard N. Longenecker, "Introduction," *Into God's Presence: Prayer in the New Testament* (W.B. Eerdmans Publishing, 2002).
2. The "Lord's Prayer" does occur chronologically in Matthew prior to this point, but it does not appear in Luke's Gospel until after this point. This particular prayer, however, appears to be primarily Jesus' teaching about prayer more than it is Jesus actually at prayer. For this reason, I have not included the Lord's Prayer in the list of ten prayers of Jesus. I will, however, demonstrate how some of Jesus' ten prayers find echoes in the Lord's Prayer.
3. Walter Brueggeman, *The Message of the Psalms* (Augsburg Publishing House, 1984) and *Spirituality of the Psalms* (Fortress Press, 2002).
4. Henri J. M. Nouwen, *Reaching Out: The Three Movements of the Spiritual Life* (Doubleday & Company, 1975).
5. Richard J. Foster, *Prayer: Finding the Heart's True Home* (Harper San Francisco, 1992).
6. Khaled Hosseini *A Thousand Splendid Suns* (Riverhead Books, 2007).

Chapter 2

An Inward Prayer of Complaint:
I Am Despondent (Matthew 26)

Our Reluctance to Lament

The excitement of my teenage daughter Jordan finally getting a new "smart phone" crackled like a fire. But the steady stream of problems we encountered as we readied it for use doused those flames like water. First, a software glitch required a two hour download to resolve. Next, a dad-glitch resulted in Jordan losing dozens of previously purchased "apps." Then, a hunting trip to the hippest electronics store in town bagged not a single case for the phone. Finally, a key feature of the phone, Jordan's favorite, kept crashing.

Jordan had been waiting half a year for this phone—ever since her previous one morphed into a disobedient child, refusing to do even the simplest task asked of it. But this was like opening that long-awaited present on Christmas morning only to find that batteries are not included and the instructions are missing.

Jordan, not surprisingly, voiced frustration and disappointment. Sighs, groans, crossed arms, rolled eyes, and hands thrown up in surrender surfaced all afternoon and evening.

But as Jordan's expressions of anger and despair grew, so did my own. Only mine was not directed at the phone. Mine were directed at Jordan. As her irritation with the phone increased, my irritation with her increased. Finally, I told her to be quiet. "Stop being so dramatic!" I commanded. Even though she had legitimate reasons to grumble, I didn't want to hear any more of it.

Sadly, I got what I asked for. The rest of that evening Jordan wouldn't talk to me—about anything. All communication came to a jarring stop. And in the silence I realized what an insensitive and uncaring father I had just been.

Some of us have an image of God which looks a little like the poor father I was to Jordan that day. When we face frustrations and disappointments we keep silent. We don't voice those dark feelings to the Father. Why?

Because we fear that God doesn't want to hear them. We suspect he will respond, with "Stop being so dramatic!" or "If you don't have anything good to say, don't say anything at all." Sometimes we envision a Father who might snap back with "If you want something to complain about, I'll give you something to complain about!" Thus, rather than say something bad in prayer, we just don't say anything at all.

In fact, according to Richard Beck—a professor at Abilene Christian University—many of us assume that lament or complaint in our prayers is a sign of immaturity.[1] Specifically, some of us operate with a "polar model" of prayer in which "faith" is one end of a continuum and "lament" is the opposite end. As lament and complaint in our prayers increase, we move farther and farther away from faith and trust in God. But as faith and trust in God increases in our prayers, we move farther and farther away from lament and complaint. Only the spiritually immature and those of puny faith groan or moan in prayer.

Writing about the church's reluctance to pray or sing psalms of lament (disorientation) in favor of praying and singing psalms of praise (orientation), Old Testament scholar Walter Brueggemann comments[2]

> It is a curious fact that the church has, by and large, continued to sing songs of orientation in a world increasingly experienced as disoriented. That may be commendable. It could be that such relentlessness is an act of bold defiance in which these psalms of order and reliability are flung in the face of the disorder..... It is my judgment that this action of the church is less a defiance guided by faith and founded in the good news, and much more a frightened, numb denial and deception that does not want to acknowledge or experience the disorientation of life.....I think that serious religious use of the complaint psalms has been minimal because we have believed that faith does not mean to acknowledge and embrace negativity. We have thought that acknowledgment of negativity was somehow an act of unfaith.

When it comes to prayer, we often view negativity as an act of unfaith. Rather than say anything bad in prayer, we don't say anything at all.

Christ and Complaint

But if this view of prayer is correct, we would expect to find only positive and praise-filled prayers falling from the lips of Jesus. We would expect his prayers to be the most mature prayers in Scripture and thus the prayers most absent of complaint, lament, grumbling, and despair. Surely the ten prayers of Jesus are the perfect model of hope-filled and faith-full words.

They are not.

Of the ten prayers saved for us by Matthew, Mark, Luke, and John, three are laments or complaints. Thus, almost one-third of Jesus' prayers are acts of unfaith—if we rely on a polar model in which faith and lament are opposite ends of a continuum.

This presents a problem. Either some of the prayers of Jesus reflect spiritual immaturity or our polar view of prayer reflects spiritual immaturity. The latter seems more likely. These portraits of Jesus in prayer as one who groans, moans, and despairs force us to consider an alternative paradigm for prayer.

Richard Beck argues that our polar model should be replaced with a circumplex model in which faith and complaint are no longer opposites. In this model a high level of complaint can also accompany a high level of faith. It is possible for lament to be a natural part of a healthy relationship with God and not necessarily a sign of an unhealthy distance from God.

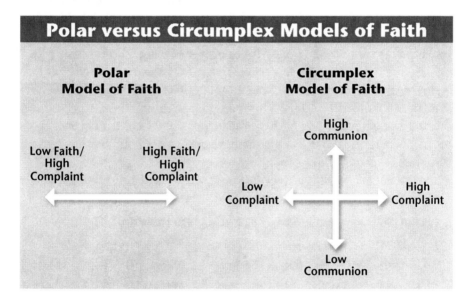

The Gethsemane prayer of Jesus best illustrates how trust and complaint can coexist in one prayer:

> Then Jesus went with them to a place called Gethsemane, and he said to his disciples, "Sit here, while I go over there and pray." And taking with him Peter and the two sons of Zebedee, he began to be sorrowful and troubled. Then he said to them, "My soul is very sorrowful, even to death; remain here, and watch with me." And going a little farther

he fell on his face and prayed, saying, "My Father, if it be possible, let this cup pass from me; nevertheless, not as I will, but as you will." And he came to the disciples and found them sleeping. And he said to Peter, "So, could you not watch with me one hour? Watch and pray that you may not enter into temptation. The spirit indeed is willing, but the flesh is weak." Again, for the second time, he went away and prayed, "My Father, if this cannot pass unless I drink it, your will be done." And again he came and found them sleeping, for their eyes were heavy. So, leaving them again, he went away and prayed for the third time, saying the same words again. Then he came to the disciples and said to them, "Sleep and take your rest later on. See, the hour is at hand, and the Son of Man is betrayed into the hands of sinners. Rise, let us be going; see, my betrayer is at hand" (Matthew 26:36-46).

Because I am guided by a polar model of prayer, I rush immediately to the second half of Jesus' thrice-repeated prayer: "...your will be done." I want to hold up Jesus as the one who sacrificially and serenely bowed to God's will. I want to celebrate Jesus' surrender and obedience in prayer. Jesus prays "your will be done." It is a prayer of tremendous trust.

And that is worthy of celebration. That is how the prayer ends. But that is not how the prayer begins. We cannot get to the sacrificial and serene surrender ("your will be done") without going through the disturbing and disquieting despair ("My Father, if it be possible, let this cup pass from me..."). We cannot hear Jesus' statement of trust without first hearing his statement of lament.

And what a lament it is! Notice the descriptions from Matthew:

◆ Jesus is "sorrowful and troubled" (Matthew 26:37).

◆ Jesus confesses being "very sorrowful, even to death" (Matthew 26:38).

◆ Jesus falls on his face (Matthew 26:39).

◆ Jesus prays not once, but three times for the cup to pass (Matthew 26:44). There is deep passion driving this prayer. It's the only prayer we know of which Jesus repeated multiple times.

Matthew's peers agree with his assessment of the emotional state of Jesus. Mark describes Jesus as "greatly distressed" (Mark 14:33). Luke, the doctor, diagnoses Jesus as "being in agony" and observes that Jesus' "sweat became like great drops of blood falling down to the ground" (Luke 22:44).

There is nothing calm or cool about this scene. The word "Gethsemane" suggests an "oil press" where olives are squeezed until their insides turn out.[4] In the same way, Jesus is now being squeezed until his insides turn out. This is lament at its most painful.

The source of Jesus' agony is "this cup"—"let this cup pass from me." Elsewhere, Jesus speaks of his impending death on the cross as a "cup" to be drunk (Matthew 20:22). The image is rooted in the biblical picture of God's "cup of wrath."[5] It is a terrible thing to contemplate consuming the wrath of God. And tonight, in the garden of "oil press" where cups are filled with a juice that is produced by crushing forces, Jesus feels pressed by a cup he will soon consume on the cross. That cup—the cross—has become a circumstance which Jesus now desperately wishes were different: "Let this cup pass from me."

Rather than counterfeiting a smile, cleaning up his emotions, or cloaking his anxiety, Jesus lifts it all up messily to God in prayer. Not once, but three times. Three times Jesus prays: "My Father, if it be possible, let this cup pass from me!" Three times Jesus groans: "I am despondent! I cannot stand this circumstance! I do not want things to be this way!"

"My Father, if it be possible, let this cup pass from me!"

"My Father, if it be possible, let this cup pass from me!"

"My Father, if it be possible, let this cup pass from me!"

That is not how the prayer ends. But it is how the prayer begins.

Perhaps this Gethsemane prayer was the prayer remembered by the Hebrew author when he wrote this summary of the prayers of Jesus: "In the days of his flesh, Jesus offered up prayers and supplications, with loud cries and tears..." (Hebrews 5:7). There are many qualities of Jesus' prayers which the Hebrew author might have recalled: their frequency, their other-centeredness, or their intimacy. But what he remembers most is that Jesus prayed "with loud cries and tears." What he finds most important is that Jesus lamented.

These loud cries and tears were not the result of a lack of faith. They were the fruit of deep faith. Jesus' appeal for altered circumstances flows not from the fact that he is unspiritual or unhealthy. Just the opposite—it flows from the fact that he has never been more spiritual or more healthy.

This is so contrary to our traditional perspective on prayer that some through the ages have dismissed the Gethsemane prayer. They argue that Jesus could not have prayed this prayer. Jesus would not have stooped to such complaining. Yet New Testament scholar Craig Keener writes that this prayer must be considered authentic because it meets "the authentic criterion of embarrassment." That is, no Christian would have contrived this account because it could have brought embarrassment upon the Christian faith. The portrait of Jesus facing death anxiously is vastly different from the image of pagan heroes like Socrates or Jewish heroes like the Maccabean martyrs who all faced death calmly.[6] Jesus deeply dislikes his circumstances and desperately begs God to change them. He does not piously pretend nothing is wrong. Instead, he is honest with the Father about his feelings. He puts the trouble into words and groans them out:

"Change this situation!"

"Stop this from happening!"

"Make things better!"

The prayer doesn't end there. But it does begin there.

Desperate for Something Different

Is your heart beginning to connect with this prayer? Haven't you been despondent about a situation or circumstance and longed for things to be different? We have Jesus' permission to sob in our supplications.

A friend named Ken texted me a few days ago: "Kate's been in a terrible wreck. We're at the hospital." I immediately called. An emotional Ken shared how his college-aged daughter Kate had suffered a severe leg injury, fractures to the pelvis, and a broken back when she was ejected from her car.

How do you pray in such a situation? Do you pretend everything is OK? Do you piously thank God for this chance to grow? Do you serenely pray for God to do whatever he wills? No. You pray as Jesus prayed: Change this! Stop this! Make things better!

Alice called me last week. She is a widow and longtime member of our congregation. We meet regularly for prayer and Bible study. "I'm having a terrible time," she confessed. Money was tight. Some plans had fallen through. An important relationship was causing discomfort. "You know how sometimes you feel you are up to your neck in something?" she said. "Today, I'm in over my head!"

How do you pray in such a situation? Do you pretend everything is OK? Do you piously thank God for this chance to grow? Do you serenely pray for God to do whatever he wills? No. You pray as Jesus prayed: Change this! Stop this! Make things better!

One evening a county sheriff arrived at the Lavelle home with solemn news: their twenty-year-old daughter Liz had just died in a car accident. Dozens of us immediately filled their house and surrounded the family.

At one point in the darkening evening, a family member screamed out: "Can I just say that I hate this?!"

How do you pray in such a situation? Do you pretend everything is OK? Do you piously thank God for this chance to grow? Do you serenely pray for God to do whatever he wills? No. You pray as Jesus prayed: Change this! Stop this! Make things better!

The Gethsemane prayer doesn't end there. But it does begin there. And so can ours.

Mark Roberts teaches at Fuller Seminary. Writing about the psalmists who lamented, he offers this helpful image:[7]

> Initially, the phrase *no holds barred* had nothing to do with conversation. It was a term used in wrestling to describe a match that isn't constrained by official rules. If you've ever seen a serious wrestling match, in the Olympics, for example, you know that many holds are prohibited. You won't see any strangleholds, unlike what you might observe in a "professional" wrestling free-for-all. Our typical approach to God brings to mind Olympic wrestling, in which every move is governed by detailed rules. Our communication with God is cautious, controlled, disciplined, and relentlessly boring. Fearful that we'll do something wrong or that God won't accept our true selves, we tame our prayers to the point that we actually hide ourselves from the Lord. We pray without energy, without passion, and without honesty.... Whether crying out in agony, complaining with bitterness, begging for deliverance, or praising with joy, the psalmists consistently accepted God's invitation to bold prayer. Whether desperate with need or bursting with thanks, they didn't hold anything back.

Like the psalmists, Jesus held nothing back. He accepted God's invitation to bold prayer. He prayed with energy, passion, and honesty. Jesus gives us permission to say to God, "Let this cup pass. Let this cup pass. Let this cup pass.

Despair and Dad

What made such honesty possible in prayer? In his volume, *Praying With Jesus*, George Martin argues that Jesus' view of God as "Abba, Father" gives him the ability to lament in this way.[8] The Gethsemane prayer is the only prayer in which Jesus addresses God as "Abba"—a term of endearment. This intimacy gives rise to Gethsemane's honesty. Mark provides the details:

> And going a little farther, he fell on the ground and prayed that, if it

were possible, the hour might pass from him. And he said, "Abba, Father, all things are possible for you. Remove this cup from me. Yet not what I will, but what you will" (Mark 14:35-36).

Jesus could cry "Remove this cup from me!" because he could also cry "Abba, Father." Only the intimacy of his relationship with God as "Abba, Father" made possible the intensity of his request to God, "Remove this cup from me!"

This view of God was the foundation upon which Jesus built prayer. In his immensely helpful study, *The Prayers of Jesus*, Joachim Jeremias writes that in the Judaism of Jesus' day it was common for religious groups to have their own customs and practices regarding prayer.[9] For example, the Pharisees and Essenes each had prayer practices unique to their groups. It appears that John's disciples did as well (Luke 11:1). Thus, it makes sense that eventually Jesus' disciples asked Jesus to teach them a unique prayer: "Lord, teach us to pray, as John taught his disciples" (Luke 11:1). Jesus' disciples wanted a prayer that would set them apart from the other religious groups. They literally wanted a "Jesus Prayer."

But what was the "Jesus Prayer"? What prayer would distinguish followers of Christ from everyone else? Here is the prayer Jesus gave in response to the request: "Father, hallowed be your name..." (Luke 11:2-4). Jeremias argues that one word makes this prayer uniquely suited to Christ-followers. One word sets this prayer, and all of Jesus' prayers, apart from the known prayers of other religious groups—the word "Father."[10]

Jeremias indicates that only fifteen times is God directly called Father in the Old Testament (although there are more instances of God being compared to a father).[11] In addition, in ancient Palestinian Judaism, God is only described as Father in four passages of the Apocrypha and there are only two prayers from ancient Palestinian Judaism which addressed God as Father.[12]

In contrast, Jesus uses the word "Father" at least 170 times to address, describe, or refer to God. More importantly, in almost every one of his recorded prayers, Jesus addresses God as Father. Even more surprisingly, Jesus addresses God as "my Father" and as "Abba." Jeremias finds no evidence of "my Father" being used by others in early Palestinian Judaism and suggests this address set Jesus' prayers apart from all others of the time.[13]

Only the intimacy of his relationship with God as "Abba, Father" makes possible the intensity of his request from God, "Remove this cup from me!"

In the Old Testament, which is about three times the length of the

New Testament, the word "Father" is used over 1,200 times. In the New Testament, the word is used over 400 times. These figures are about what we would expect since the Old Testament is three times the length of the New and therefore has about three times as many references to "Father". But if we count only the number of times that "Father" is used with reference to God, then we find that only 40 (3%) of the occurrences of the word in the Old Testament refer to God. In the New Testament 260 (63%) of the occurrences refer to God.[14] The New Testament takes a giant leap from the Old Testament in speaking about God as Father. How do we explain this leap? What happened from the Old Testament to the New Testament?

New Testament scholar, I. Howard Marshall, suggests that what happened is Jesus.[15] Jesus frequently referred to God as Father in his teaching. In addition, Jesus often spoke to God as Father in his prayers. While this was not necessarily new, Jesus' laser-like focus on God as Father in his teaching and in his prayers led to the word "Father" becoming the dominant way of understanding God in the New Testament and the dominant way of talking to God in prayer.

Jesus was able to so honestly express his frustrations because he daily experienced God as Father. Jesus could confidently utter his anger because he constantly understood God as "Abba."

One summer many of us followed the saga of Sky—the eleven-year-old son of Chris Seidman. Sky had been hospitalized for weeks with meningitis, staph, and a vicious rash. On day forty-five, Sky was, in Chris' words, "in a rage." He was filled with anger and despair. He couldn't stand his present circumstance. What was Chris to do? He said, "I told him he could let God have it." And Sky did. Chris wrote to us that he stood beside Sky while the boy hollered at God. Later, Chris wrote this: "Confessing one's doubts about God to God is still an expression of faith in God." It's when we come to relate to God as Abba Father that we finally are freed to share with him our deepest hurts and fears. We are finally freed to let God have it.

Practicing This Prayer

This week practice a "no holds barred" type of prayer. Practice a prayer characterized by brutal honesty. Let God have it. When you are faced with situations that disturb you, get vocal in prayer about them. Put your deepest and darkest feelings into words. As you do, remember that the one to whom you speak is not just Creator or Lord, but Father. He welcomes your lament because of the intimacy you share together as child and Father.

If it helps, use this formula with all circumstances that you trouble you this week: "Father, let _____ pass." In addition, consider praying Psalms 13—a brief but passionate lament prayer—once a day during the week. It may provide the words for those feelings you cannot quite put into words yourself.

---

1. Richard Beck, "The Psychology of Christianity: Part 5," (7/12/2010).
2. Walter Brueggeman, *Spirituality of the Psalms*, (Fortress Press, 2002), 25-26.
3. Beck.
4. "Gethsemane," D. R. W. Wood and I. H. Marshall, (1996). *New Bible Dictionary* Third Edition, (Intervarsity Press, 1996), 407.
5. Ps. 11:6; 60:3; 75:8; Is. 29:9-10; 51:17, 21-23; Jer. 25:15-29.
6. Craig S. Keener, *A Commentary on the Gospel of Matthew* (W.B. Eerdmans Publishing, 1999), 633.
7. Mark D. Roberts, *No Holds Barred: wrestling with God in prayer* (Waterbrook Press, 2005), 4-7.
8. George Martin, *Praying With Jesus: what the Gospels Tell Us About How to Pray* (Loyola Press, 2000), 96.
9. Joachim Jeremias, *The Prayers of Jesus* (Fortress Press, 1978), 63.
10. Ibid.
11. E.g., Deut. 32:6; 2 Sam. 7:14 (par. 1 Chr. 17:13; 22:10; 28:6); Ps. 68:5; 89:26; Is. 63:16; 64:8; Jer. 3:4, 19; 31:9; Mal. 1:6; 2:10.
12. Jeremias., 12, 15, 24.
13. Ibid., 57.
14. I. Howard Marshall, "Jesus—Example and Teacher of Prayer in the Synoptic Gospels," *Into God's Presence: Prayer in the New Testament* (W.B. Eerdmans Publishing, 2002).
15. Ibid.

Chapter 3

An Inward Prayer of Complaint:
I Am Deserted (Mark 15)

Crying for Help in a Hole

When I was in kindergarten, Charlotte Griffin's ranch made the ideal location for our field trip. About twenty five-and-six-year-olds were scampering among the goats, the hens, and the hay like crazed ants. After a long morning, we were hot, dusty, and grinning from ear to ear. Our teachers and chaperones signaled for us to get back on our bus, but I was in the barn climbing on the stacked bales of hay. I was at the top and turned to join my friends scurrying to the bus. Suddenly I stepped out into air where hay should have been. The bales had not been pushed together when stacked. And my feet had found one of those places where the spaces in between were just large enough to swallow a little boy.

Freefall. A blur of light. Then darkness. Suddenly I found myself upside down in a hole—head at the bottom, feet lodged at the top.

"Help!" I screamed. "Help!"

My screams went unanswered. Every friend and adult had already left the barn. They were upright and comfortable in the sunny bus while I was hanging uncomfortably in the frightening darkness of a hole in the hay.

My screams grew higher and more frantic. They left me! They forgot me! They deserted me!

But just when the fear was more than my five-year-old heart could handle, I felt a strong hand on my foot. I began to float upward, toward the top of the hole. As the darkness faded and the light grew, I could make out a dirty cowboy boot, then jeans, then a belt buckle, then a plaid shirt, then a wide-mouthed grin on the face of the man who had just rescued me.

I couldn't believe it! Rescued! I was so relieved to be out of that hole.

There's nothing worse than being deserted. There's nothing better than being delivered.

But what happens when no rescue is in sight? What happens when the prospect of deliverance remains distant?

As I was working on this chapter a close friend of mine was tending to her young husband in the hospital when she learned that he had been having an affair. When confronted, the husband didn't hesitate to produce a confession—he told his wife that he wanted out of the marriage immediately. She has three young children and no job. I caught her on the phone as she was limping to her mother's house for refuge. Abandoned. Rejected. And no likelihood of reunion.

There's nothing worse than being deserted. There's nothing better than being delivered. But what happens when it seems like you're stuck in that hole forever?

Forsaken

The Gospel of Mark provides an unforgettable image of just such a dark time:

> And when the sixth hour had come, there was darkness over the whole land until the ninth hour. And at the ninth hour Jesus cried with a loud voice, "Eloi, Eloi, lema sabachthani?" which means, "My God, my God, why have you forsaken me?" And some of the bystanders hearing it said, "Behold, he is calling Elijah." And someone ran and filled a sponge with sour wine, put it on a reed and gave it to him to drink, saying, "Wait, let us see whether Elijah will come to take him down." And Jesus uttered a loud cry and breathed his last. And the curtain of the temple was torn in two, from top to bottom. And when the centurion, who stood facing him, saw that in this way he breathed his last, he said, "Truly this man was the Son of God!" (Mark 15:33-39).

There's never been a hole deeper than Jesus' hole. There's never been darkness thicker than Jesus' darkness. And there's never been one so utterly alone as Jesus.

His loneliness is complete. Jesus is deserted by his greatly esteemed pals. Peter, James, and John alone witnessed Jesus raising the dead daughter of Jairus. Only this trio accompanied Jesus at his transfiguration. Only these three received teaching about the end of the age on the Mount of Olives. And these three men alone, though sleepy, kept company with Jesus as he wrestled in prayer in the Garden of Gethsemane. But on this day, Jesus is in the hole alone. James, we must assume, has fled. Peter, we know for certain, has rejected his master no less than three times. John remains (John 19:26). The trio is reduced to a solo.

But Jesus is deserted by more than just his closest friends. Craig S. Keener, author of a dozen books and professor of New Testament at Palmer Seminary, says the whole world abandoned Jesus at the cross.[1] In Jesus' day "the whole world" was comprised of two people-groups: Jews and Gentiles. At the cross, we see Roman soldiers—that is, Gentiles—mocking and rejecting Jesus. While they waste time before the crucifixion these Gentiles take a soldier's cloak and place it on Jesus like a royal robe. They take the bamboo cane, previously used for beating Jesus, and place it in his hands like a royal scepter. They take a thorny plant and weave a crown of it.[2] Clearly the Gentiles reject Jesus. And so do the Jews. Jewish leaders conspire to trap Jesus. Jewish rulers condemn Jesus. Jewish crowds ridicule Jesus. Both groups of people reject him.

Yet it's not just these two ethnic groups who abandon Jesus. It's the elite and the marginalized as well. Among Jews and Gentiles there is high society and low society. Both ends of the class structure abandon Jesus. We watch as men in the highest Roman and Jewish positions judge Jesus. And we watch as a criminal dying on his own cross snaps at him too.

Jesus' esteemed pals and the entire planet—Jew and Gentile; high and low—reject and abandon him. There's not a human left in the barn. They've all gotten on the bus.

But it gets worse.

Because not only has every human deserted Jesus—so has every deity. The absence of the other two members of the Holy Trinity to which Jesus belongs pains Jesus more than the abandonment of Peter, James, and John. Jesus feels forgotten by the Father. He feels cast aside by the Spirit. The Trinity is down to two. Just as you have never known life without oxygen, blood, and bones, Jesus has never known life without the Trinity—except now, when he needs them the most. That community is as vital to his life as air is to ours. And as Jesus spiritually asphyxiates on the cross, he cries out, "Why have you forsaken me?"

Accepted. Received. Embraced. These are the words that should be coming out of the mouth of God's only Son. These are the words that describe his daily life in the Trinity. But not today. Today he is forsaken.

It is a dark hole. Mark records, "And when the sixth hour had come, there was darkness over the whole land until the ninth hour." Three hours of darkness to accompany the loneliness and despair. It is an appropriate image. In the Bible, discouragement almost always seems paired with darkness. For example, the authors of the Psalms use the word "pit" to describe those times when life is discouraging. David writes "Let not the flood sweep over me, or the deep swallow me up, or the pit close its mouth over me" (Psalm 69:15). Another psalmist states, "You have put me in the depths of the pit, in the regions dark and deep" (Psalm 88:6). This is the dark and deep pit in which Jesus is crucified. Only darker. Only deeper.

Deserted by friends. Abandoned by the world. Forsaken by the Father and the Spirit.

A few days ago the daughter of a friend emptied her medicine cabinet into her stomach. She had endured three years of an abusive marriage which finally dissolved. Then she fell in love with another man—only to discover that man was cheating on her. At the bottom of that pit, so dark and so discouraging, her father told me she was angry at God. Where had God been? Why had he permitted such pain?

There's nothing worse than being deserted. Especially when it feels as if God himself is the first one out the door.

Praying in the Pit

And the question is this: How do you pray at the bottom of such a pit? What do you say to a God with whom you're not on speaking terms? As I've been with people in dark times, it seems that many of us pray in one of two directions.

First, some of us pray *irregularly*. The river of prayer dries up or is restricted to an occasional trickle. We get so hurt, angry, and disappointed that we barely or rarely pray. A friend of mine who is working through the grief of losing a loved one was at this point recently. He told me that he hadn't prayed in weeks. He was so traumatized that he could not talk to God. Sorrow becomes a stone which dams up all supplication.

Second, some of us pray *dishonestly*. The river of prayer keeps flowing, but it's forced. The pain inside is not permitted to show itself outside. We pray about everything—except what is most on our mind. In the morning we speak to God about our bowl of cereal, our day ahead, and that breaking news on the TV. In the afternoon we speak to God about our coworker's divorce or our classmate's upcoming move. In the evening we speak to God about our family and friends. But the ache in our heart is like the elephant in the room. We know it's there. More importantly God knows it's there. But we refuse to say anything about it.

How do you pray at the bottom of a pit? What do you say to God when you're not on speaking terms?

The Perfect Imperfect Prayer

Jesus shows us the way: "And at the ninth hour Jesus cried with a loud voice, 'Eloi, Eloi, lema sabachthani?' which means, 'My God, my God, why have you forsaken me?'" (Mark 15:34). In Matthew and Mark these are the only words spoken by Jesus from the cross. The only words from the cross which caught these chroniclers' attention were these words.

If your last prayer was going to be permanently recorded, would you utter this prayer? If I knew a journalist was going to write my final prayer, I'd try to make it positive and polished. Something that might inspire others. Something like the last words in the movie *Braveheart*.[3] The movie is based on the true story of William Wallace, a Scottish rebel who leads an uprising against an English ruler named Edward the Longshanks. Wallace is captured and tortured before his public death. He is made a spectacle. Wallace tries to speak. Those presiding over the torture urge the crowd to be silent. It's the darkest moment of Wallace's life. What will he say? Wallace sums up the entire rebellion perfectly with his dying breath: "Freedom!"

It is the perfect last word. It's what I'd like to think I'd say or pray with my final breath. And compared to this, what Jesus gives us sounds so imperfect: "My God, my God, why have you forsaken me?" Yet his line turns out to be the perfect imperfect prayer.

It is perfect because of its honesty. Jesus does not pretend the pain isn't painful. Jesus doesn't make believe the darkness isn't dark. He doesn't ignore what's on his heart and go through a hollow prayer list. Instead, Jesus prays with brutal honesty: "My God, my God, why have your forsaken me?"

This compelling candor characterizes Jesus throughout the crucifixion. Matthew notes that "they offered him wine to drink, mixed with gall, but when he tasted it, he would not drink it" (Matthew 27:34). The drink offered here is probably wine laced with a kind of narcotic designed to numb the pain of the cross. An ancient Jewish book called the Talmud tells of women in Jerusalem who provided condemned criminals a drink of wine mixed with a narcotic to deaden their senses.[4] Jesus, however, closes his lips to the offer. He does not blunt the burden. His senses remain sharp. He drinks deeply of the pain of the cross.

In the same way, Jesus' prayer does not detour around the darkness. Instead, the prayer drives straight into its heart: "My God, my God, why have you forsaken me?"

This prayer was perfected long before Jesus speaks it. Its original supplicant was the Old Testament hero David who writes down these lines in Psalm 22. Jesus borrows line one of David's prayer to express his own feelings.

Psalm 22 is part of the family of psalms known as "laments." They are surprisingly frank pleas from folks at the bottom of inky black holes. Sometimes it is one person praying:

How long, O LORD? Will you forget me forever? How long will you hide your face from me? How long must I take counsel in my soul and have sorrow in my heart all the day? How long shall my enemy be exalted over me? Consider and answer me, O LORD my God; light up my eyes, lest I sleep the sleep of death, lest my enemy say, "I have prevailed over him," lest my foes rejoice because I am shaken (Psalm 13:1-4).

At other times, it's a whole group lamenting:

But you have rejected us and disgraced us and have not gone out with our armies. You have made us turn back from the foe, and those who hate us have gotten spoil. You have made us like sheep for slaughter and have scattered us among the nations (Psalm 44:9-11).

When Jesus searches for a way to put his wounds into words, his search results in a psalm of lament like these. Twice in his ministry Jesus prays through a psalm, and in both cases, it is a lament (the other time being Luke 23:46). They are the perfect prayers for imperfect moments.

Praying Our Way Out

What does this mean for us? First, with the prayer "My God, My God, why have you forsaken me?" Jesus teaches us to pray *honestly*. As I noted earlier, lament psalms like the one Jesus leans on here are an "act of bold faith about reality." They insist that we experience the world as it really is, not as we might wish it to be. They insist that nothing is out of bounds when it comes to prayer.[5] God is big enough to handle your harshest words and your darkest emotions. If the lament prayers like the one Jesus uses here teach us anything, they teach us to bring it all out on the table.

Second Jesus teaches us to pray *hopefully*. The lament psalms—including the one Jesus groans—don't leave us in the dark. They ultimately point us to God who is still there and who still cares. Psalm 22 begins with a direct statement about God being absent. But near its conclusion it includes a hope-filled statement about God being present: "For he has not despised or abhorred the affliction of the afflicted, and he has not hidden his face from him, but has heard, when he cried to him" (Psalm 22:24). Jesus must have this second statement in his heart even as he utters the first statement from his mouth. Just because it's dark does not mean God is distant. Jesus certainly recognizes that in the end, God hears and is near. Jesus gives us permission to speak the unspeakable. But he also gives us courage to consider the unimaginable. God does not desert. God does not abandon. Despite all appearances, he is standing nearby.

Third, and most importantly, Jesus is teaching us to pray—*simply to pray*. The dark holes in life should not suppress prayer. They should unleash prayer. If your Bible has the words of Christ in red, you'll notice that in Matthew's account of the crucifixion, there's only one occurrence of red words—this prayer. In Matthew's gospel, the only time Jesus verbalizes anything is in a prayer to God. Not in a conversation with his mother. Not in an instruction to the criminals crucified alongside him. But in a prayer to God. Even at the bottom, Jesus looks up. He prays hard words. He prays raw words. But the important thing is that Jesus prays. He does not let go just because he feels the Father has.

The best thing you can do when you and God are not on speaking terms is speak. Even if it's ugly. Even if it's crude. Even if it's hard. Just speak.

Author Madeleine L'Engle once offered this prayer: "Dear God. I hate you. Love, Madeleine.[6]" Jesus' prayer from Mark 15 teaches this same duality. In the dark, his prayer empowers us to voice our hurt in forceful ways. He enables us to say, if we must, "Dear God, I hate you." Yet Jesus' prayer does not leave us there. It also fuels our ability to rediscover faith. It energizes our capacity for trust and hope. Jesus enables us to say, if we can, "Love, Madeleine."

Practicing This Prayer

Have you fallen in a hole and as a result just stopped talking to God? Is there a pain, an injury, or a wound that you no longer even bring up with God because you don't even think he's listening? Jump-start your communication with God—even if you have to use hard and raw words. Just start talking again. Make a commitment to pray at least one time every day. Even if it's a short prayer, commit to praying something to God every day.

Specifically, this week commit to praying honestly and hopefully. Close each day this week with a two fold prayer. First, at day's end share with God as honestly as possible one way in which he seemed painfully absent to you that day. Second, share with God one way in which he seemed refreshingly present to you that day. In this way, you'll be praying ideas inspired by Psalm 22 which Jesus quotes in his heart-breaking prayer from the cross: "My God, my God why have you forsaken me?"

---

1. Craig S. Keener, *A Commentary on the Gospel of Matthew* (W.B. Eerdmans Publishing, 1999).
2. Ibid., 674-675.
3. *Braveheart* Dir. Mel Gibson. (Icon Productions, 1995)

4. Keener, 674; Leon Morris. *The Gospel According to Matthew* (W.B. Eerdmans Publishing, 1992), 715.

5. Walter Brueggeman *Spirituality of the Psalms* (Fortress Press, 2002), 27.

6. Gary Thomas *Sacred Marriage: what if God designed marriage to make us holy more than to make us happy?* (Zondervan Publishing House, 2000), 157.

Chapter 4

An Inward Prayer of Complaint:
I Am Deprived (John 19)

Thirsty

You'd think we Americans were dying of thirst. You'd think we were dangerously deprived of liquid. Twenty years ago the average size of an ice-cold soda was six and a half ounces. Today the average size is twenty ounces. We can't seem to guzzle enough of the fabulous fizz. The story is even bigger regarding our hot beverage of choice—coffee. Twenty years ago the average serving consisted of one hundred and forty calories. Today's cup of joe is so grand it carries three hundred and fifty calories. We're swigging down what once used to require only sipping.[1]

For the last forty years we've demanded increasing amounts of fluids like soda and coffee. Yet by satisfying those thirsts, we've endangered ourselves. The added gulps pack on the pounds and corrode our canines. Supersize drinks translate into supersize drinkers.

Worse, while fulfilling these dangerous cravings we sometimes forget our body's real thirst. A friend and I recently took a co-worker to a Memphis eatery called Huey's. It was our co-worker's last meal in this Memphis original before moving to Washington D.C. for a new job. We placed our drink orders and my friend requested only water. I've eaten with him numerous times and never heard him order only water. It's usually a Coke or Dr. Pepper or an Orange Crush.

"What's with the water?" I asked.

"My mom just went into the hospital with kidney stones," he explained. "I realized I've not been drinking enough water. I don't want to go through what my mom just went through."

We give in too readily to our thirst for sweet soda and creamy coffee. But we ignore our body's more important thirst for pure water—until circumstances force us to take notice.

One thirst we obey without question. The other we rarely recognize.

A Tale of Two Thirsts

This condition is seen in the woman at the well. A weary Jesus plops down beside the watering hole outside of a Samaritan village named Sychar. The town's name may mean "liar" or "drunkard."[2] It is providential, then, that at the well near the village of "Drunkard," we meet a woman who insists on satisfying the wrong thirst in the wrong way. Near the township of "Liar" we watch a woman who's been deceived about the true nature of thirst.

The noon sun spotlights this lone woman who has come to draw water from the well where Jesus rests. "Give me a drink," Jesus requests. But as justifiable as his own thirst is, Jesus' real interest is in her thirst. He tells her, "If you knew the gift of God, and who it is that is saying to you, 'Give me a drink,' you would have asked him, and he would have given you living water" (John 4:10). Translated into prayer-language, Jesus says, "If you realized who I am, you could pray to me 'I thirst,' and I would say to you, 'I quench.' I can satisfy your true thirst."

But the craving Jesus identifies in the woman is one she seems to rarely recognize. Instead, she's been rapidly succumbing to another thirst. Jesus knows that she's married five men and is now involved with a sixth. This woman does not feel her need for living water. But she does feel a desire for men. Thus she's been consuming guys like a drunkard on a binge. One. Two. Three. Four. Five. And now, six.

Yet the woman is no pagan. She is religious. Later, she says, "Sir, I perceive that you are a prophet," and "Our fathers worshiped on this mountain, but you say that in Jerusalem is the place where people ought to worship," and "I know that the Messiah is coming (he who is called Christ). When he comes, he will tell us all things" (John 4:19-20, 25). The woman has deep spiritual roots. It's not hard, therefore, to imagine that she's even prayed for God to quench this all-consuming thirst. "I'm so thirsty God, for a man who'll really love me." She's likely done everything she can to quench her thirst.

But while abandoning herself to her craving for men, she's avoided her true inner thirst. She's overlooked what she most needs. Perhaps she's rarely, if ever, prayed about that which she desperately requires—that which Jesus envisions when he invites her to ask for "living water."

She's a woman obsessed with quenching the wrong thirst in the wrong way. He's a Savior longing to fill her right thirst in the right way.

If she'd only ask.

If she'd only pray.

In his nonfiction book, *Sahara Unveiled*, William Langewiesche writes of traveling four thousand miles in the Sahara. He tells of a truck which breaks down while crossing the desert as it carries an Algerian named Lag Lag and a companion:[3]

> The sun forced them into the shade under the truck, where they dug a shallow trench. Day after day they lay there, watching their water dwindle and waiting for God's will. They turned inward to Islam and talked about the afterlife. They had food, but did not eat, fearing it would magnify their thirst. Dehydration, not starvation, is what kills wanderers in the desert. And thirst is the most terrible of all human sufferings. The physiologists who specialize in thirst seem never to have experienced it. This surprises me. You would think that someone interested in thirst would want to stop drinking for a while, especially since for short periods it can be done safely. But the physiologists pursue knowledge, not experience. They use words based in Greek, which soften the subject. For instance, they would describe the Sahara—the burning sand and relentless sky—as *dipsogenic*, meaning "thirst provoking." In discussing Lag Lag's case, they might say he progressed from *eudipsia*, meaning "ordinary thirst," through bouts of *hyperdipsia*, meaning "temporary intense thirst," to *polydipsia*, by which they mean "sustained, excessive thirst." We can define it more precisely: since poly means "many," polydipsia means the kind of thirst that drives you to drink anything. There are specialized terms for such behavior, including *uriposia*, "the drinking of urine," and *hemoposia*, "the drinking of blood." For word enthusiasts, this is heady stuff. Nonetheless, the lexicon has not kept up with technology. Blame the ancients for not driving cars. I have tried, and cannot coin a suitable word for "the drinking of rusty radiator water."

We can experience thirsts so controlling that they force us to consume poison in order to satisfy them. We can find ourselves drinking rusty radiator water just to find relief. That's what this woman has done. Dehydrated for purpose and passion, she turns to the poison of men who will use and abuse her. But she may as well be drinking rusty radiator water.

She's a woman obsessed with quenching the wrong thirst in the wrong way. He's a Savior longing to fill her right thirst in the right way.

If she'd only ask.

If she'd only pray.

Thirst Denied

Even Jesus thirsts. But in contrast to the woman, Jesus models a better response to the multiple cravings we encounter. At the cross we witness Jesus turn down the opportunity to satisfy one thirst. It is a thirst he recognizes should not be filled. Then we watch as Jesus prays for the satisfaction of another thirst. It is a thirst he believes should be filled.

Ironically, the first thirst is for something we'd judge large and substantial—a thirst worthy of attention and energy. Yet Jesus does not fill it. The second is for something we'd judge small and trivial—a thirst not worthy of prayer. Yet Jesus prays for God to fill it.

First, Jesus is "offered wine mixed with myrrh" (Mark 15:23). This liquid is a kind of sedative. Offered by compassionate women from Jerusalem, it is designed to take the sharpest edge off of the pain the condemned men are about to endure.[4] A stiff drink before leaping into the boxing ring. A prescription painkiller before grueling physical therapy. A heavy dose of anesthesia before surgery.

As men sentenced to crucifixion anticipate the agony and slow death ahead of them, they yearn for some assistance with their anxiety. They thirst for some distraction from their despair. And caring women quench this thirst with the wine mixed with myrrh.

Jesus, however, will not consume it. He refuses to suck in the soothing cocktail. Why? His denial does not stem from the possibility that he feels no pain. Jesus is not immune from the agony of the crucifixion. Some dry patch of his soul longs for this anesthetic liquid. This thirst registers strongly on his radar. We cannot explain his refusal to drink by saying that he did not feel the need to drink.

Why then does Jesus turn away from the anesthetic? Jesus wishes to embrace the full suffering offered by the spikes. He desires to experience the total torture made possible by his timbers. Jesus has not come to this moment to bear some of our sin. He has come to bear all of our sin. His passion is not to receive some of our punishment. His passion is to receive all of our punishment. Jesus will not avoid the despair with drugs. He will not escape the misery with elixir. He will take the full swing of God's wrath so there is none left for you and me. This thirst he will deny. It's such a large and substantial thirst we'd not blame him for satisfying it. But this thirst he will deny. He will not drink the wine mixed with myrrh.

I Thirst

A second thirst, however, he will satisfy. There is one thirst Jesus does attend to at the cross. But in comparison to the first thirst which he refuses, this second thirst seems trivial. Not worthy of attention. And certainly not worthy of prayer. Yet of the few prayers from the dying lips of Jesus, one prayer centers on this second craving.

John writes "After this, Jesus, knowing that all was now finished, said (to fulfill the Scripture), 'I thirst'" (John 19:28). Jesus is deeply and painfully thirsty. He's not craving drugs or elixir. He's already walked away from that thirst. Now he's craving a simple soothing for his dry throat. He just wants the equivalent of a sip of water. D. A. Carson, a New Testament scholar and author of over fifty books, reports that, "...a man scourged, bleeding, and hanging on a cross under the Near-Eastern sun would be so desperately dehydrated that thirst would be part of the torture."[5] Jesus is experiencing a deep and primal thirst. He groans for this refreshment just as he gasps for air. It's not going to dull the searing pain or end the excruciating agony. It will merely relieve his parched lips and refresh his dusty mouth for a few seconds.

Notice what Jesus does with this thirst. Whereas the first thirst was rejected and not even deemed worthy of attention, this thirst is elevated so high that it makes Jesus' prayer list. How do we know "I thirst" is a prayer and not just a cry from a desperate man? When John tells us that Jesus says, "I thirst" in order "to fulfill Scripture," John is telling us that Jesus allowed Scripture to guide him regarding this need. Faced with a legitimate thirst he is helpless to fill, Jesus turns to Scripture for direction. And according to Scripture, in that circumstance, one would lift the thirst up to God in prayer. Jesus' prayer of "I thirst," fulfills Scripture because that is how others in Scripture addressed similar needs. They lifted their thirst to God. If John had not included the phrase "to fulfill the Scripture," we might imagine this is Jesus just crying out to anyone who will listen. But the phrase "to fulfill Scripture" narrows the intended audience of his address. Jesus has one listener in mind as he cries "I thirst." It's the same listener to whom people in Scripture spoke. Jesus has his Father in mind.

What Scripture then does "I thirst" fulfill? Where in Scripture do we find people praying about their thirst? Jesus probably has in mind a Psalm, specifically Psalm 22.[6] Psalm 22 has just been quoted by John as he describes the way the soldiers divvied up Jesus' garments (John 19:24; Psalm 22:18). In addition, we've heard another of Jesus' prayers which originated from Psalm 22: "My God, My God, why have you forsaken me?" (Matthew 27:46; Psalm 22:1). Psalm 22 is filling Jesus' mind in these final moments. It is the text which carries him through this terror. And now, as Jesus experiences dehydration, he is perhaps reflecting on Psalm 22:15: "my strength is dried up like a potsherd, and my tongue sticks to my jaws; you lay me in the dust of death." Here the psalmist's tongue sticks to his mouth from desperate thirst. And what does the psalmist do? He talks to God about it.

As Jesus experiences his own agonizing thirst, he remembers what a seasoned prayer-warrior in Psalm 22 did. Jesus recalls how his father David responded in a time of personal drought. He lifted the need up to God. He begged God to quench that thirst.

And like a chip off the old block, Jesus follows suit. "I thirst," he prays.

In his book, *Mornings on Horseback*, David McCullough writes about the dark days when a twenty-something Teddy Roosevelt watched his father die after a grueling bout with stomach cancer.[7] Theodore Roosevelt Sr. had been the sun of the large family's solar system. Teddy called him "Lion Heart." Now, the Lion roared no more. Perhaps in searching for the words to pray, Teddy wrote the date of his father's death next to one verse of Scripture. The verse? It was Psalm 69:3 "I am weary with my crying out; my throat is parched."

"I thirst," Teddy Roosevelt prayed. "I thirst."

It's what Jesus did. He turned to Scripture and found his direction. "I thirst," he prayed. "I thirst."

On the list of things the Son of God might pray about in his last moments, this item may seem miniscule. We could imagine Jesus praying for world peace, for an end to all violent regimes, for unity among his followers, or for God's kingdom to come. Those would be worthy thirsts for prayer. But here, Jesus just petitions God for a drink. It's not lofty. It's not "spiritual." But it's what he needs. "I thirst."

And God answers. He nudges those tending the cross to lift up a sponge drenched in sour wine. For a very brief moment, Jesus' cracked lips are moistened and his dry throat is soothed.

Bringing Prayer Down to Earth

Like the woman at the well, there are times when we are thirsty and we identify that thirst as something deep and important. So we strive to fill that thirst. We even plead for God to quench it. We pray for a long and slow drink from a new relationship, a new possession, or a new career. Yet God refuses. He urges us to walk away. He knows what we don't—satisfying that thirst will work against his will for our lives.

Like the caregivers at Golgotha, there are times when we have certain conviction about thirsts and the best way to fill them. Yet if we could wear the eyes of God, we'd notice that what we're seeking is ultimately just an escape. A drug. An elixir. We would understand that satisfying that thirst in that way will only force us outside the Father's will.

But like Jesus on the cross, there are times when we become aware of a deep and legitimate thirst. There are moments when we do indeed need the very thing we believe we need. It may be a small thing in the eyes of others. A simple thing. A less than "spiritual" thing. But it is something we can hardly do without.

And what do we do in those moments? What do we do with a craving which we believe is genuine yet which we are helpless to fill? We lift it to God in prayer.

Eugene Peterson notes: "[This] is the only prayer in which Jesus expresses physical agony. Think of it: seven prayers prayed across those three hours on the cross and only one of them out of physical pain."[8] In the list of Jesus' prayers, "I thirst" is a rare prayer. Yet this prayer about physical thirst survived the cut. This plea for a cup of water got in. Think of all that Jesus might have prayed. Think of the heavenly and extraordinary things he might have cried out to God. But in this instance, we hear something earthly and ordinary. "I thirst."

That prayer is often the one prayer we don't pray. We are quick to pray about the magnificent things we want. Yet we are slow to pray about miniscule things we actually need. We are ready to petition God for the rousing things of heaven. Yet we are reluctant to lobby God for the routine things of earth. Jesus' prayer "I thirst" remedies this. It keeps us from spiritualizing and romanticizing our prayers. It brings our prayers back down to earth.

I recall talking recently to a woman about a problem she had encountered. I don't remember the specific problem. It was something routine. Something common. Something so plain it didn't even lodge in my memory. I suggested we pray about it. "Do you really think we can pray about *that*?" she asked. It was as if "that" was not big enough, not sacred enough, and not spiritual enough to bring before God. She had forgotten that one day on the cross, Jesus' prayed about *that*. "I thirst."

In his book, *Traveling the Prayer Paths of Jesus*, John Indermark writes, "Sometimes prayer comes down to basics. I am..., with little more than a word or a phrase following, can express to God all we are in that moment.... For Jesus, this brief phrase *I am thirsty* expresses his most pressing need to God and to anyone who might act in the name of decency to slake that thirst.... To follow Jesus' prayer path in this instance reminds us that we do not leave our humanity behind when we approach God in prayer. As God fashioned us human, so we fashion our prayers, crying out for the meeting of our basic human needs and those of others."[9]

Bread and Water Prayers

It should not surprise us that Jesus prayed this simple prayer. After all, the one who called out the prayer "I thirst" also commanded us to pray "Give us this day our daily bread" (Matthew 6:11). The Lord's Prayer is certainly filled with "big" and "spiritual" things: "hallowed be your name," "your kingdom come," "forgive us our debts," and "deliver us from evil." Those are the kinds of prayers which frequently echo through church buildings and spill out of pious mouths. Yet the Lord's Prayer also includes this line: "Give us this day our daily bread."

Philip Yancey tells of conducting research on prayer for a book he was writing. His wife, a veteran of inner city ministry, told him, "If you're writing a book about prayer, you should hang around the homeless for a while. Street people pray as a necessity, not a luxury."[10] Yancey wisely took his wife's advice. He started hanging around the homeless and listening to their prayers. He writes, "I was struck by the prayers' down-to-earth quality—indeed, their resemblance to the Lord's Prayer. 'Give us this day our daily bread': They all had stories about running out of food, praying, and then finding a burrito or uneaten pizza."

Perhaps that's the greatest consequence of finding yourself on the street, in a pit, or on the cross. You once again experience prayer as a necessity not a luxury. Things you might have only rarely considered praying now come rapidly to your lips. You not only pray for the big and spiritual things. You also pray for the small and material things. Bread for the day. Water for the moment. Your prayers come back down to earth. "I thirst" suddenly becomes your life-sustaining plea.

While I was working on this book, a friend of mine named Kate was involved in a near-deadly accident. Her car flipped while rounding a corner. Kate was ejected from the driver's seat. Her small-town Oklahoma hospital could do little to put the pieces back together. Thus Kate was flown quickly to Memphis and its better equipped hospitals. Kate was in excruciating pain when I entered her room three days later. Her pelvis was fractured. She had lumbar injuries. The bottom half of her right leg was shredded. For three days she had been lying in bed in agony. Waiting for surgeries. Waiting for treatment. Waiting for miracles. While I visited with her, she broke down: "I feel so helpless. I can't even get up and look out my window. I can't do anything for myself. I'm so used to being independent. Now I can't do anything. I can't even get a drink of water!" In between her tears, I reminded her about Jesus on the cross. After six hours he too was in excruciating pain. He also couldn't do anything. Like her, Jesus couldn't even get a drink of water. So in total helplessness, he cried out to God, "I thirst." I think that on that day, prayer for Kate moved from luxury to necessity. I think that on that day her prayers came back down to earth.

Practicing This Prayer

This week bring your prayers down to earth. Do not pray for a single magnificent or heavenly thing. Instead, pray every day this week only for mundane and earthly things. Pray for clean water to drink and hot food to eat. Pray for physical health and emotional stability. Pray for an upcoming test. Pray about that trip you'll be taking in a couple of weeks. For one week only, eliminate all praying that focuses on the "big" and "spiritual" things of life. Instead, fill your days with prayers about the "small" and "earthly" things of life.

One way to do this is to begin every day this week by finishing this statement: "I am..." Perhaps hungry is what you are. Discouraged is what you are. In need of help on a project at work is what you are. Answer that statement each day, and then allow that answer to form the focus of your prayer for that day.

---

1. Statistics *National Heart, Lung and Blood Institute* (2010).
2. M. Easton, *Easton's Bible Dictionary* (Logos Research Systems, Inc., 1996).
3. William Langewiesche, *Sahara Unveiled: a Journey Across the Desert* (Pantheon Books, 1996), Chapter 5.
4. D. A. Carson, *The Gospel According to John* (Intervarsity Press, 1991), 620.
5. Carson, 619.
6. Carson, 619.
7. David McCullough, *Mornings on Horseback* (Simon and Schuster, 1982).
8. Eugene Peterson, *Tell It Slant: A Conversation on the Language of Jesus in His Stories and Prayers* (W.B. Eerdmans Publishing, Co., 2008), 256.
9. John Indermark, *Traveling the Prayer Paths of Jesus* (Upper Room Books, 2003), 155.
10. Philip Yancey, "The Word on the Street: What the homeless taught me about prayer." *Christianitytoday.com*. (7/20/2010).

Chapter 5

An Upward Prayer of Confidence:
You Still Rule (Matthew 11)

The date: 1992.

The place: Barcelona, Spain.

The race: 400 meter.

Derek Redmond had previously broken the British record. He was a favorite to medal that day. The gun sounded and Redmond sprang from the blocks. His form was perfect. His stride was flawless. Few could compete with this athlete.

But fifteen seconds into the race, Redmond stumbled and then stopped. He had pulled a hamstring. Unable to continue, he watched helplessly as every runner sprinted past him.

Redmond finished dead last.

It was one of the most shocking events of the 1992 Summer Olympics. It must have been one of the most disappointing moments in Redmond's life.

Strong start, a stumble, and then a stop.

By the time we reach the events of Matthew 11, we find Jesus in a similar situation.

Strong Start

If the Gospel of Matthew is a second-by-second replay of Jesus' race, then the first ten chapters show a remarkably strong start.

- Jesus' preaching was perfect. For example, in Matthew 5-7 Jesus gave a sermon that left people amazed. Its content and delivery are so astounding that it's still known as the greatest sermon ever preached. Here's how the crowds responded: "And when Jesus finished these sayings, the crowds were astonished at his teaching..." (Matthew 7:28). Jesus' preaching was perfect.

- And his practice was flawless. For example, in Matthew 8-9 Jesus launched a tour of miracles and healing. We witness ten miracles in two chapters:

- Man with leprosy—made clean.
- Paralyzed servant—healed.
- Mother with a fever—made well.
- Storm on the lake—stilled.
- Two men filled with demons—freed.
- Paralyzed man—walks.
- Woman who's bled for twelve years—cured.
- Little girl who's died—raised to life.
- Blind men—sight restored.
- Mute man—now speaks.

It was a strong start for Jesus.

Stumble and Stop: Doubt

But in Matthew 11 Jesus hits the back stretch and seems likely to stumble. It appears he may falter due to three rocks strewn across his path—the rocks of doubt, disappointment, and desolation.

The first sign of trouble comes when John, one of Jesus' greatest supporters, begins showing signs of doubt. John's been thrown in jail—thrown there for public remarks he made about a politician's love life. In this dungeon, John seems to doubt: "Now when John heard in prison about the deeds of the Christ, he sent word by his disciples and said to him, 'Are you the one who is to come, or shall we look for another?' And Jesus answered them, 'Go and tell John what you hear and see: the blind receive their sight and the lame walk, lepers are cleansed and the deaf hear, and the dead are raised up, and the poor have good news preached to them. And blessed is the one who is not offended by me'" (Matthew 11:2-6).

When Jesus' ministry began, John the Baptist was the first one in front, applauding and telling others about Jesus: "I baptize you with water for repentance, but he who is coming after me is mightier than I, whose sandals I am not worthy to carry. He will baptize you with the Holy Spirit and fire" (Matthew 3:11). No one believed in Jesus more than John.

But now, doubt appears: "Are you the one who is to come, or shall we look for another?" Some scholars are so alarmed by this question that they propose it wasn't John who doubted. It was his followers who doubted. And John is asking on behalf of those doubting followers.[1]

But make no mistake—John doubts.[2] John had predicted that Jesus was coming to "clear his threshing floor and gather his wheat into the barn, but the chaff he will burn with unquenchable fire" (Matthew 3:12). John predicted that Jesus would come with flames of judgment. Jesus would burn up all this chaff in the religious and political world. But now, John's been tossed in prison by the same political establishment he expected Jesus to blaze away. Jesus hasn't unseated or punished anyone in political power or religious power. All he's done is help the nobodies—a fact that Jesus affirms. After all, Jesus doesn't say, "Go and tell John what you see and hear: the Son of Man sits on the throne in Jerusalem; Rome has fallen; the Pharisees have been run out of town." Instead, Jesus says, "Go and tell John what you hear and see: the blind receive their sight and the lame walk, lepers are cleansed and the deaf hear, and the dead are raised up, and the poor have good news preached to them." Jesus has helped some needy individuals at the margin of society, but he's done nothing to address the larger political and religious institutions which are the cause of so much suffering.

John doubts.

Eugene Peterson writes, "John and Jesus were different in the ways they went about their work. John preached in thunder to popular acclaim; Jesus told stories over meals and with friends on the road. John was a public figure confronting the high profile sin of Herod Antipas in the public square; Jesus worked for the most part inconspicuously in the small villages in Galilee. John was an ascetic in diet and clothing; Jesus enjoyed a glass of wine, even at times in the company of disreputable outsiders. It is understandable that John would wonder what exactly was going on."[3] Thus John, once Jesus' closest ally, has become "undecided."

Strong start. But here, a stumble.

Stumble and Stop: Disappointment

After his strong start, not only does Jesus face the doubt of John, he also faces the disappointment of the crowds. Earlier in Matthew 5-7 the crowds were astonished at Jesus. But in Matthew 11, they demonstrate a different reaction: "But to what shall I compare this generation? It is like children sitting in the marketplaces and calling to their playmates, 'We played the flute for you, and you did not dance; we sang a dirge, and you did not mourn.' For John came neither eating nor drinking, and they say, 'He has a demon.' The Son of Man came eating and drinking, and they say, 'Look at him! A glutton and a drunkard, a friend of tax collectors and sinners!' Yet wisdom is justified by her deeds" (Matthew 11:16-19).

Jesus pictures groups of children sitting in the marketplace. They are complaining because one group won't do what the other group wants.[4] They are frustrated because each group disappoints the expectations of the other. The crowds' recent reactions to Jesus and to John the Baptist remind Jesus of these children.

"We played the flute for you, and you did not dance." Some wanted a joyful spiritual leader but found John the Baptist too stern and serious— why, he wouldn't even eat or drink!

"We sang a dirge, and you did not mourn." Some wanted a serious and stern religious leader but found Jesus too joyful—why, all he does is eat and drink! At one time the crowds were astonished at Jesus' teaching. Now, they complain because Jesus doesn't meet their expectations. The once devoted crowds are now disappointed.

Strong start. But here, another stumble.

Stumble and Stop: Desolation

Not only does this fast-off-the-blocks Jesus face the doubt of John and the disappointment of the crowds, he finally faces the spiritual desolation of the cities in which he has ministered: "Then he began to denounce the cities where most of his mighty works had been done, because they did not repent. 'Woe to you, Chorazin! Woe to you, Bethsaida! For if the mighty works done in you had been done in Tyre and Sidon, they would have repented long ago in sackcloth and ashes. But I tell you, it will be more bearable on the day of judgment for Tyre and Sidon than for you. And you, Capernaum, will you be exalted to heaven? You will be brought down to Hades. For if the mighty works done in you had been done in Sodom, it would have remained until this day. But I tell you that it will be more tolerable on the day of judgment for the land of Sodom than for you'" (Matthew 11:20-24).

On the positive side, Jesus' ministry has held major campaigns in three Jewish cities: Chorazin, Bethsaida, and Capernaum. We're told in verse 11 that "most of his mighty works" had been performed in these places. The best miracles. The best healing. The best preaching. These cities should now be bearing abundant spiritual fruit. They ought to be places of enormous spiritual harvest filled with changed lives and transformed cultures.

But here's the harsh reality: the cities are dry deserts of spiritual desolation. Jesus preached his finest sermons and conducted his most powerful miracles but these cities remained as unjust, corrupt, and dark as Sodom. It's like Billy Graham came to town and not a soul in the fifty-thousand seat stadium responded to his evangelistic invitation. It's like

Beth Moore held a workshop in the city and not a single woman purchased the workbook or read the material. City after city: Chorazin, Bethsaida, and Capernaum.

Jesus didn't simply find indifference in these cities. He found outright rejection. These people treated Jesus and his volunteers so badly Jesus says those Jewish cities will be worse off on judgment day than three pagan cities: Tyre, Sidon, and Sodom.

Strong start, stumble, and stop. It must have been one of the most disappointing moments in Jesus' life.

I know what I would have done. I would have complained. I would have cried. I would have quit.

But notice what Jesus does.

Jesus prays.

And what a prayer!

You Are in Charge

On the heels of the doubt of the one who used to have his back, the disappointment of the fickle crowds, and the desolation of the people whom he's tried to serve, Jesus prays this prayer: "At that time Jesus declared, 'I thank you, Father, Lord of heaven and earth, that you have hidden these things from the wise and understanding and revealed them to little children; yes, Father, for such was your gracious will'" (Matthew 11:25-26).

Don't those words—"I thank you, Father"—seem out of place? Jesus' greatest supporter almost withdraws his endorsement. The crowds are acting like whiny kids. And despite monumental efforts, Jesus hardly has anything to show for his work. Yet Jesus prays, "I thank you, Father." At other dark times Jesus does pray prayers of complaint. But here, Jesus prays one of those upward prayers of confidence. What makes it possible for Jesus to pray with thanks on such a thankless day?

Two things.

First, notice how Jesus addresses God: "Lord of heaven and earth." Jesus envisions the one to whom he prays as the CEO, President, King, and Lord of everything in heaven and on earth. Prayer is what enables Jesus to remember that the Father is in control. External circumstances like John wondering, crowds being childish, and cities not responding may seem like evidence that God is *not* in control. But prayer is how Jesus grounded himself in this fundamental fact—God is still in charge. God is still Lord of heaven and earth. And because of this fact, Jesus can still pray, "I praise you." He can pray "Thank you" simply because he recognizes who God is—Lord of heaven and earth. God is still in charge. God still rules over all things which seem to challenge his sovereignty.

You Are at Work

Jesus praises God not simply for who God is but also for what God is doing. Not only does Jesus realize through prayer that God is still in charge. He also realizes that God is still at work.

Based on the events of the day, it may seem that God is doing nothing. How could God be active when allies are dropping like flies, the crowds are becoming wishy-washy, and perfect ministry brings pathetic results? Surely God has taken a break.

Yet in this prayer, Jesus recognizes that God is still at work: "I thank you, Father, Lord of heaven and earth, that you have hidden these things from the wise and understanding and revealed them to little children; yes, Father, for such was your gracious will." Through prayer, Jesus is able to view the events of the day through a new lens. This lens allows him to see things more clearly. Through prayer, Jesus remembers that God generally doesn't work in a way that is high profile or with methods that persuade the sophisticated and the elite. Instead, Jesus remembers that God works in humble ways, in unseen ways, and in ways that impact the lowly and unsophisticated.

Jesus may not be able to see much fruit being borne among the notable and noteworthy. But God's doing a great work through Jesus among the nobodies. Jesus is able to recognize that God is still at work. God still rules over all things which seem to challenge his mission and ministry.

And for this, Jesus can say, "I thank you, Father." Even on a bad day, Jesus teaches us to pray with thanksgiving, because God is still in control and God is still working. God still rules.

Praying with Confidence

Larry McKenzie is a long time minister at our congregation. If you ask Larry how he's doing, he always says, "I'm grateful." It doesn't matter what's going on. The rain could be falling in sheets and the wind could be blowing seventy miles an hour.

"Larry, how are you today?"

"I'm grateful."

Larry may have just finished one of the most difficult funerals he's ever conducted.

"Larry, how're you doing?"

"I'm grateful."

Does Larry not see the bad things going on? Is Larry blind? No, of course he sees. He's seen more bad days than most of us due to the nature of his ministry. But Larry also sees something else. He sees a God who is still Lord of heaven and earth. He sees a God who is working in humble and hidden ways. He believes in a God who still rules. As a result, he's able to say every day, "I thank you, Father."

My wife Kendra and I were talking with a woman named Julie one recent Sunday. Julie's husband had lost his job just days earlier. We asked her how he was doing. "He's calm and confident," she reported. "He just believes that God's going to take care of everything. He trusts that God knew this was going to happen and is going to work in the midst of it." Kendra and I marveled at the way he peacefully accepted that God was still in charge and still at work.

Michel Quoist was a priest and a French writer. In his thirties he wrote a book of poems called *Prayers*.[5] One of the prayers, entitled, "Thank You," stands as a compelling example of what our prayer can be when inspired by this prayer of Jesus. As we read Quoist's prayer, we follow him through his entire day. And all day long, Quoist finds reasons for thanks.

- As he wakes he thanks: "Thank you for the water that woke me up, the soap that smells good, the toothpaste that refreshes. Thank you for the clothes that protect me, for their color and their cut."

- As he works, he thanks: "Thank you for the metal in my hands, for the whine of the steel biting into it, for the satisfied look of the supervisor and the load of finished pieces."

- As he walks home he thanks: "Thank you for the boy I watched playing on the sidewalk opposite."

- As he eats dinner and relaxes he thanks: "Thank you for the roof that shelters me, for the lamp that lights me, for the radio that plays, for the news, for music and singing. Thank you for the bunch of flowers, so pretty on my table."

- And as he falls asleep he thanks: "Thank you for the tranquil night. Thank you for the stars. Thank you for the silence."

Quoist was able to note what Jesus noted. Every day, in every way, God was still in charge. God was still at work. God still ruled. This made every occasion an occasion for thanks.

In 1994, Mother Theresa spoke at a National Prayer Breakfast. She said, "One evening we went out, and we picked up four people from the street. And one of them was in a most terrible condition. I told the sisters, 'You take care of the other three; I will take care of the one who looks worst.' So I did for her all that my love could do. I put her in bed and there was such a beautiful smile on her face. She took hold of my hand as she said two words only: 'Thank you.' Then she died."

This poor woman had many reasons to despair. She was homeless. She was dying. She was abandoned. But her final breath was "Thank you."

This is what Jesus teaches us to do in prayer. Jesus teaches us that even on the very worst day, we can say "Thank you." God is still in charge. God is still at work. God still rules. And for this, every day, we must pray: Thank you.

Practicing This Prayer

This week, carry a threefold prayer with you into every situation: "You are still in charge. You are still at work. You are still worthy of praise." Especially as you encounter challenges or trials, every day this week pray this prayer, "You are still in charge. You are still at work. You are still worthy of praise." As you stumble upon doubt, disappointment, or desolation, pray this threefold prayer.

---

1. Leon Morris, *The Gospel According to Matthew* (W. B. Eerdmans Publishing, 1992), 274-275.
2. Frederick Dale Bruner, *Matthew: a commentary* (Word, 1987), 408ff.
3. Eugene Peterson, *Tell It Slant: A Conversation on the Language of Jesus in His Stories and Prayers* (W.B. Eerdmans Publishing Co., 2008), 199.
4. Morris, 284-285.
5. Michel Quoist, *Prayers* (Sheed and Ward, 1963), 61-63.

Chapter 6

An Upward Prayer of Confidence:
You Still Listen (John 11)

The Need to Be Heard

Several years ago I fell headlong into a pit. Chaos was creeping into our congregation due to an impending relocation, the retirement of a beloved staff member, and other congregational stressors. One day the crisis climaxed with a meeting in my office during which some people whom I deeply respected questioned my leadership and competency. It was as if the ground beneath my feet suddenly gave way and before I knew it, I was in a pit of despair.

After the meeting, I needed to talk. To vent. To process. Thankfully, with providential timing, two long-time friends reached out to me. We met for lunch and I poured out my heart. I verbalized every vile emotion I was feeling.

But I didn't just need to talk. I could have grabbed a stranger and accomplished that goal. I could have opened my mouth and talked to the walls if speaking was the only objective. What I ultimately needed was to be heard. I longed for someone who knew and loved me to pay attention to everything I was wrestling with inside. I wanted someone whom I trusted to really listen to my woes.

Sometimes what we most need is to know we are heard.

When engaged couples contact me for pre-marital counseling, one of the things we discuss is a skill called "active listening." Research finds that healthy couples regularly engage in active listening in which the listener can paraphrase back to the speaker what he/she heard: "So what I hear you saying is that you want me to..." At first, as engaged couples practice the skill, it feels funny and formal. But after some rehearsal, it begins to feel natural. Most couples find it beneficial. Why? Because much of the time a wife or husband just wants to know the spouse is truly listening. Even if the wife or husband disagrees with what the partner says, frequently what matters most to the one speaking is just knowing that the other is listening.

Sometimes all we need is to know we are heard.

On August 5, 2010, thirty-three miners were trapped 2,300 feet underground when the main ramp into the San Jose mine in Chile collapsed. For seventeen days rescuers could not locate anyone below. For seventeen days the miners survived on small bits of fish and tiny amounts of water. For seventeen days there was no contact with anyone on the surface. The silence must have been frightening. I can imagine the miners tapping the walls and doing anything possible to send word to the surface. I can envision them straining their ears for any clink, buzz, thud, or hum to indicate that someone up there was listening.

Finally, on August 22 one of the exploratory rescue drills from above found the roof of the shelter in which the miners were living. The miners managed to attach a note to the drill as it reversed course and returned up top. The note read "We are fine in the shelter, the thirty-three of us." What a relief it must have been after four hundred hours of isolation to know that someone up there was listening. Someone up there finally heard.

Sometimes all we need is to know we are heard.

Trapped in a Pit

In John 11, Jesus and some of those closest to him are swallowed by an even deeper pit in the village of Bethany. Here, about two miles from Jerusalem, live three of Jesus' most intimate friends—Lazarus and his sisters, Mary and Martha. Jesus frequents their home as often as an extended family member would. At each visit, Martha seems to be the dynamic one, fretting over whether Jesus has enough to eat or drink and wanting to make sure he has the perfect place to sit. Mary seems to be the reflective one, looking for the chance to sit near and listen to Jesus. During one of Jesus' many visits, Martha runs through the house finishing her preparations while Mary sits quietly listening to Jesus (Luke 10:38-42). On another visit Martha again runs herself ragged serving a meal while Mary opens the jar of their most pricey perfume and anoints Jesus' feet with it (John 12:1-8).

Their house was such a home for Jesus that during his final week it serves as a kind of headquarters (Matthew 21:17; Luke10:38–42; John 11:1–12:11). With Jesus' campaign now in its Jerusalem-phase, Lazarus' home is the ideal command post. In land wars, the commanding officers will often take over a local home to plot war strategy for that region. For example, after the defeat of German forces, when Truman, Stalin, and Churchill met in Potsdam Germany, they each stayed in local homes. In that case, however, Russian troops had forcefully ejected the owners and taken possession of the homes. In Jesus' case, he is invited into Lazarus' dwelling and treated as an honored guest. The brother and his sisters are happy to host Jesus' climactic campaign.

Their's is about as intimate a relationship as is portrayed anywhere in the Gospels. The two sisters describe Lazarus to Jesus as "he whom you love" (John 11:3). John states outright "Now Jesus loved Martha and her sister and Lazarus" (John 11:5). The house of Mary, Martha, and Lazarus is one of those places where Jesus can truly relax. It is that rare safe-place filled with friends who only seek his success and who are wholeheartedly devoted to his mission. No matter what religious leader critiques him or what local group denounces him, Jesus knows that this trio always has his back.

But on this day Mary and Martha send an alarming word to Jesus: "Lord, he whom you love is ill" (John 11:3). Apparently the illness is severe because within days, Lazarus is dead. It's one of those "I-can't-believe-this-is-happening" situations. It's like a healthy forty-year-old who goes to the doctor about an unrelenting headache and dies six days later from brain cancer. Before anyone even has time to process the fact that Lazarus is ill, he is dead. The circumstances are so shocking that "many of the Jews" from Jerusalem "come to Martha and Mary to console them" (John 11:19).

Their beloved brother is gone. His death leaves a tremendous hole in their hearts. Their social world shudders from the earthquake of Lazarus' death. But not only does his passing radically change their social circle. It deeply affects their social security. Two single women will not fare well in a culture like this. In Lazarus they had not only a brother but a backer. They had not only a sibling but a sponsor. Lazarus could speak up for the needs and rights of Mary and Martha in this male-dominated culture. But now both advocate and adoring brother are gone.

At first glance, what Jesus does in response to their plight appears to contradict his feelings for them. John writes, "Now Jesus loved Martha and her sister and Lazarus. So, when he heard that Lazarus was ill, he stayed two days longer in the place where he was" (John 11:5-6). These two sentences are as mismatched as a bulky overcoat and a July afternoon. The two sentences would seem to repel one another like the north poles of two magnets. I expect to read, "Now Jesus loved...them...so...he rushed immediately to their side." But instead of dashing, he delays. "Now Jesus loved...them...so...he stayed two days longer." Instead of sprinting, Jesus stays.

Why? Jesus tells his disciples, "This illness does not lead to death" (John 11:4). Jesus knows that he has the power to overturn the disease's deadly consequence. In fact, after two days, having allowed the virus to do its violence, Jesus states "Our friend Lazarus has fallen asleep, but I go to awaken him" (John 11:11). Jesus later proclaims, "I am the resurrection and the life. Whoever believes in me, though he die, yet shall he live" (John 11:25). Jesus delays so that he might have the chance to demonstrate that his power to save his friend is just as great as his passion for his friend.

But his delay leads to despair. When Martha sees Jesus finally arriving, she seems bitter: "Lord, if you had been here, my brother would not have died" (John 11:21). It's as if she is asking, "Jesus, where have you been? Jesus, why didn't you come sooner?" Even devout and dedicated Mary seems distraught. She too spits at Jesus: "Lord, if you had been here, my brother would not have died" (John 11:32). It's as if she is accusing, "Jesus, you could have stopped this. Jesus, why didn't you save Lazarus?"

John reports that Mary is weeping at this point, as are all who have come to console her and Martha (John 11:33). But they are not the only ones. John tells us "When Jesus saw her weeping, and the Jews who had come with her also weeping, he was deeply moved in his spirit and greatly troubled" (John 11:33). A few moments later, Jesus is "deeply moved again" (John 11:38). And suddenly Jesus is weeping (John 11:35).

Always-on-the-go Martha is stopped in her tracks by her tears. Devout and dedicated Mary is deeply depressed. A mob of well-dressed well-wishers are wailing. And Jesus' vision is blurred from the water welling up in his eyes. Because of the fallout from Lazarus' death, this whole crowd—including Jesus—has landed at the bottom of a deep pit of despair.

He Heard

But then Jesus prays. "And Jesus lifted up his eyes..." (John 11:41). Jesus looks upward from the floor of that fissure. And he begins to pray: "Father, I thank you that you have heard me. I knew that you always hear me, but I said this on account of the people standing around, that they may believe that you sent me" (John 11:42).

"Father, I thank you that you have heard me..."

What has the Father heard? It's as if Jesus is referring to some other prayer which he's already prayed and he's now praising God for hearing that prayer. But that cannot be. This is the first prayer recorded in this tragic tale.

What has the Father heard?

It's as if Jesus has just raised Lazarus by the power granted him through some divine appeal and Jesus is now thanking God for hearing that prayer and answering it so absolutely. But Lazarus is still four-days-dead.

What has the Father heard?

Perhaps this is a thanksgiving of anticipation—an acknowledgment that God will enable Jesus to raise Lazarus from the dead in a few moments. A sort of "Thank you for hearing the prayer I'm about to pray." Jesus is so close to the Father that perhaps he gives thanks now because he knows, in just a moment, that God will hear his request to raise Lazarus.

But Jesus does not pray, "Father, I thank you that you will hear me." He prays, "Father, I thank you that you have heard me." At some point during this distressing situation, Jesus has communicated in some way to God. And God has assured Jesus that he received the message. Thus Jesus thanks God for hearing what he communicated. Jesus praises God because he is certain God has heard him.

But what has the Father heard?

In his examination of the Jewish roots of the prayers of Jesus, Timothy Jones argues that what God heard was Jesus' weeping: "When [Jesus] found himself in the shadow of his friend's tomb, he couldn't put his prayers into words, so he put them into tears instead. And his Father heard his cries."[1] In other words, what catches God's ear is the sound of Jesus' tears. Jesus thanks God because the Father has heard his heart breaking.

Such an interpretation of Jesus' prayer becomes more and more likely when we read the prayers of others who also thanked God simply because God heard their cry:

"LORD, you hear the desire of the afflicted" (Psalm 10:17).

"From his temple he heard my voice, and my cry to him reached his ears" (Psalm 18:6).

"For he has not despised or abhorred the affliction of the afflicted, and he has not hidden his face from him, but has heard" (Psalm 22:24).

"This poor man cried, and the LORD heard him" (Psalm 34:6).

"I cry aloud to God, aloud to God, and he will hear me" (Psalm 77:1).

When people in pain go to God, what they almost always thank God for is the simple fact that he hears their hurt. The sound of a sob thunders loudly through God's hallowed halls.

This seems to be what drives Jesus' prayer of thanksgiving in Bethany. God has heard the sound of his weeping. In fact, Jesus' circumstance and prayer closely mirror the circumstance and prayer of David in Psalm 6. Jesus is portrayed as "deeply moved in his spirit and greatly troubled." David pictures himself as "greatly troubled." We are told that "Jesus wept." David writes, "I drench my couch with my weeping." Jesus praises, "Father, I thank you that you have heard me." David remarks, "For the LORD has heard the sound of my weeping."

Could it be that as Jesus faces this trial, he is reminded of one of the similar trials his forefather David faced? Could it be as Jesus searches for the words to pray, he remembers the words David prayed? Could it be that just as David was grateful simply for the way God heard his grief, so now Jesus rejoices in the fact that his Father has heard his grief?

"Father, I thank you that you have heard the sound of my weeping."

God has heard the unspoken cries of Jesus. Jesus lifts up his eyes, looks into his Father's face, and says, "Father, I thank you that you have heard me. You heard the sound of my weeping."

He Hears

Jesus' prayer at the tomb of Lazarus draws us back to one of those basic elements of prayer. Timothy Jones writes, "at the heart of all our prayers, what we really want is not an answer but an assurance—an assurance that our Father is listening."[2] Even more than God's "I will" in answer to my prayer, I need his "I hear."

Sometimes all I need to know is that I am heard.

And Jesus takes steps to ensure we know this very thing. Notice that he doesn't whisper his gratitude to God. Jesus speaks it loud enough for the rest to overhear: "I knew that you always hear me, but I said this on account of the people standing around, that they may believe that you sent me." This prayer could have remained just between Son and Father. Instead, Jesus brings those nearby into the intimate encounter. He allows us to eavesdrop on gratitude. Why? Because he wants us to know this basic truth: God hears. John Indermark writes that Jesus speaks out loud so "they may hear that God hears."[3]

As I write this chapter a friend of a friend lies dying of breast cancer in Searcy, Arkansas. It's her third meeting with this monster. This time, it's won. I can imagine that there have been times when she or those close to her have prayed, only to feel that heaven's doors were shut, that the Lord was on leave. And for her, and her family and friends, Jesus prays, "Father, I thank you that you have heard me. I knew that you always hear me, but I said this for the sake of my sister in Searcy, that she too may believe that you still hear." Jesus prays aloud so we may hear that God hears.

I know a woman who's been caught in the midst of worship-wars in her church. I spoke to her recently and she said, "I don't feel like God's around anymore. I feel like he's left." These kinds of disappointments make her feel that God just doesn't care and that God can't be reached. But for her, Jesus prays, "Father, I thank you that you have heard me. I knew that you always hear me, but I said this for the sake of this woman wounded by worship-wars, that she too may believe that you hear." Jesus prays aloud so we may hear that God hears.

William White writes of a seminary professor named Hans who is devastated by the death of his wife Enid.[4] Overcome with grief, he stops eating and barricades himself within his home. The seminary president and three friends strive to intervene. Together they pay Hans a visit. Hans confesses to them that he has lost his faith. "I am no longer able to pray to God," he admits. "In fact, I am not certain I believe in God anymore." With great sensitivity, the president responds: "Then we will believe for you. We will pray for you." The four of them begin to meet daily for prayer—the three praying while Hans sits silently. After several months, Hans gratefully shares, "It is no longer necessary for you to pray for me. Today I would like you to pray with me."

This, I believe, is what Jesus does at the tomb of Lazarus. For those of us who struggle to believe God is still there, Jesus believes for us. For those of us who struggle to pray, Jesus prays for us. "Father, I thank you that you have heard me. I knew that you always hear me, but I said this for the sake of my struggling friends, that they too may believe that you hear them."

Sometimes all we need is to know we are heard.

Jesus wants you to know that you are.

Practicing This Prayer

Each day this week bring to mind an issue you believe God has ignored. You feel like he's not engaged in this issue. You wonder if he's even paying attention to this issue. Now picture God speaking to you: "I am listening. I have heard. Nothing you've said or felt about this issue has escaped my notice." Then, give thanks to God, praising him for listening to your plea.

In addition, each day this week intercede for others using this prayer. There are others who feel God is ignoring them or not hearing them. For them, each day this week, pray something like this: "Father, I thank you that you hear them. I know that you always hear them. But help them to know that. Help them to believe what I believe—that you are truly the God who hears."

---

1. Timothy P. Jones, *Praying Like the Jew, Jesus: Recovering the Ancient Roots of New Testament Prayer* (Lederer Books, 2005), 71.

2. Ibid., 73.

3. John Indermark, *Traveling the Prayer Paths of Jesus: a sourcebook for Christian storytellers* (Upper Room Books, 2003), 58.

4. William White, *Stories for the Journey* (Augsburg Publishing House, 1988).

Chapter 7

An Upward Prayer of Confidence:
You Still Reveal (John 12, 17)

His Hour Has Come

About a decade ago I taught a workshop at Abilene Christian University called, "The Church of Oprah." The workshop explored the spiritual influence of the famous talk show host and entertainer Oprah Winfrey. A few years later I wrote a book based on the workshop. Then one day, not long ago, a reporter reached me at my church office. She was writing an article on Oprah and she had read my book. "Could you give me a quote for my article?" she asked. I shared with her some of the material I had previously taught and written on the topic. After fifteen minutes, we hung up. I didn't think of it again—until four months later. That's when I unfolded a *USA Today* and saw an article about Oprah. The article included my quote. I was stunned. I had been referenced in a national newspaper! I immediately drove to a nearby bookstore, purchased five copies of the newspaper, and mailed them to family members.

That evening as I shared the story with a friend, he said, "Well, looks like you finally got your fifteen minutes of fame." "Fifteen minutes of fame" is a phrase that describes a brief time in the spotlight. A few moments of attention. A few seconds out of the shadows. It's usually a pleasant and desirable experience.

Jesus and the Gospel of John use a similar image of time to describe a much different experience. Rather than fifteen minutes, John writes and Jesus speaks about an "hour." But Jesus' hour is more about pain than it is about fame:

> So Jesus proclaimed, as he taught in the temple, "You know me, and you know where I come from? But I have not come of my own accord. He who sent me is true, and him you do not know. I know him, for I come from him, and he sent me." So they were seeking to arrest him, but no one laid a hand on him, because his hour had not yet come (John 7:28-30).

These words he spoke in the treasury, as he taught in the temple; but no one arrested him, because his hour had not yet come (John 8:20).

Now among those who went up to worship at the feast were some Greeks. So these came to Philip, who was from Bethsaida in Galilee, and asked him, "Sir, we wish to see Jesus." Philip went and told Andrew; Andrew and Philip went and told Jesus. And Jesus answered them, "The hour has come for the Son of Man to be glorified" (John 12:20-23).

Now before the Feast of the Passover, when Jesus knew that his hour had come to depart out of this world to the Father, having loved his own who were in the world, he loved them to the end (John 13:1).

We use the phrase "fifteen minutes" to refer to a pleasant and pleasing experience of fame. Jesus uses the image of an hour to refer to a dark and discouraging experience of pain. The "hour" refers to the betrayal, beating, and barbaric crucifixion of Jesus. This will be the most physically, emotionally, and spiritually challenging time Jesus has ever suffered. It will be the point at which he has to choose between walking by faith and walking by sight. Like a date on a wall calendar marked "X" in permanent ink, Jesus can see this hour coming. Like a train charging down the tracks, Jesus knows this hour will hit with ferocity.

Your Hour Has Come

No human has faced or will ever face a similar hour. This is one of the bedrocks of the Christian faith—Jesus embraces what we would not. Jesus endures what we could not. There is no hour like Jesus' hour. It will never come for us in quite the same way as it does for Jesus.

Yet most of us still endure our own kinds of hours. We encounter times of physical, emotional, and spiritual challenge. We are sometimes thrust into intersections at which we have to choose between walking by faith or by sight. In fact this hour of pain will be far more common an experience than fifteen minutes of fame. It may be an instant when doing the right thing comes with a radical cost. It may be a time when a doctor's diagnosis makes our heart beat heavily. It may be a moment when a phone call carries word that a dear one has departed. It may be an occasion when the cycle of life brings challenging changes—the first break up, a new school with no friends, the first lost job, a first child with less sleep and more diapers than you thought possible, the stunning silence on your first day as an empty-nester, or the "what now?" of retirement.

Thankfully, none of us will ever meet an hour like Jesus' hour. But we do often collide with times of difficult decisions, moments when we must either walk on the water or stay in the boat, seconds when life drops us from a peak into a pit.

My in-laws, Ken and Nelda, faced an hour about five years ago. They had purchased a dream retirement home on a Texas lake. Ken had repaired and renovated every square inch of the house and property. It was a perfect place to relax, entertain grandchildren, and blissfully spend the remainder of their days. But then Nelda's health declined. Multiple sclerosis, cancer, and other maladies chopped away at her vigor and vitality. It became clear that they needed help. But the only way to secure that assistance was to sell the dream home and move closer to family. It was as challenging a time as they'd ever faced. Their hour had come.

Our congregation supports an organization called HopeWorks. Unemployed people can come to HopeWorks and gain life skills and job skills. They even get placed in internships which can lead to full-time employment. Virtually every HopeWorks student has faced an hour. They wouldn't need HopeWorks if they hadn't. One student named Polly had encountered a particularly difficult hour. As a youth from East Tennessee, Polly was involved in what she'd only call "a freak accident" involving her daughter. The price was a ninety-nine-year sentence. She was paroled after thirty years. That's when I met her. We spoke together on a panel at a local women's prison. "Your time doesn't have to be hard," she told the women. But you could tell that her time had been just that–hard. "I was involved in all kinds of homosexual relationships and things I shouldn't have been when I was in prison," she confessed. "I thought my life was over. You don't know what it's like to have the shame of a ninety-nine-year sentence on your back." She held the tears back as an inmate handed her some tissue. Polly's hour had come—and gone. But she was still deeply affected by it.

Save Me from This Hour

As Jesus faces his hour, we hear him praying. Twice John records moments when the imminence of Jesus' hour promps Jesus to pray. In John 12, shortly after Jesus proclaims that "the hour has come" (John 12:23), we read Jesus' confession: "Now is my soul troubled. And what shall I say?" (John 12:27). The context that follows reveals that "And what shall I say?" is literally "And what shall I pray?" Jesus' hour has come. His soul is deeply troubled. And he asks: "What shall I pray?" Not long after, we find Jesus in a similar situation, only this time his prayer has already started: "When Jesus had spoken these words, he lifted up his eyes to heaven, and said, 'Father, the hour has come...'" (John 17:1). The hour has come. So Jesus prays to his Father. But what does he pray?

How do we pray when we find ourselves facing that time of testing or that moment of menace? Jesus shows there are two possible ways of praying. The first prayer sounds like this: "Now is my soul troubled. And what shall I say? 'Father, save me from this hour?'" (John 12:27). One way to pray when passing through a painful time is to say, "Save me from this hour." Rescue me. Deliver me. Save me from this hour. Jesus prays something similar to this in the Garden of Gethsemane: "Father, if you are willing, remove this cup from me" (Luke 22:42). This is another way of saying, "Save me from this hour."

And that is a legitimate prayer. Those are permissible words to say when the hour draws near. When doing the right thing is going to demand a high price, it is appropriate to want a divine discount. When a doctor delivers a tough diagnosis, it is expected that we'd ask God for a second opinion. When a phone call brings fearful news, it is OK to beg God for this to be the wrong number. And when slipping into one of life's tough transitions, it is fitting that we'd ask God to keep it from happening.

Save me from this hour. That is one way to pray as the hour approaches.

Glorify Yourself

But there is a second possibility. One that is rarely taken. One demanding deep faith. Yet one that can change everything about our experience in moments of misery. This is the path Jesus takes as he prays about his hour. We hear it first in John 12: "Now is my soul troubled. And what shall I say? 'Father, save me from this hour'? But for this purpose I have come to this hour. Father, glorify your name" (John 12:27-28). Facing his hour, Jesus says, "Father, glorify your name." Jesus repeats this prayer later in John 17: "When Jesus had spoken these words, he lifted up his eyes to heaven, and said, 'Father, the hour has come; glorify your Son that the Son may glorify you'" (John 17:1).

Jesus changes the subject of prayer from his salvation to the Father's glorification. Jesus' prayer is not "Save me from this hour." Instead it is "Glorify your name," and "Glorify your son that the Son may glorify you." Jesus changes the object of prayer from self to God. The prayer is not "May I be saved," but "May you be glorified." Jesus' greatest concern in this prayer is not himself, but his Father. He begs for God to glorify himself through this hour.

But what does this mean? What is the significance of asking for God to be glorified in the midst of a horrendous hour? The word "glorify" is a sibling of the word "glory."[1] Glory crops up early in John's gospel. He introduces the story of Jesus with these words: "We have seen his glory, glory as of the only Son from the Father, full of grace and truth" (John 1:14). John then discloses what this glory is: "No one has ever seen God; the only God, who is at the Father's side, he has made him known" (John 1:18). Jesus' glory is the means by which he reveals God to us.

This God-revealing glory shined brightly through the miracles of Jesus. For example, after Jesus changed water to wine John records, "This, the first of his signs, Jesus did at Cana in Galilee, and manifested his glory" (John 2:11). Regarding the raising of Lazarus, Jesus states, "'This illness does not lead to death. It is for the glory of God,'... 'Did I not tell you that if you believed you would see the glory of God?'" (John 11:4, 40).

Through the miracles, Jesus revealed God. He showed the power and majesty of God. These miracles were like spotlights illuminating God. We see something about God we would not have seen without them.

And Jesus believes that his hour can do something similar. His suffering on the cross can shed light upon God. We will be able to see something about God we would have not seen without this hour. Thus, as Jesus awaits his agony, he prays for God to be glorified. He asks that the darkness of the hour provide the perfect setting for God to be illuminated. Jesus requests that God publicize something about his person through the misery of this moment. Rather than, "Save me so that I will be safe," Jesus prays, "Show yourself so that you will be seen."

Jesus embraces this hour because he knows that others will see God in a way they would not have seen without this hour. Humanity will observe God's love and faithfulness in ways they could not without this hour. This trial will become a viewfinder through which others will more clearly picture the heart of God. Thus rather than run from it, Jesus runs toward it. He prays that in this hour of risk and cost, the light will shine upon God in a way it never has before.

John Ortberg writes about Kathy, Ralph, Doug, and Kim.[2] Kathy has been committed for years to a man who is only half-heartedly committed to her. Everyone else sees what she remains blind to. They tell her to leave him. But she won't. She's frightened of life without him. Ralph ministers in an unhealthy church. The leaders are demanding. The members are divisive. Ralph knows he should speak prophetically into their dysfunction. But he can't. He's too scared of rocking the boat. Doug is addicted to pornography. But he's afraid of confessing it. He's frightened of addressing it. He can't imagine his life without it. And Kim's life revolves around her dad. Everything she does is done to please him. Sadly, nothing pleases him. But the thought of crossing her dad gives Kim a heart attack.

Each is faced with an hour. Each is wrestling with a difficult decision or a time of suffering. We'd understand if they prayed, "Father, save me from this hour." But Jesus challenges them to pray, "Father, glorify yourself." Or in other words, "As I take this risk, as I take this step of faith, as I embrace this suffering, use it to show yourself to others. Use it to reveal yourself to others. Use it to shine a light on the kind of God you are."

There is something about God that people will only see if we faithfully embrace our hour. There is a feature of the Father people will only glimpse if we bear our burden. The darkness of our hour provides the perfect setting for God to illuminate himself. Thus, rather than, "Save me so that I will be safe," we can pray, "Show yourself so that you will be seen." We can embrace our hour because we know that others will see God in a way they would not have seen without this hour.

I was recently in the home of a mother whose child had just been killed in a car accident. The grief was unimaginable. This mother's hour had come like few hours I've ever seen. But in the midst of that hour, the mother did the unbelievable. She said, "Will someone please get me the name of the truck driver who hit Liz? I know he feels terrible. I want to pray for him." That comment became a beacon of light that shattered the shadows. It revealed to us something of the compassion and graciousness of God—because only God could have led a grieving mother to say something like that. I don't know if she had just prayed, "Father glorify your name." But I do know that's exactly what God did. In the darkness, God shined a light upon himself. I saw something about God in a way I would have not seen without this mother's hour.

That's the very best we can hope for. That's the very best we can pray for.

Not "Save me." But "Show yourself." Not "Rescue me." But "Reveal yourself."

Praying This Prayer

You may be facing an hour or two this week. Take some time to make a short list of all the challenges, obstacles, or difficulties waiting for you at school, home, or work this week. Each day this week, pray this prayer over that list: "God reveal yourself through this painful time. Let people see something about you they never would have seen had I never entered this challenging moment."

Perhaps this week finds you free from such hours. If so, spend time each day this week praying this prayer on behalf of others. Make a short list of people whom you know are facing an hour: a disease, a death in the family, job instability, family concerns, emotional difficulties, or health issues. Each day pray this week for them: "God reveal yourself through their painful time. Let people see something about you they never would have seen had these never entered this challenging moment."

---

1. R. B. Zuck, *A Biblical Theology of the New Testament* (Moody, 1994), 194.
2. John Ortberg, *If You Want to Walk on Water, You've Got to Get Out of the Boat* (Zondervan Publishing House, 2001), 17-18.

Chapter 8

An Upward Prayer of Confidence:
You Still Matter (Matthew 26)

When God Says No

An uncle e-mailed me a few days after his young niece had died in a car accident. The niece was a godly girl raised in a God-fearing home. Her mother and father are spiritual giants in our congregation—people of prayer and of great faith. An hour or so before her death, the niece and her mother had prayed together for traveling mercies as the girl left Memphis for Nashville. But she never made it to Nashville. The uncle e-mailed me asking, "We pray for our children and their safety. And then something like this happens. Why?"

Why did God say no to these prayers for safety?

A man I know has a father who has endured chronic health issues for decades. The son and his family have prayed continuously for the father's healing. Recently, the father suffered another setback. "I'm praying for your Dad," I told the son. The son said, "Thanks. But you know how I feel about prayer. We've prayed for years for Dad, and God hasn't done a thing in response to all those prayers."

Why did God say no to these prayers for healing?

Several years ago *Newsweek* magazine ran a cover story on prayer. The article included many inspiring stories. Each recounted astonishing answers to prayer. A week later the editor received this letter from a reader: "I could hardly believe it—devoting eight pages plus the cover to such drivel in a news magazine! Life is a crap shoot—some people luck out and some don't.... There is no evidence of any kind that prayer has any effect whatsoever on the outcome." Sometimes we hear no to our prayers so often that we might arrive at the same conclusion as this irate reader: there is no evidence of any kind that prayer has any effect whatsoever on the outcome.

When God Said No

Our struggle with divine no's is not unique. We may be tempted to view

Scripture as a record of those rare and remarkable people who heard yes from God every time they asked. But that's not true. The Bible actually chronicles prominent person after person hearing no from God.

At the sunset of Moses' life, after what must have seemed an eternity of leading a rebellious people, Moses prays. What he desires most deeply is to arrive at the final destination of this forty-year journey. He asks God to let him live long enough to get to the Promised Land. But God says no: "Enough from you; do not speak to me of this matter again. Go up to the top of Pisgah and lift up your eyes westward and northward and southward and eastward, and look at it with your eyes, for you shall not go over this Jordan" (Deuteronomy 3:26-27).

David dreams of constructing a temple for God. His passion is to provide a perfect place for God. But God says no: "Hear me, my brothers and my people. I had it in my heart to build a house of rest for the ark of the covenant of the LORD and for the footstool of our God, and I made preparations for building. But God said to me, 'You may not build a house for my name, for you are a man of war and have shed blood'" (1 Chronicles 28:1-3).

Elijah's is as mystical and magnificent a ministry as there ever will be. It climaxes that day on Mount Carmel when Elijah faces hundreds of Jezebel's prophets in a prayer showdown. The first group to get their god to answer yes to a plea for fire from heaven prevails. Despite dances and desperation, Jezebel's prophets can't even win a whisper from their gods. But when Elijah prays, God sends fire so furious it persuades all present that Elijah's God is the true God. Days later a spiteful Jezebel puts a price on Elijah's head. She marshals her vast resources to bring an end to this troublesome sage. In response, Elijah prays. He prays for God to provide an immediate and permanent way out. But God says no: "'It is enough; now, O LORD, take away my life, for I am no better than my fathers.' And he lay down and slept under a broom tree. And behold, an angel touched him and said to him, 'Arise and eat'" (1 Kings 19:4-5).

One particularly very-bad-no-good-day, a massive fish has Jonah for lunch. Unbelievably, Jonah survives and prays from the bowels of the beast. He pleads for God to save him. And God answers with a yes. The nauseous fish lurches to shore and heaves until Jonah is ejected. Not long afterwards, someone else is in danger of dying. Now it's the people of Nineveh. God's about to swallow them up for their immorality and idolatry. In desperation, they pray. They plead for God to save them. And God answers with a yes. But Jonah can't stand it. Nineveh is the city everyone loves to hate. They deserve destruction not deliverance. So Jonah prays one more time. He doesn't plead for God to save his life. He begs God to end his life. But God says no: "'Therefore now, O LORD, please take my life from me, for it is better for me to die than to live.' And the LORD said, 'Do you do well to be angry?'" (Jonah 4:3-4).

Finally, Paul receives a divine no to a particularly thorny problem in his life: "Three times I pleaded with the Lord about this, that it should leave me. But he said to me, 'My grace is sufficient for you, for my power is made perfect in weakness'" (2 Corinthians 12:8-9). Not only have you probably heard a heavenly no, Scripture abounds with key characters struggling with the same answer.

When He Heard No

Even Jesus is denied. And on more than one occasion. At least three times we hear the Son fail to receive the answer he desires from the Father.

Prayer #1: "I do not ask for these only, but also for those who will believe in me through their word, that they may all be one, just as you, Father, are in me, and I in you, that they also may be in us, so that the world may believe that you have sent me" (John 17:20-21). There is no greater unity than that between Father and Son. The two are one. Here, Jesus prays for that same unity to be granted to "those who will believe in me through their word." That's you, me, and all who have believed in Jesus in the last two thousand years. Jesus prays that we "may all be one." Yet, the answer to this prayer appears to be on "pause." At times, there is no greater disagreement than that between Christian and Christian, or church and church. Though intended for accord, we often display discord. This is a prayer still begging for a yes.

Prayer #2: "Simon, Simon, behold, Satan demanded to have you, that he might sift you like wheat, but I have prayed for you that your faith may not fail" (Luke 22:31-32). Immediately prior to his arrest, Jesus shares that he's been in prayer for Peter. Jesus has been on his knees pleading with God to keep Peter faithful. Yet moments later, Jesus' prayer falls as flat on its face as Peter's faith: "Then they seized him and led him away, bringing him into the high priest's house, and Peter was following at a distance. And when they had kindled a fire in the middle of the courtyard and sat down together, Peter sat down among them. Then a servant girl, seeing him as he sat in the light and looking closely at him, said, 'This man also was with him.' But he denied it, saying, 'Woman, I do not know him'" (Luke 22:54-57). Jesus requests divine strength for Peter, yet Peter remains weak.

Prayer #3: "And going a little farther he fell on his face and prayed, saying, 'My Father, if it be possible, let this cup pass from me; nevertheless, not as I will, but as you will'.... Again, for the second time, he went away and prayed, 'My Father, if this cannot pass unless I drink it, your will be done'.... So, leaving them again, he went away and prayed for the third time, saying the same words again" (Matthew 26:39, 42, 44). Jesus prays, "Let this cup pass." Jesus begs God to modify the plan, to call an audible, to stop what is about to start. Jesus asks God to manufacture an alternative to the cross. And God says no. Within hours Jesus hangs dead on that very cross. Even Jesus faced the no from above.

Two Extremes Regarding No

But there is something unique about Jesus' last prayer—the let-the-cup-pass prayer. While transparently confessing his wish ("let this cup pass"), Jesus is also humbly surrendering to God's will ("not as I will, but as you will"). These two extremes, and Jesus' unique way of blending them in Gethsemane, can enable us to deal properly with those times when God says no.

The Gethsemane prayer balances two extremes: I seek my wish and I seek your will. Each taken by itself leads to a prayer-perspective that is ineffective. Brought together, the two outlooks empower us to deal appropriately with God's no's.

One extreme is this: I seek my wish. Jesus indeed seeks his wish. He boldly prays, "Let this cup pass." His heartfelt wish is for the cup to pass. But his prayer-life does not exist solely at this edge. Another extreme is added to his prayer. Another perspective modifies this perspective.

However, too often our prayers perch only on this end of the continuum. Too frequently, this is the only ingredient in our petitions. Our sole focus becomes this: I seek my wish. What matters most to us is our need. Prayer is generally about getting God to grant our wish.

Philip Yancey writes about a Japanese friend who visited him in the United States.[1] The friend told Yancey that he was shocked by the directness of our prayers. The American who prays, he told Yancey, "resembles a person who goes to Burger King and orders a 'Whopper well-done, but hold the pickle and lettuce—with extra ketchup, please.'" By contrast, the friend told Yancey, the Japanese are "more like the tourist who walks into a foreign restaurant unable to read the menu. He finally communicates, with gestures and reference to a phrase book, that he would like the house specialty." In other words, he cannot ask for what he really wants so he just tells the host to bring what he thinks is best.

There is something direct about our prayers in America. Directness isn't always wrong. It can be appropriate when paired with the opposite perspective illustrated in the Gethsemane prayer. But our directness often results from the fact that our prayers have one exclusive focus: I seek my wish. Too often prayer is about me getting exactly what I want in exactly the way I want it.

Not only is this outlook inappropriate, it is ineffective. When God says no we are devastated. When prayer is only me seeking my wish, a wish denied leads to discouragement with prayer and disillusionment with God. If our heart is devoted only to our wish, when God says no our heart gets broken. This type of prayer is unable to cope with the reality of prayers answered in the negative.

Thankfully, Jesus' prayer in Gethsemane displays a second extreme. Jesus does seek his wish. But he also seeks God's will. He prays, "Let this cup pass." But he also prays, "Your will be done." For Jesus prayer is not merely I seek my wish. It is also I seek your will.

But for some of us, prayer can move too far in this other direction. Surrender becomes the only ingredient in our petitions. We cease confessing our wishes and only seek God's will. Here, we are more like the Japanese person praying in Yancey's story. We don't ask for the dish we truly desire. Instead we just ask God to bring whatever serving he believes superior.

A woman once shared her prayer perspective with me. "I've just stopped praying about things like the physical healing of family members, or things I need at work. I no longer even ask God for things like the repairing of a friend's marriage. Because I know God has a will for all of those things. And I think God's going to do his will whether or not I pray about them. So I just entrust all of those things to him rather than bothering him with what I want." She stopped asking for what she wants. Instead, she just asked for what God willed.

Just as with the first extreme, there is something inappropriate and ineffective about this extreme when it is practiced in isolation. Several days ago I was studying in my office. I overheard some of my co-workers outside my closed door talking about going out for lunch. Then I watched them through my window get into a car and drive off together. They hadn't even asked if I wanted to go out to lunch with them. It's not that they didn't want me with them. It's that they knew what my answer would be if they asked. Based on my routine, they knew I was busy studying and would turn down an invitation to interrupt the study. They knew my will and thus didn't bother to ask. But my feelings were a little hurt. I would have liked the opportunity to say no. Why? Because that situation had to do with more than just lunch. It had to do with our relationship. I want to be a part of the lives of those with whom I work. I want connection with them. That day, I felt disconnected.

Perhaps this is similar to what God experiences when our prayers dwell at the extreme of "I seek your will." If we reach a point where we rarely request intervention because we think we already know God's will, we are forgetting the relational aspect of prayer. We may believe that God's going to say no to our appeal. And he may. But God would like the chance to say no. He wants that connection. He desires a bond. For God, prayer is never just about a request. It's always about a relationship.

Neither of these two extremes deals effectively with unanswered prayers. The first—"I seek my wish"—can't handle it when God says no. The second—"I seek your will"—doesn't even give God a chance to say no.

The Middle Ground

There is a third way. It is the way illustrated by Jesus in his Gethsemane prayer: "And going a little farther he fell on his face and prayed, saying, 'My Father, if it be possible, let this cup pass from me; nevertheless, not as I will, but as you will'.... Again, for the second time, he went away and prayed, 'My Father, if this cannot pass unless I drink it, your will be done'.... So, leaving them again, he went away and prayed for the third time, saying the same words again'" (Matthew 26:39, 42, 44).

In this painful prayer Jesus brings the two extremes together. Neither stands alone. Both are vital. On the one hand, Jesus seeks his wish: "let this cup pass from me." But Jesus also seeks God's will: "nevertheless, not as I will, but as you will." For Jesus, prayer is not either "I seek my wish" or "I seek your will." It is both. Jesus finds a way of praying which permits him to ask for exactly what he wants yet also enables him to honestly leave the final decision up to God. This third way is the only way to come to terms with God's no.

Because God is fundamentally relational, God wants to hear our prayers. He wants us to ask for what we wish. Sometimes God will respond to those requests positively. At other times he will respond negatively. But he wants us to ask for what we wish.

This freedom, however, comes with a price. The price is the no which may come our way after opening up and sharing our heart's desire. That's why the other extreme of prayer is essential. When we not only seek our wish but God's will, we place ourselves in a safer position to handle the no. When our prayers are focused on both our wish and God's will, we are ready to rejoice at the yes answers and ready to receive humbly the no answers. Jesus models the best way to deal with God's no.

When We Say Yes

Ultimately, the Gethsemane prayer is about learning to say yes to God. Even though God may occasionally say no to us, prayer is always an opportunity for us to say yes to God. Every time we combine "I seek your will" and "I seek my wish," we are telling God that he matters more to us than anything else. We are communicating to him that our answer to him will always be yes regardless of his answer to us.

This outlook empowers us to handle a "no." But more importantly, it enables us to walk more fully in the way of Christ. My colleague Chris Seidman says, "Jesus died at Gethsemane before He died at Golgatha." What enables Jesus to embrace the world-changing but life-ending cross is the fact that in his Gethsemane prayer Jesus says yes to God. Jesus shares what he wants, but he also commits to what God wants. Eugene Peterson writes that before the agony of the cross, Jesus experiences the agony of prayer. Both agonies are the same.[2] Because Jesus says yes in Gethsemane, he is able to say yes at Golgatha. And because he dies first in prayer, he is able to die later on the cross.

John Indermark suggests that the prayer in Gethsemane moves from "tension" to "trust."[3] I think these two words are helpful. Because Jesus is willing to boldly state what he wants, there is initially tension as he wrestles with God over the cup he must drink. Such tension is the inevitable part of a healthy prayer life. The absence of any tension in our prayers should be a warning that perhaps we are not as transparent and honest with God in prayer as we ought to be.

But the tension soon gives way to trust. Jesus trusts that the Father's way is the best way. Jesus trusts that God's will matters more than his own wish. This trust empowers him to surrender at Gethsemane and ultimately at Golgatha.

In one prayer, Jesus says things we often won't say because we fear offending the Father ("Let this cup pass from me'…"). He also says things we often can't say because we fear surrendering to the Father ("Nevertheless, your will be done…"). Our spirit longs for us to submit our will to God's, but the flesh is so often weak. Our flesh longs for us to be honest and transparent with God, but the spirit so often refuses. In this one prayer, Jesus brings it all together. He teaches us a better way. If we hope to one day surrender to a world-shaping and life-changing opportunity from God, we will first need to learn to surrender in every prayer we lift to God.

Let this cup pass. Your will be done.

Praying This Prayer

Each day this week bring to your mind a discouraging circumstance in your life or in the life of someone you care about. For a few moments, pray nothing but "Let this cup pass...Let this cup pass...Let this cup pass...." After some silence, begin praying again. This time, however, pray nothing but "Nevertheless, your will be done...Nevertheless, your will be done...Nevertheless, your will be done."

---

1. Philip Yancey, *Prayer: Does It Make Any Difference?* (Zondervan, 2010), 107.
2. Eugene H. Peterson, *Tell It Slant: A Conversation on the Language of Jesus In His Stories and Prayers* (Eerdmans, 2008), 231.
3. John Indermark, *Traveling the Prayer Paths of Jesus* (Upper Room Books, 2003), 128.

Chapter 9

An Upward Prayer of Confidence:
You Still Hold (Luke 23)

Out of Our Hands

While growing up in New Mexico, my brother and I skied regularly with our dad. Each winter we'd drive a couple of hours to Sierra Blanca and ride the gondola nearly to the top of the twelve-thousand-foot mountain. Even on clear and sunny days, temperatures at that elevation were cold. On cloudy and snowy days, they were bone-chilling. After the initial ascent in the gondola, most of our other uphill transportation during the day consisted of a series of chairlifts. Sometimes we'd be on a chairlift in freezing temperatures and steady wind for fifteen minutes. We often used that time to replenish ourselves with some peanut butter and crackers or energy bars which we kept in a small backpack. In order to unzip the backpack, pull out the food, and tear away the packaging, one of us had to take our gloves off. They were so stuffed with insulation that no one could perform a task requiring fine motor skills while wearing them. Usually, my dad would say, "Let me hold your gloves while you get the food." I would place my gloves in his outstretched hands making sure he had a firm grip on them before I released them. If he dropped them, my skiing day was done. Without the gloves, my fingers would get frostbite. I'd have to spend the rest of the day alone in the lodge at the base of the ski area while my dad and my brother enjoyed the slopes. But in all those years, my dad never dropped my gloves. We performed this chairlift ritual hundreds of times. But he never dropped my gloves. Each time, having unzipped the backpack, pulled out the food, and opened the packaging, I'd find my gloves firmly in his grasp. Relieved, I'd pull them back on and we'd eat together in silence, taking in the grandeur of the mountain before us.

What started as a seemingly insignificant ski-day custom has given way to a very significant daily necessity. Every six months I place the care of my teeth in the hands of my dentist. Every two weeks I place my paycheck in the hands of my local bank teller. Each morning I place my children in the hands of teachers at school. Life is filled with the necessity of placing what is precious into the palms of others.

And some things are harder to let go of than others. I recall the first time Kendra and I handed over our first child, Jordan, to baby-sitters. She was a one-year-old and we hadn't left her side since her birth. So, it was time for a date—our first in Jordan's lifetime. Yet despite our need for couple time and the fact that the baby-sitters were her own grandparents, they had to pry Jordan out of our hands when we dropped her off at their home. The whole time Kendra and I were gone (only about sixty minutes) we were worried: "What if...?" "Did we tell them...?" "I wonder if they will remember..." "You don't think they'll...?"

That's the real challenge isn't it? You simply cannot live without regularly putting valued things into the hands of others. But what we place in those hands we often want immediately returned. We cannot personally accomplish every project requiring attention at the workplace. So we delegate to co-workers. But sometimes we pull those projects right back because we want to make sure they are completed correctly. We hire a neighborhood kid to watch the family dog while we're on vacation. But we end up sick with worry, wondering if the kid will actually feed the dog and keep the back gate closed. We wind up thinking we should have just brought the dog with us. Life necessitates our handing things over. But we regularly want them handed back to us.

We all know this is a trust issue. Specifically, it's a trust issue regarding competency and character. Can I trust the competency of the one whose hands now hold my treasures? Are those hands strong enough? Are they skilled enough? Can those hands do any better than mine? Competency was the primary matter in our minds when we turned our son Jacob over to doctors for his tonsillectomy. We'd never had a child undergo a significant medical procedure. What we needed to know without any doubt was the competency of the hands that wheeled him away and cut into his throat. It was only when we were convinced that these doctor's skills were superior that we were able to let Jacob go with some amount of peace.

We worry about competency. We also wonder about character. Can I trust the character of the one whose hands now hold the things most precious to me? Maybe they have strong muscles and fine skills. But do they also have strong ethics and fine morals? With speculative investing, ponzi schemes, and corruption in some levels of the financial markets, I sometimes worry about all the hands my retirement investments pass through on their way (hopefully) to higher yields. Can I trust those hands?

The Competency of God's Hands

Unfortunately, we have the same trust issues when we pray. They are the very issues Jesus addresses in one of his prayers from the cross: "It was now about the sixth hour, and there was darkness over the whole land until the ninth hour, while the sun's light failed. And the curtain of the temple was torn in two. Then Jesus, calling out with a loud voice, said, 'Father, into your hands I commit my spirit!' And having said this he breathed his last" (Luke 23:44-46).

Jesus is exposed. Physically, of course, he is displayed on a cross wearing nothing but an undergarment, but also emotionally, spiritually, and psychologically Jesus is exposed. People curse him. People mock him. Almost everyone he once counted on has deserted him. And from all appearances, it would seem that even God has proven himself unworthy of Jesus' trust. Despite this, Jesus prays a prayer of childlike faith. It's similar to the familiar prayer of childhood: "Now I lay me down to sleep, I pray the Lord my soul to keep; If I should die before I wake, I pray the Lord my soul to take."[1] Though faith has every reason to be absent, in this petition it is present. Jesus prays a prayer of tremendous trust.

The trust is rooted in Jesus' deep and intimate knowledge of the competency and character of God's hands. First, the prayer focuses on competency: "into your hands I commit my spirit!" In the Bible the human hand is an expression of power and control. When Israel triumphed over an enemy, we are told that God gave Israel's enemy "into their hands." And when Israel lost to an enemy, we are told that Israel fell into the "hands" of that enemy (Judges 11:21; 13:5). This expression reveals how humanity leverages their strength and might, and how humanity is given the ability to shape another's destiny. The human hand is the symbol of power and control.

The same is true regarding God's hands. When the Philistines capture the ark and then suffer discipline from God, the writer says that the "hand of God was very heavy there" (1 Samuel 5:11). When people are delivered or protected in the Bible, is it by the hand of God. God brought the Israelites out of Egypt with a "with great power and with a mighty hand" (Exodus 32:11). When Moses retells the exodus story, he speaks repeatedly of God's "mighty hand" (Deuteronomy 3:24; 4:34; 5:15; 7:19; 9:26; 11:2). Joshua looks back on the exodus and says that God rescued Israel so that "all the peoples of the earth may know that the hand of the LORD is mighty" (Joshua 4:24). In the Bible, the hands of God are synonymous with the greatness and might of God.

Jesus has witnessed God's hands for an eternity past. He knows beyond any doubt that these hands are the most skilled and most powerful hands that exist. He knows these hands are greater than the hands which placed him on the cross. He believes these hands are superior to the nails which pierced his hands. Jesus trusts completely in the competency of God's hands.

Rusty and Stephanie are friends of mine. Rusty's construction company built our church building. During one Thanksgiving week, Rusty's ten-year-old son, Lee, suffered an unusual migraine. The boy has wrestled with migraines for years, but they've been managed through medication. This one, however, would not subside. It was worse than any they'd ever seen. Thankfully, they were able to take Lee to LeBonheur Children's Hospital in Memphis, a preeminent teaching hospital and a leader in pediatric care. LeBonheur's neuroscience unit has gained national attention for the treatment of childhood brain tumors. Literally, Lee could not be in better hands. At one of the finest children's hospitals, some of the finest specialists were able to diagnose the problem and perform brain surgery on Lee—a move, as it turned out, that saved his life. As difficult as the situation was, Rusty and Stephanie could trust in the skill of those human hands. They could trust there were no more competent human hands than the ones caring for Lee.

Jesus believes the same about God. There are no more competent, mighty, and powerful hands than God's hands.

The Character of Father's Hands

But Jesus not only points to the competence of God's hands in his prayer, he also points to the character of those hands. His prayer comes from Psalm 31. But Jesus adds a word to this ancient prayer. He adds the word "Father."[2] In the original, David prays, "Into your hands I commit my spirit" (Psalm 31:5). In Jesus' version we hear this important addition, "Father, into your hands I commit my spirit!" Jesus envisions not merely the grand hands of God or the controlling hands of the Creator. Jesus envisions the loving, caring, and adoring hands of the Father. These are the hands that have applauded, hugged, and held Jesus. Jesus knows the character of these hands as only the Son can know the hands of the Father.

Scripture not only speaks of God's hands as mighty and magnificent. It also speaks of God's hands as caring and compassionate. The psalmist appeals to this character when he cries out: "Arise, O LORD; O God, lift up your hand; forget not the afflicted" (Psalm 10:12). This is not a prayer about God's might. It's a prayer about mercy. The psalmist sees God's hands as the source of help and kindness for the afflicted.

Later, the psalmist praises God's hands for a similar reason: "For he is our God, and we are the people of his pasture, and the sheep of his hand" (Psalm 95:7). God's hands are the hands of a shepherd. They are not the hands of a hunter. Both the hands of a hunter and the hands of a shepherd are strong and skilled. But when it comes to the sheep, the hunter's hands lead to slaughter while the shepherd's hands lead to safety. God's hands are the hands of a shepherd: kind and compassionate, a safeguard.

Each year as Israelites traveled to Jerusalem for festivals, they celebrated God's caring hands. In one of their Songs of Ascents they remembered, "Behold, as the eyes of servants look to the hand of their master, as the eyes of a maidservant to the hand of her mistress, so our eyes look to the LORD our God, till he has mercy upon us" (Psalm 123:2). The hands of the master and the mistress were not merely competent—they were compassionate. The male servant looked to the master's hand for sustenance and kindness, as the female servant looked to the mistress' hand for mercy and compassion. The Israelites used these images to describe the way that they looked to God's hands. The Israelites not only trusted in the ability of God's hands. They trusted also in their integrity. God's hands would always bring mercy to his people.

It's not hard to imagine that Jesus has these images in mind when he prays his prayer. After all, his prayer is a quote from the Psalms. Jesus knows how the psalmists celebrate the kindness and mercy of the hands of God. Thus he does the same on the cross.

My friend Brishan and his family recently travelled out of town to see his extended family. They couldn't bring their dog, a young puppy the kids adore. As a result, they had to find someone to watch the dog. Finally, they connected with Michael and Jesslyn—two enthusiastic dog lovers. Brishan dropped his dog off at their house and then left town. Upon returning, he discovered that Michael and Jesslyn had so nurtured and cared for his dog that for a week his dog was in mourning. Brishan's dog moped around just longing to go back to Michael and Jesslyn's house. Their hands had been so caring that they made a lasting impression on the dog. And Brishan now knows exactly who to ask for dog care the next time he leaves town.

When it comes to those things that are special to us, what we most need are caring hands. We want hands of a person with integrity and compassion. We need hands of mercy and power. That's exactly what Jesus had in his Father. The character of those hands enabled Jesus to surrender himself to them.

Our Spirit

And because of this trust, rooted in his conviction about the competency and character of God's hands, Jesus is able to place something priceless in those hands. Jesus prays, ""Father, into your hands I commit my spirit!" The word "spirit" refers to the innermost part of Jesus. Spirit here is the critical energy by which the body is animated.[3] This is Jesus' core. This is the most fragile and vulnerable piece of himself. This is the battery which fuels the rest of the machine. Jesus entrusts into God's hands not just something important or someone important. Jesus entrusts his spirit—the most fundamental part of himself.

When we genuinely understand the competency and character of God's hands, we are able to entrust those hands with what is most important. Not just the superficial. Not just the merely significant. But those matters around which our life revolves, those matters we live and die for, those matters which give meaning and purpose to our existence.

Timothy Jones, author of *Prayers Jesus Prayed*, proposes that the original prayer from Psalm 31 was spoken by the priest at the temple as the invocation for the evening sacrifice.[4] Here, Jesus uses it as an invocation for his own sacrifice. He offers to God that which is most valuable and he places it in the hands of God. Just as the priest would lift the slaughtered animal to God saying, "Into your hands I commit this offering," so now Jesus lifts himself to God saying, "Into your hands I commit my spirit." Because of his trust in the Father, Jesus can lay not just an offering, but himself in those hands.

Greg Gilbert writes about trying to teach his one-year-old son to swim.[5] His son didn't even like getting his face wet in the bathtub. There seemed to be no way he was going to jump into a swimming pool at the coaxing of his father. Still, Greg set him on the side of the pool, stepped into the water a few inches away, and invited, "Come on, jump!" His son looked at him as if his father was crazy. He frowned and said, "No. I go see Mommy." Greg chased him down, set him on the side of the pool again, and urged, "Come on, jump!" This time he added, "I'm right here. I'll catch you. I promise!" With a skeptical look in his eye, the son did a little wind up and then jumped. As he promised, Greg caught him. That experience made a convert out of his son. His son squealed, "Doot 'gain, Daddy! Doot 'gain!" And for half an hour, the son jumped and Dad caught—over and over.

Later, Greg's wife worried that their son was a little too enthusiastic. What if he jumped into the pool when Greg wasn't there to catch him? But over the next few days, they watched their son. Not once did he even consider leaping into the water—unless Greg was standing in front of him to catch him. Greg wrote this: "You see, despite all his apparent successes, my son's trust was never in his own ability to handle the water. It was in his father, and in his father's promise: 'Come on kiddo. Jump. I promise I'll catch you.'"

That is the same promise Jesus hears. Standing nearby, the Father urges Jesus: "Jump! I promise I'll catch you." Jesus knows the promise is true. Jesus knows those hands. There are no stronger hands. There are no more caring hands. So through prayer, Jesus jumps.

Henri Nouwen writes of attending a circus performance in Germany.[6] He particularly enjoyed the trapeze artists called the Flying Rodleighs. After the performance, Nouwen asked the leader of the troop about their craft. Rodleigh said, "As a flyer, I must have complete trust in my catcher. The public might think I am the star, but the real star is my catcher.... The secret is that the flyer does nothing and the catcher does everything. When I fly I have simply to stretch out my arms and hands and wait for him to catch me. The worst thing I can do is to try to catch the catcher. A flyer must fly and a catcher must catch and the flyer must trust, with outstretched arms, that the catcher will be there for him."

Jesus has complete trust in his catcher. Through prayer Jesus stretches out his arms and flies. He knows the Father will catch him. There is no doubt in his mind.

Sometimes there is nothing we can do but trust that those hands still hold. We may not be able to change a thing about our situation. We may have no control over the source of our suffering. We may not be able to pause the pain. But one thing we can do: fall into the Father's hands. We can entrust what is most valuable and most endangered into his hands.

When the brain surgery was completed for ten-year-old Lee, I visited his parents in the hospital. His mom said, "All through this ordeal, I've been trying to just place Lee in God's hands. It's been hard. I'll put him there in prayer, but then I'll walk away and take him right back. I just can't help it. But I think God finally got through to me. I've finally been able to just leave Lee there. I know without a doubt that all of this is out of my hands. There's nothing I can really do. So I'm finally just leaving it all in God's hands."

There comes a moment when we are finally able to trust our catcher. We realize that there's nothing we can really do. So we just stretch out our arms, offer what is most precious to us, and let God do what he does best: catch and hold.

Praying This Prayer

Jesus' prayer is a powerful one to utilize on those occasions when something precious seems endangered. Consider your life this week. Is something threatened—a dream?—a plan?—a relationship?—a desire?—an important person? Every day this week picture that endangered person or possession in your mind and then pray: "Father, into your hands, I commit my _____."

This prayer is also beneficial for praying over all the things which are important to us—whether or not they seem endangered. Prayed daily, this petition becomes a habitual way of surrendering everything and every person in our lives to God. Make a list of the most important people in your life, the most important possessions in your life, and the most important plans you have for life. Each day this week, one by one, day by day, pray: "Father, into your hands, I commit _____."

---

1. Eugene Peterson, *Tell it Slant : a Conversation on the Language of Jesus in His Stories and Prayers.*" (William B. Eerdmans Publishing Co., 2008), 251-253.
2. David Neff "'Father, Into Your Hands I Commit My Spirit': Jesus' important addition to David's cry" *Christianity Today.*
3. Strong, J. *The exhaustive concordance of the Bible : Showing every word of the text of the common English version of the canonical books, and every occurrence of each word in regular order.* Ontario (Woodside Bible Fellowship).
4. Timothy P. Jones, *Prayers Jesus Prayed: Experiencing the Father through the Prayers of His Son* (Vine Books, 2002), 151.
5. Greg Gilbert, *What Is the Gospel?* (Crossway, 2010), 71-72.
6. Henri J. Nouwen, *Our Greatest Gift: a meditation on dying and caring* (Harper San Francisco, 1994), 66-67.

Chapter 10

An Upward Prayer of Confidence:
You Still Stop (John 19:30)

Finally Finished

Though it occurred over two decades ago, my high school graduation ceremony is still a vivid and cherished memory. In our robes, six of us gathered in the school cafeteria to be photographed together. All six had journeyed from kindergarten through twelfth grade together. With eyes still blinded from camera flashes, we then marched slowly and solemnly into our school gym with the other seniors. I listened to the valedictorian give her speech and silently "booed" her because her GPA had beaten mine by one-tenth of a grade point. I gave my speech as salutatorian and watched my parents cry with joy as I spoke. We strode across the stage and shook the hand of Mr. Lane, our superintendent. Finally, twenty-six graduation caps were launched into the air in a symbolic gesture of victory.

There had been some challenging days during high school. The afternoon we buried Mrs. Cox, a much-loved teacher who died of cancer. The day we learned a fellow student had perished in a car accident. The night I was transported by ambulance to a hospital after a nasty hit during a football game. Sometimes it seemed high school would last forever. But no matter how hard or challenging, I knew that one day graduation day would arrive. Finally it was over!

When I think back to that day, I struggle to find one word that captures the rich experience. But I recently stumbled upon a Greek word that fits the need nicely. The word is "tetelestai." It means "It is finished" or simply "Finished." It's the perfect word for using when tossing a graduation cap into the air. Tetelestai! It is finished!

This is, I think, a word many mothers might stuff into the bag they keep ready for that moment when the water breaks and they rush to the hospital. Whether this is her first or fifth baby, that moment is the end of months of waiting. Months of anticipation. Months of endless questions: How much longer? How are you feeling? How far along are you? Is it a boy or a girl? Although there are joys which often accompany pregnancy, there are also challenges. Swollen feet. Worry over the baby's health. The backaches. Fluctuating hormones. Waddling like a duck. Heartburn. Leg cramps. Morning sickness. Stretch marks. False labor. But no matter how hard or challenging, mothers know that one day birth-day will arrive. And I can see why a mother might, as a doctor hands her the newborn, whisper gratefully, tetelestai. It is finished. Sometimes (I'm told) it seems like pregnancy will last forever. But finally that day comes. Finally it is finished. Tetelestai.

This is an appropriate word for any difficult time in life. A few years ago a friend of mine named Sally spoke at a fundraiser for a charitable organization. Sally was undergoing treatment for breast cancer. Dozens of us were following her progress. It was a tense time of praying and waiting. As she took the stage at that morning's fundraiser, Sally beamed and said that she had just completed her last chemo treatment. She said, "I'm finished." We stood and clapped. Had Sally spoken Greek that morning, she might have said, Tetelestai. It is finished. Sometimes a treatment regimen can feel like forever. But finally that day comes. Finally it's finished.

I can picture the slaves who passed through the Underground Railroad uttering this word of relief. In Memphis, the stop on the Underground Railroad was Slave Haven. Slaves found rest and refreshment as they travelled north to freedom. Imagine what it must have been like when, after respite at Slave Haven and similar stops, continuing northward, they finally got freedom. Can you hear them shouting, crying: Tetelestai! It is finished. The oppression and injustice must have felt as though it would last forever. But for those escaping by the Underground Railroad, that day had come. Finally it was finished.

This word certainly could have been in the mouths of some ancient slaves. For hundreds of years Egyptians had enslaved the Hebrew people. The Egyptians worked the Hebrews "ruthlessly" and made the lives of the Hebrews "bitter with hard service" (Exodus 1:13-14). The Israelites, we are told, "groaned because of their slavery…" (Exodus 2:23). Finally, God stepped in. He turned the water to blood, made frogs appear, sent swarms of gnats, then flies, caused a plague to fall on the Egyptian livestock, made festering boils appear on the Egyptians and their animals, rained down hail, brought in ravenous locusts, and caused darkness to fall. Each plague was a step closer to freedom. Then the last plague arrived, and with it, deliverance. To protect themselves from this final curse, God commanded the Hebrew slaves to slaughter a lamb, dip a makeshift brush of hyssop into the blood, then paint the blood on the doorframe of their house. They were to eat the lamb, along with bitter herbs and bread made without yeast with their belts fastened, sandals on their feet, and staffs in hand—ready for liberation. This would become an annual rite, a yearly celebration called Passover, marking the moment when God passed over the houses of the Hebrew slaves. After that first Passover meal, Pharaoh summoned Moses and begged him to take his people and go. The enslavement was over. I can imagine those Hebrew slaves, having slaughtered the Passover lamb and painted its blood on their doorposts, and having been told by Pharaoh to go, now shouting Tetelestai! It is finished.

Finished on the Cross

In John's account of Good Friday, the day of Jesus' death, this Greek word is the last word on Jesus' lips. Throughout Passion Week, we've welcomed Jesus into Jerusalem as the long-awaited king (Monday), watched him fight for the temple to be a sacred place of prayer (Tuesday), witnessed him being anointed extravagantly (Wednesday), and listened to him call us to be a foot-washing community (Thursday).

Today, Friday, Jesus is on the cross: "After this, Jesus, knowing that all was now finished, said (to fulfill the Scripture), 'I thirst.' A jar full of sour wine stood there, so they put a sponge full of the sour wine on a hyssop branch and held it to his mouth. When Jesus had received the sour wine, he said, 'It is finished,' and he bowed his head and gave up his spirit" (John 19:28-30). Three times John uses a form of the word "tetelestai": twice in vs. 28 (translated once as "fulfilled") and once in vs. 30. John literally writes that Jesus knew everything was "finished"; and so that Scripture would be "finished"; and then Jesus said, "finished." John wants there to be no mistake. Jesus' death on the cross was the finish. Up there on the cross tetelestai is found three times.

But what did Jesus' death finish? An important clue is found in one detail revealed only by John. As the other Gospel authors do, John notes that someone takes a sponge, soaks it with wine, and lifts it up for Jesus to drink. This is the second time a drink has been offered to Jesus. At the beginning of the crucifixion, wine is offered to Jesus but he refuses it. This first offering involves a strong wine that would have been used as a sedative to dull the pain of the cross.[1] Jesus refuses that drink. He will not enter this crucial moment with his mind clouded by drugs. But later, as John recounts, another drink is offered to Jesus. This one is a cheaper wine used merely for quenching thirst. And John is the only author to indicate that this drink was lifted to Jesus on a hyssop plant: "A jar full of sour wine stood there, so they put a sponge full of the sour wine on a hyssop branch and held it to his mouth" (John 19:29). Only John includes the small detail that this drink was lifted to Jesus on a hyssop plant. Why did John think this was significant?

Without a doubt, the most noteworthy biblical reference to hyssop comes at the place where God commands that the hyssop plant be used to spread the blood of the Passover lamb on the doorposts of the Israelite homes (Exodus 12). Perhaps John is struck by the appearance of the hyssop plant at the cross because of its appearance at the Passover. The same hyssop that was used to spread the Passover lamb's blood is now used to lift up a drink to Jesus. Earlier in John's Gospel, Jesus is explicitly connected to the Passover Lamb: "The next day he saw Jesus coming toward him, and said, 'Behold, the Lamb of God, who takes away the sin of the world!'" (John 1:29). Perhaps John includes the detail about the hyssop plant because he wants us to think of the lamb's blood painted on those ancient doorposts. By means of that blood God brought an end to the slavery and oppression of the Hebrews. Similarly, through Jesus' blood God is now bringing an end to the slavery and oppression of all humanity.

And that's why Jesus shouts Tetelestai! Our enslavement, our captivity to sin and its power is now finished. Our Passover has come. Our deliverance has come. Tetelestai! It is finished.

Finished Prayer

But what is this cry? To whom is it addressed? When we finish high school "Finished!" may be a word we shout to our parents and friends. When the baby finally arrives, "tetelestai" might be a word whispered to a nearby husband or doting grandmother. When the cancer is cleared, it could be a word cried to faithful friends who've followed our progress. And when freedom finally arrives, it could be a word proclaimed to all those who also were once enslaved.

Sometimes, however, it is more. Sometimes words like these are spoken as much with God in mind as anyone else. Sometimes the word is a miniature prayer. Its heavenly orientation is betrayed by the fact that such phrases are often accompanied by "Thank God!": Thank God, it's finished. Thank God, it's over. Tetelestai can function as a prayer.

It seems to play this role for Jesus. Jesus may be proclaiming tetelestai for the benefit of the soldiers, his mother, Mary Magdalene, and John—all of whom are within earshot. He might be speaking this statement so they can participate in his grateful completion of his work. Yet upon closer examination, tetelestai seems to be more. It seems to be directed not to the people below the cross but the Father above it.

This direction becomes clear in John 17. Jesus' cry in John 19 has a twin in John 17. And where there is a hint of it being a prayer in John 19, it's undeniable in John 17. There Jesus speaks to God: "I glorified you on earth, having accomplished the work that you gave me to do" (John 17:4). The word "accomplished" is the word "finished." Jesus uses the same verb in John 17 as he does in John 19. Jesus actually prays the "Finished!" prayer twice. In John 17 it is "I have glorified you on earth by finishing the work you gave me to do." In John 19 the prayer is "It is finished."

Finished Work

My first inclination is to view this prayer from the perspective of what is now finished for me. I want to hear about what Jesus completed on my behalf. My captivity to sin is finished. The burden of guilt from my horribly selfish choices is finished. The frustratingly strong power of sin in my life is kaput. I hear Jesus saying to God, "It is finished. Chris' enslavement to sin is over." That is very good news—news I have to remind myself of every day. And perhaps this is part of what Jesus prayed. I hope so. I need that confident statement from Jesus on my behalf.

But there is another layer to the prayer. Let's consider tetelestai from the perspective of what is now finished for Jesus. This prayer reflects not only something that's taken place in my life. It reflects something that has just been completed in Jesus' life. Something has been resolved for Jesus. And that something now prompts this prayer.

This cry takes us back to Genesis.[2] Upon the completion of God's cosmic creating, the author tells us, "Thus the heavens and the earth were finished, and all the host of them. And on the seventh day God finished his work that he had done, and he rested on the seventh day from all his work that he had done" (Genesis 2:1-2). The note of completion that sounded on Creation Friday in Genesis 1 is now sounded on Good Friday in John 19. Just as God completed his work of creation, so now Jesus completes his work of salvation. He has finished the work he was given to do. Jesus is straining toward the Father saying, "Father, I'm done. This work is over. I've finished it all."

Were there moments, in his humanity, when it seemed this labor of salvation would take forever? Were there times, at his lowest, when it seemed this work would never end? Were there occasions, at the darkest, when he thought he could not endure the effort any longer? No doubt. Yet what may have seemed unending, finally ended. God brought resolution and completion. That moment came when the work was finally finished. What Jesus had been sent to accomplish was finally accomplished.

It is such an unparalleled accomplishment that Jesus prays about it twice. In John 17 the prayer is anticipatory. By the time the marathon prayer of John 17 arrives, everything has been settled in Jesus' mind. The cross, the single greatest work given to him by God, is a necessity. There is no way around, under, or over it. There is only the pathway through it. At other times Jesus has wrestled with his course of action. He's prayed for the cup to pass. In John 12 his soul was troubled because of the cross. But by John 17, his mind is at peace. He will go through with it. He will embrace this work, knowing that it is from the Father, knowing that what is about to begin will also eventually end. His resolve is so strong that he can pray in John 17 as if the cross has already been completed: "I have finished the work you gave me to do." Then, in John 19, Jesus puts the Amen on the prayer: "It is finished."

"Finished!" is the prayer Jesus chooses as bookends around the cross. One prayer appears prior to the cross. The other prayer appears upon the cross. One comes with the work of the cross before him. The other comes with the work of the cross behind him. One prayer looks forward. The other prayer looks backward. "Finished!" becomes a kind of inauguration and benediction surrounding the cross.

Expectation and Exultation

Prayed in John 17, "Finished!" is a prayer of expectation. Even before the final note sounds, Jesus has such expectant trust and hope in God that he knows without a doubt that God will bring this long and hard salvation work to completion. That's why he can pray "Finished!" before the crucifixion begins. Here, his prayer has this sense: "I know that this work is as good as done, because I know that you will ensure its completion." It is a prayer of expectation.

Prayed in John 19, "Finished!" is a prayer of exultation. This work is truly over. Jesus expresses his gratitude to the Father. He praises. He shouts. He rejoices. Here, his prayer has this sense: "I thank you for bringing this work to a conclusion. I praise you for seeing it through with me to the very end." It is a prayer of exultation.

Expectation and exultation are the appropriate prayer parentheses to the work God gives us—especially when that work is hard, dark, or overwhelming. Overwhelmed described me when I took my first full-time preaching position after seminary. The elders of this five hundred member congregation with a storied past and a vibrant campus ministry called me to be their preacher. I had one preaching class under my belt, had preached no more than fifteen or twenty sermons to that point, and was only twenty-six years old. On Sunday mornings I was so anxious I developed a nervous cough. During weddings and funerals I stuttered, stammered, and stumbled through the duties. Some days I could hardly catch my breath. Yet I had no doubt this was the work to which God had called me (especially since it was the only preaching position I was offered).

And for such moments Jesus teaches us this prayer of expectation: Finished! Jesus' John 17 version of the prayer, uttered with my first job in mind, might sound like this: "I know you've called me to this work. I know it will be challenging. But I know you will walk through it with me. I know, at the appropriate time, you'll bring it to an end. You'll see it through with me." Jesus' prayer teaches us to approach these moments with expectant trust and hope. His prayer urges us to believe that what may seem like a long and winding road will eventually reach its divinely appointed destination.

Faye is one of the most loved members of our congregation. Several years ago doctors discovered cancer. She faced it bravely and faithfully. After weeks of treatment and days of prayers, the cancer was gone. Her physical and spiritual family rejoiced. A few months ago, however, a doctor brought bad news. Faye had cancer—again. As expected, the family wept some and worried some. But I was shocked at the peace with which Faye met the news. I visited her in the hospital after one of her treatments. Expecting to find her solemn and still on her back in her hospital bed, I found her sitting upright with a smile on her face and eyes full of light. I sat down next to her to offer consolation but realized there was no need for it. She was as lively and happy as if I was visiting her in her own home during a holiday. She talked again and again of God. Though I never heard her say the word, the spirit of tetelestai invaded our conversation. As these events began to unfold, Faye faced them knowing that God would bring it all to his desired resolution. She knew this was work God had given her to do and that he would walk with her through it to the very end. She had an expectant spirit of hope and trust which allowed her to meet this work with peace.

But "Finished!" is not merely a prayer of expectation we ought to pray at the beginning of a work to which God has called us. It is also a prayer of exultation we ought to pray at the conclusion of a work to which God has called us. From his perch on the cross Jesus teaches us the importance and necessity of exultation. When that work given to us by God reaches its end, when that finish line is crossed, celebration and thanksgiving are in order. Sometimes, perhaps in an effort to be the stoic hero of the storyline given to us by God, we cross celebration and jubilation off the lines of our script. Yet Jesus' life ends, as tragic a setting as it is, with a note of celebration: Finished!

John Indermark points out that tetelestai can be either a statement of resignation and defeat or a statement of fulfillment and joy.[3] Those looking up at Jesus hanging shamefully on the cross could have cried out "Finished! He's done for. He's defeated." But ironically, it was Jesus who shouted "Finished!" Not as a cry of resignation. But as a shout of celebration.

Sometimes we get this—we understand how important it is to mark the end of something with exultation. The parents throw an all night party for the group of seniors who've just completed high school. Sisters throw a homecoming for the sibling who's just completed her chemotherapy treatment. But more often than not, we miss this—especially when it comes to prayer. At least for many of us who follow Jesus, the notion of exultation is uncomfortable. Some of us just aren't sure we should celebrate or commemorate. It may be some strain of rigid Puritanism or Protestantism deep in our souls that makes us pause our partying. Yet as awkward as this sight is, I believe there on the cross—bloody, sweaty, and hurting—one of the last things Jesus does is pray a prayer of praise. It is a kind of "Hallelujah!" And his prayer prompts us to do more of the same.

Mark Galli writes that "Paul was a thanksgiving junkie."[4] Giving thanks is a frequent topic of Paul's letters. To the Ephesians Paul writes that we should be "giving thanks always and for everything to God the Father in the name of our Lord Jesus Christ" (Ephesians 5:20). To the Colossians Paul says, "May you be strengthened with all power, according to his glorious might, for all endurance and patience with joy, giving thanks to the Father" (Colossians 1:11-12). To the Thessalonians Paul jots down, "Rejoice always, pray without ceasing, give thanks in all circumstances; for this is the will of God in Christ Jesus for you" (1 Thessalonians. 5:16-18).

Paul not only preaches thanksgiving, he practices it. To the Romans, Paul writes, "I thank my God through Jesus Christ for all of you" (Romans 1:8). To the Corinthians he proclaims, "I give thanks to my God always for you because of the grace of God that was given you in Christ Jesus" (1 Corinthians 1:4). To the Ephesians Paul states, "I do not cease to give thanks for you, remembering you in my prayers" (1:16).

Paul, Galli writes, is a thanksgiving junkie. Perhaps he learned this from his experience with and study of Jesus. At a moment when few of us could even contemplate thanksgiving, Jesus does just that. "Thank you for bringing this to an end. Thank you for seeing this through. Thank you that this journey is finally over." Finished. No matter the work God's given us, when it reaches its end, a shout is called for. A celebration is demanded. A party must be planned.

Practicing This Prayer

Consider something you are just beginning, or maybe already in the middle of. Some work God has called you to. Some effort you are being required to make. You know there is no way to remain loyal to God and to whom he's called you to be without embracing this work. You cannot go around, over, or under it. Following Jesus requires you to go right through it. Perhaps it is something pleasant like the start of a degree program or the early stages of a new relationship. Perhaps it is daunting like the first steps into a challenging project at work or a decision about seeing your marriage through despite the difficulties. Pray every day this week about that issue. Pray with expectation that what God is beginning, he will also bring to an end. Pray with anticipation that the God who's called you to this work will indeed walk through it with you. Pray with conviction that he will see it to the end. Pray the tetelestai prayer of expectation every day this week.

Now consider some small or significant task you've recently completed or a matter in which you've experienced resolution. Perhaps you just completed your first year at a job. Maybe you've just ended a season of particularly exhausting parenting problems at home. Perhaps you've just buried a dear friend or family member for whom you provided encouragement and care in the final days. Pray every day this week about that matter. Pray with exultation for the way God brought fulfillment to that task. Pray with thanksgiving and praise for the way that season of winter is now over and spring is becoming visible. Pray with gratitude for the way God has brought completion to the work. Pray the tetelestai prayer of exultation each day this week.

---

1. D. A. Carson *The Gospel According to John* (Intervarsity Press, 1991), 620.
2. Eugene Peterson, *Tell It Slant : A Conversation on the Language of Jesus in His Stories and Prayers.* (William B. Eerdmans Publishing Co., 2008), 258; N. T. Wright, *The Challenge of Easter* (IVP, Books, 2009), 33.
3. John Indermark, *Traveling the Prayer Paths of Jesus* (Upper Room Books, 2003), 157.
4. Mark Galli, "The Impossibility of Thanksgiving," *Christianity Today* (11/25/09).

Chapter 11

An Outward Prayer of Compassion:
Mind Their Mission (John 17)

Under Attack

Israeli intelligence analyst Ronen Bergman writes of the time in 1962 when Egyptian leaders announced the successful test of missiles that gave Egypt the ability to decimate Israel.[1] Israeli military intelligence learned of a secret facility in the Egyptian desert—Factory 333—which was staffed by East German scientists. The factory aimed to build nine hundred missiles—all pointed at Israel. These were the same minds which gave birth to the German V1 and V2 rockets that demolished London. In response to this threat, the Israeli's devised a fear campaign designed to frighten the German scientists into quitting. Assassins were sent to take out key scientists. The assassins, however, were to make it clear that Israel was behind the hit. The hope was that when the other Factory 333 scientists heard of an assassination of one of their own, they would conclude that they could be next. The plan worked. Factory 333 personnel realized that an attack on one was an attack on them all. They rightly concluded that what happened to their colleague could very likely happen to them. The enemy which had their co-worker in its sights had all of them in its sight. Thus, when West Germany offered the scientists jobs in West Germany, nearly all accepted the offer. Egypt was left without the means to complete its plot.

Something similar motivates part of Jesus' prayer in John 17. Jesus' words, especially in John 17:6-18, are driven by danger. Jesus speaks about the way the world has responded to him and his followers: "...the world has hated them because they are not of the world, just as I am not of the world...They are not of the world, just as I am not of the world" (John 17:14, 16). The prayer takes place in the context of hatred and threats. In addition, Jesus begins the prayer with "Father, the hour has come." As we've previously seen, this "hour" refers to the hour of Jesus' death. The entire prayer is prompted by the reality that there were human enemies on the way, ready to assassinate Jesus. But Jesus thinks not only of imminent threats from the world. In verse 15 he talks to God about "the evil one."

Behind the human faces of Jesus' mortal enemies is the inhuman face of his immortal enemy. The devil himself has Jesus in his sights. Natural and supernatural powers are arrayed against the Christ and his followers. Thus this section of his prayer is filled with military language: "keep/guard them" (John 17:11); "I kept/guarded them" (John 17:12); "I have guarded them" (John 17:12); "keep/guard them" (John 17:15). Jesus knows that he's the target of a human and demonic assassination plot. He knows that a foe is coming, armed to the teeth.

But Jesus recognizes that the enemy threatening him also threatens his disciples. He grasps that what's happening to him can happen to his followers. Jesus knows that the enemies that have him in their sights also have those devoted to him in their sights. This attack on Jesus is an attack on them all. No doubt the enemy hopes to frighten off the Christians with this ploy against the Christ. Strike the shepherd—scatter the sheep.

Jesus' prayer is therefore not merely focused on himself. His prayer is also focused on the others who will eventually face what he is now facing. In an earlier chapter, we listened to and learned from the part of this prayer in which Jesus prays for himself (Chapter 7). In this chapter and in the following chapter, we'll listen to and learn from the part of this prayer in which Jesus prays for others. John 17 is the longest recorded prayer from the lips of Jesus and it comes immediately prior to the most excruciating assault he would endure. While none of us would blame Jesus if every word of this prayer was in first person singular (me, my, I), two-thirds of the prayer is third person plural (they, theirs, them). One thing Jesus models so well when in the pit is the importance of praying for others rather than merely praying for ourselves:

> "Holy Father, keep them in your name, which you have given me, that they may be one, even as we are one. While I was with them, I kept them in your name, which you have given me. I have guarded them, and not one of them has been lost except the son of destruction, that the Scripture might be fulfilled. But now I am coming to you, and these things I speak in the world, that they may have my joy fulfilled in themselves. I have given them your word, and the world has hated them because they are not of the world, just as I am not of the world. I do not ask that you take them out of the world, but that you keep them from the evil one. They are not of the world, just as I am not of the world. Sanctify them in the truth; your word is truth. As you sent me into the world, so I have sent them into the world. And for their sake I consecrate myself, that they also may be sanctified in truth" (John 17:11b-19).

Notice to whom Jesus prays: "Holy Father." This is the only time recorded by John when Jesus addresses God in this way. The name "Holy Father" combines the intimacy of "Father" with the reverence and awe of "Holy."[2] What Jesus needs in this moment of menace is a God who is not only willing to help due to the nature of his love and compassion (Father), but a God who is also able to help due to the nature of his power and presence (Holy). This is the God to whom Jesus prays.

But Jesus does not pray "keep/guard me." Over and over he prays "keep/guard them." Jesus prays for the disciples who will remain behind when he ascends to the Father. He prays for the apprentices he's invested in and trained. As "Father," this God loves Jesus' followers as he loves Jesus. As "Holy," this God guards Jesus' followers as he guards Jesus. Jesus begs the Holy Father to move heaven and earth to rescue those who now wear the name of Jesus. Just as Jesus is soon to be attacked, so they too will be attacked.

Specifically, Jesus prays three things: "keep them in your name" (John 17:11b); "keep them from the evil one" (John 17:15); and "Sanctify them" (John 17:17). As Jesus considers his closest followers and the cunning foe they will face, he prays his followers will be kept in the Father's presence, kept from the devil's power, and kept for their global purpose.

Kept in the Father's Presence

First, Jesus prays they will be kept in the Father's presence: "keep them in your name" (John 17:11b). The Father's name is an important part of this prayer. Jesus reminds God, "I have manifested your name to the people whom you gave me out of the world" (John 17:6). He states "I kept them in your name" (John 17:12), and that "I made known to them your name" (John 17:26). In Scripture, "name" is synonymous with "identity," "person," or "presence." Names were chosen because they communicated something about the individual. They revealed the person's identity. To know a name was to know the essence of the person named. In addition, a person's name could carry the same authority as the personal presence of that individual. To come "in the name" of a ruler or a king was to come with the same authority as if that ruler or king were present himself. Jesus earlier stated that he came in the Father's name (John 5:43; 10:25)—that is, he came with the authority of the Father, as if the Father himself were present. Here, Jesus rehearses in prayer how he manifested God's name or made known God's name—that is, Jesus made God's identity known. This is another way of stating what John says at his Gospel's introduction: "No one has ever seen

God; the only God, who is at the Father's side, he has made him known" (John 1:18). Jesus made God known—he revealed God's name and made known God's name.

Thus when Jesus asks God to "keep them in your name," he is praying for God to keep Jesus' followers under his care, under his authority, and by his power; to be present to them and with them; and to keep them close by him. In a word, Jesus prays for God to keep them in his "presence." This is the presence of the "Holy Father" and is thus a place of power.[3] But it is also a place of intimacy and compassion. Jesus prays his followers will remain under the Father's powerful and passionate care. "Don't let them out of your sight," Jesus prays. "Keep them close to your heart and hold them in your hands," Jesus begs. "Let them live every day close to your bosom," Jesus petitions. All of this is included in his petition "keep them in your name."

The Lord's Prayer provides an echo of this John 17 prayer. Earlier in his ministry Jesus taught us to pray, "Our Father in heaven, hallowed be your name." That is, "Our Father in heaven, may your people come to know the holiness of your name. May your people come to know your true identity. May you be powerfully present to your people." Similarly Jesus prays now, "May my followers be kept in your name."

On the first Sunday night of this year, our congregation held a prayer session regarding the New Year. This followed a similar prayer session that morning hosted by my Sunday School class. The temptation at such times is to pray for ourselves. As we looked into the New Year, each of us saw threats, possible obstacles, potential pitfalls, and problems we might encounter in the days, weeks, and months ahead. But we realized these challenges were not ours alone. They also affected the people who lived in our metro area. They further affected even our missionaries in places like Ukraine, Papua New Guinea, and the Philippines. Thus, while we did indeed pray for ourselves, we also spent two-thirds of our time praying for others. And while we never clearly articulated it this way, the thought was there: "Keep them in your presence, Father. Be as present to them this New Year as you are to us."

After the prayer session, an elderly member of our congregation approached me. He placed his hand around me and looking into my eyes said, "I pray every day for you. I want you to know that. I pray every day for you." That meant a great deal to me. There's hardly anything I appreciate more than knowing someone else is interceding for me. John Indermark writes, "The act of being prayed for by another is an extraordinary gift."[4] It is indeed. And I suppose if I could make a request of that gentleman who is praying so faithfully for me, it would be this: pray that I would be kept in the Father's presence. Pray that I will remain under God's powerful and passionate care. Pray that God won't let me out of his sight. Pray that God will let me live every day close to his bosom.

There is no greater gift we can offer than to intercede for those who face the challenges we ourselves face. There is no greater blessing than to pray for others, "Keep them in your presence. Keep them in your powerful and passionate care."

Kept from the Devil's Power

But Jesus not only prays "keep them in your name" (John. 17:11b). He also prays "keep them from the evil one" (John 17:15). Jesus not only asks that his followers will be kept in the Father's presence. He begs that they also be kept from the devil's power.

Jesus' prayer is guided by a kind of magnetic worldview. On the one hand, he believes in a Father to whom all should be drawn and in whom all should be kept. On the other hand, Jesus believes in a devil from whom all should be repelled and from whom all should be kept. Jesus' prayer has a push and a pull. He asks that those he deeply loves will be pushed closer to the Father and pulled farther from the devil. Jesus believes in real evil which emanates from a real devil. And his concern now is that his servants be protected from that dark power.

Satan's black presence is so prevalent that John summarizes the entire ministry of Jesus in this way: a light shining in the darkness (John 1:5). Jesus promises that whoever follows him will not walk in darkness (John 8:12; 12:46). Jesus warns the religious leaders of the day that the prince of this darkness is so crafty that even they have fallen under his influence (John 8:54). Later, John will reveal that the betraying work of Judas was actually the work of this dark devil (John 13:2, 27).

And Jesus knows that he is not the lone figure at the center of the devil's target. That bull's-eye is also filled with the name of every person wearing the name of Jesus. Just as the devil labored to derail Christ, so he is laboring to derail Christians. This leads Jesus to pray passionately that they will be kept from the devil.

As with the first petition, we hear this second petition echoed in the Lord's Prayer. In it, Jesus taught us to pray "Deliver us from evil." That is, "Our Father in heaven, protect us from the evil one. Deliver us from his tricks and temptations." Similarly, Jesus now prays, "Keep them from the evil one. Deliver them from his tricks and temptations."

A few years ago *The Atlantic Monthly* ran a story about the guidelines followed by writers, editors, and illustrators who prepare textbooks and tests for K-12 students in the United States.[5] Among the words expressly forbidden are "devil" and "Satan" (along with "God"!). Children in the United States are fed a worldview which denies that the devil is real and is engaged in warfare against them. Jesus prays from the opposite worldview. His example calls us to do the same.

Mario Sepulveda, one of the thirty-three Chilean miners trapped underground for two months in 2010, commented to reporters: "I was with God, and I was with the devil. They fought, and God won."[6] That's the essence of Jesus' prayer. Jesus finds himself in a deep pit with God and the devil. He finds himself locked in a supernatural battle. But he realizes that he is not the lone person impacted by the conflict. All who follow him are impacted as well. Thus he prays not only that they will be kept in the Father, but that they will be kept from the devil.

Kept for Their Global Purpose

Finally, Jesus prays, "Sanctify them" (John 17:17). Upon first hearing, this petition seems out of place. There appears to be no line to draw between this dot and the two prior to it. Is there any connection at all between the first two petitions and "Sanctify them"? The linkage becomes clearer when we listen to the full prayer: "Sanctify them in the truth; your word is truth. As you sent me into the world, so I have sent them into the world. And for their sake I consecrate myself, that they also may be sanctified in truth." Jesus is reflecting upon his mission and theirs. Jesus is meditating upon his purpose and theirs. He's pondering how he's been sent into the world to accomplish a greater purpose and how his followers are similarly being sent into the world.

In John 17 "sanctify" and "sent" are almost synonymous. The word "sanctify" is literally "make holy." At its most basic level, "holy" is an adjective for God, meaning that he is other, distinct, and separate from his creation (Isaiah 6:3; Revelation 4:8). When applied to people and things, "holy" refers to them being reserved for God and his use.[7] Jesus has been sanctified. He's been reserved for God and his use. He's been sent into the world for God's purposes. Now Jesus prays the same for his followers. Just as Jesus was set apart for the purpose of being sent into the world, so now he prays for the disciples to be set apart for the purpose of being sent into the world. Jesus prays about their mission. He begs the Father to set these men apart for the task of continuing Jesus' mission. He prays that they might fulfill their purpose in life.

It is a purpose that is global in nature. Listen to how much of Jesus' prayer centers upon the world (emphasis added):

"And now, Father, glorify me in your own presence with the glory that I had with you before the *world* existed" (John. 17:5).

"I have manifested your name to the people whom you gave me out of the *world*" (John 17:6).

"I am praying for them. I am not praying for the *world* but for those whom you have given me, for they are yours" (John 17:9).

"And I am no longer in the *world*, but they are in the *world*, and I am coming to you" John 17:11).

"But now I am coming to you, and these things I speak in the *world*, that they may have my joy fulfilled in themselves" (John 17:13).

"I have given them your word, and the *world* has hated them because they are not of the *world*, just as I am not of the *world*" (John 17:14).

"I do not ask that you take them out of the *world*, but that you keep them from the evil one (John 17:15).

"They are not of the *world*, just as I am not of the *world*" (John 17:16).

"As you sent me into the *world*, so I have sent them into the *world*" (John 17:18).

"...that they may all be one, just as you, Father, are in me, and I in you, that they also may be in us, so that the *world* may believe that you have sent me" (John 17:21).

"I in them and you in me, that they may become perfectly one, so that the *world* may know that you sent me and loved them even as you loved me" (John 17:23).

"Father, I desire that they also, whom you have given me, may be with me where I am, to see my glory that you have given me because you loved me before the foundation of the *world*" (John 17:24).

"O righteous Father, even though the *world* does not know you, I know you, and these know that you have sent me"(John 17:25).

The sobering reality is that Jesus' greatest concern in this, his longest recorded prayer, is not for his followers—it is for the world. The world does not exist apart from his followers or for the sake of his followers. Instead, Jesus' followers exist for the sake of the world.

Though Jesus lived long before the world, and enjoyed intimate fellowship with the Father apart from the world, it was to the world that he was nonetheless sent (John 17:5, 18, 24). Jesus' followers were chosen from the world (not from some heavenly training camp) and are now being sent into the world (not being kept from the world in some isolated heavenly retreat) (John 17:6, 18). Although the world may respond with hostility and criticism, Jesus never prays for his followers to be kept from the world, only that they be kept from the evil one while they are in the world (John 17:14, 15). Being kept in the Father's presence and kept from the devil's power are not ends in themselves. They are means toward a greater end—that the world would know of the Father's love (John 17:21, 23).

Jesus thus prays for his followers to remain sanctified—set apart for their global purpose of enabling others to know the Father and the Son. How easy it would be for them to become distracted. How quickly they would become discouraged. How soon they would get disillusioned. So Jesus prays against their distraction, discouragement, and disillusionment. He prays they would remain focused on the bigger picture—their mission to the world. Sanctify them.

In her book, *Almost Christian* Kenda Dean writes about Faith Christian School in Grapevine, Texas.[8] Grapevine has a $90,000 median family income and award-winning schools like Faith Christian School. Faith's football team has seventy players, eleven coaches, the latest equipment, and hundreds of involved parents. In November 2008, the Faith Christian School Lions were 7–2 going into a game with the Gainesville State Tornados. Gainesville State was the complete opposite of Faith Christian. Their record was 0–8. They had fourteen players who wore seven-year-old pads and dilapidated helmets. Worse, they were escorted by twelve security guards who took off the players' handcuffs before the game. Gainesville State is a prison north of Dallas and gets its students by court order. Many of their students have convictions for drugs, assaults, and robberies. Their families have disowned them. They play every game on the road. Kenda Dean writes this:

> Before the game, Faith's head coach Kris Hogan had an idea. What if, just for one night, half of the Faith fans cheered for the kids on the opposing team? "Here is the message I want you to send," Hogan wrote in an email

to Faith's faithful. "You are just as valuable as any other person on Planet Earth." The Faith fans agreed. When the Gainesville Tornados took the field, they crashed through a banner made by Faith fans that read "Go Tornados!" The Gainesville players were surprised to find themselves running through a forty-foot spirit line made up of cheering fans. From their benches at the side of the field, the Gainesville team heard two hundred fans on the bleachers behind them, cheering for them by name, led by real cheerleaders (Hogan had recruited the JV squad to cheer for the opposing team). "I thought maybe they were confused," said Alex, a Gainesville lineman. Another lineman, Gerald, said: "We can tell people are a little afraid of us when we come to the games... But these people, they were yellin' for us! By our names!" Gainesville's quarterback and middle linebacker Isaiah shook his head in disbelief. "I never thought I'd hear people cheering for us to hit their kids... But they wanted us to!" At the end of the game (Faith won, 33–14), the losing team practically danced off the field with their fingers pointing #1 in the air. They gave Gainesville's head coach Mark Williams what ESPN sportswriter Rick Reilly described as the first Gatorade bath in history for a 0–9 coach. When the teams gathered in the middle of the field to pray, Isaiah surprised everybody by asking to lead. ("We had no idea what the kid was going to say," remembers Coach Hogan.) This was Isaiah's prayer: "Lord, I don't know how this happened, so I don't know how to say thank You, but I never would've known there was so many people in the world that cared about us." As guards escorted the Tornados back to their bus, each player received a bag filled with burgers, fries, candy, a Bible, and an encouraging letter from a Faith player. Before he stepped onto the bus, Williams turned and grabbed Hogan hard by the shoulders: "You'll never know what your people did for these kids tonight. You'll never, ever know." The Gainesville players crowded onto one side of the bus, peering out the windows at an unbelievable sight—people they had never met before smiling at them, waving goodbye, as the bus drove into the night.

There's a group in whom Jesus' third petition was answered. These coaches and kids remembered that they existed for more than just football and fame. They existed for the sake of the world. Thus they turned a football game into a moment of kingdom-coming and heaven-on-earth. They lived out a greater and grander purpose.

Jesus prays for this kind of thing to happen more and more. He prays his followers will see beyond their next test, Friday's game, their cubicle or classroom, their upcoming vacation, or their new vocation. He prays they will grasp this bigger picture and give themselves fully to it. He prays they will be kept in the Father's presence and from the devil's power so they can truly fulfill their global purpose. He prays the Father will sanctify them.

And Jesus' prayer encourages us to pray similarly.

It Had to Be Love

On the second Sunday of this year, Memphis was greeted with this tragic front-page headline: "Mother, 2 babies, perish in blaze."[9] A single woman's partner was cooking and left the apartment to take food to another resident in the complex. Unattended grease on the stove ignited and when the man returned, the apartment was ablaze. The mother and four children—ages 4, 3, 18 months, and 2 months—were trapped inside. The man rushed into the apartment and rescued the two older children. He received burns on his hands, arms and head. Rushing in a second time, he was unable to save the mother and the two youngest children.

A neighbor witnessed the heroic efforts. She told reporters, "It takes love to go into a building like that. It had to be love."

It had to be love.

That's true regarding this prayer from Jesus. Jesus finds himself next to a burning apartment. He can feel the heat of the hot attacks from the devil and from the world. But Jesus knows that he's not the only one endangered. He knows all who follow him will face the same peril. And this intercessory prayer is Jesus running into the apartment to save them all, to save us all. Jesus isn't content to just save his own skin. He's not content to cry to heaven for a one-man-miracle. Instead he begs God to move heaven and earth to save our skin. Thinking of those who would come after him, he prays they will be kept in the Father's presence, kept from the devil's power, and kept for their global purpose.

Practicing This Prayer

This is the first of three prayers in which Jesus teaches us to pray for others. It is part one in a three-part school of intercessory prayer. The next two chapters in this book will survey the remaining two other-centered prayers. Of the three prayers, this one is the broadest and most comprehensive. What Jesus tutors us in here can be applied in many prayer-circumstances and prayer-situations.

Above all, this prayer in John 17 urges us simply to pray for others. It demands that intercession be characteristic of our prayer lives. It reminds us that the dangers we face are faced by others. As much as we long for assistance in dealing with our own demons, this prayer leads us to also pray about the demons confronting others.

In my family, each day is devoted to intercession for a different group. Mondays are for our congregation's staff and elders. Tuesdays are for our congregation's newest members and those most recently baptized. Wednesdays are when we pray for our friends. Thursdays are the days on which we ask God's blessings on world and urban missionaries. Fridays are devoted to praying for leaders of Christian colleges, universities, and para-church ministries. Saturdays and Sundays are dedicated to prayers for those we know who are sick, struggling, hurting, or otherwise in need.

There are, of course, many other ways to practice intercession. One of our congregation's longest serving ministers has for decades prayed page by page through our church directory and page by page through a detailed street map of our city. In this way he prays for every person in our church and in our city.

One deacon in a congregation where I served kept a notebook in which he wrote down every single person he ever became aware of who needed divine assistance. He prayed passionately through that list week by week.

How you do it doesn't matter all that much. What matters is that you do it—just start praying for others. This week, pray for others. Every day pray for others.

But Jesus offers some specific guidance in his prayer if we are willing to receive it. This week make a list of friends, family members, fellow believers, those involved in Christian ministry/para-church organizations, those serving in Christian charities, and those who are involved with Christian education. Pray through that list three times during the week.

On your first intercessory pass, pray for these men and women to be kept in the Father's presence. Pray for them to remain under the Father's powerful and passionate care. Ask God to keep them close to his heart. Beg God to hold them in his hands. Request that God be present in the midst of their peril.

On your second intercessory pass through the list, pray for these people to be kept from the devil's power. Pray that none will give in to temptation. Pray that none will fall prey to demonic tricks and traps. Pray that every plan Satan has devised against them will fail.

On your final intercessory pass, pray for these men and women to be kept for their global purpose. Pray that neither distraction, nor disillusionment nor discouragement will keep them from their kingdom calling and purpose. Pray that everything God wants to do through them this week will be done through them. Pray through your list three times this week with these three intercessory prayers.

1. Ronen Bergman, "Killing the Killers," *Newsweek* (December 20, 2010), 33.
2. D. A. Carson, *The Gospel According to John* (Intervarsity Press, 1991), 561.
3. Carson, 562.
4. John Indermark, *Traveling the Prayer Paths of Jesus* (Upper Room Books, 2003): 93.
5. Diane Ravitch, "The Language Police," *The Atlantic Monthly* (March 2003), 82-83.
6. "Perspectives 2010," *Newsweek* (Dec. 27, 2010/ Jan. 3, 2011), 18.
7. Carson, 565.
8. Kenda Dean, *Almost Christian: what the faith of our teenagers is telling the American church* (Oxford University Press, 2010).
9. Linda A. Moore, "Mother, 2 babies, perish in blaze," *The Commercial Appeal* (January 9, 2011), A1.

Chapter 12

An Outward Prayer of Compassion:
Concentrate Their Community (John 17)

Bridging and Bonding

Mary was crying to me over the phone. Plagued with multiple physical ailments and a stubborn mental illness, Mary is essentially imprisoned in her house. It's difficult for her body to make the trip outside. It's also a challenge for her mind to leave the security of her house. Thus Mary has few opportunities to connect with people other than her immediate family. And the few she can connect with often collapse from the weight of Mary's burdens. It's difficult for those who do not share Mary's maladies to bridge the gap and relate to her. The burdens that weigh her down eventually weigh them down.

And not even those who share her world successfully bond. This was the story behind tonight's call. Mary had managed to make a friend. She met another woman with challenges similar to hers, and they quickly bonded. They could empathize with one another in a way few could. They talked often on the phone and occasionally escaped their homes to meet at a store or restaurant. They grew so close they even finished each other's sentences. But then the only person Mary might even dream of calling a "BFF" called and said their friendship was finished. Her own demons were so dark that she could no longer handle exposure to Mary's.

Mary was heartbroken. "It's worse than dealing with a death!" she cried to me. She felt isolated. She felt alone. She felt cut off.

In his widely acclaimed book, *Bowling Alone*, Robert Putnam writes about experiences like Mary's.[1] Putnam argues that there are two kinds of relationships critical in a society: bridging and bonding. Bonding refers to relationships that are built between people who are similar to each other—like Mary and her new friend. Bridging refers to relationships that are built between people who are dissimilar to one another—like Mary and those who do not suffer from her challenges. Putnam argues that both bonding and bridging are necessary in a society. We need intimacy and connection with people who are just like us. But we also need unity with people who are different from us. We need to bond and bridge. We need strong ties with people like us and with people unlike us.

Disconnected

Sadly, however, bonding is a challenge for many of us. A few years ago the *American Sociological Review* reported that friendships are on the decline in the United States.[2] Over a period of two decades, researchers found an increasing number of Americans saying they do not discuss important matters with anyone. For those Americans who do discuss important matters with someone, the number of confidants was decreasing. Those who say they have no one to discuss important matters doubled during the study: one out of four. In addition, the number of close confidents Americans said they had in their lives dropped from three to two.

Increasingly, we seem disconnected.

Paul Adams is the Senior User Experience Researcher at Google. He finds that the average American has strong ties with only four people.[3] Though the average user of Facebook, the social networking site, has one hundred thirty "friends," he/she only interacts with four to six of those "friends" on a weekly basis. In addition, eighty percent of our phone calls are made to the same four people. We have lots and lots of connections. But we seem to have fewer and fewer friends.

Donald Miller suggests that such isolation is hell—literally.[4] In attempting to illustrate the essential quality of hell, Miller writes the parable of Don Astronaut:

> There once was a man named Don Astronaut. Don Astronaut lived on a space station out in space. Don Astronaut had a special suit that kept him alive without food or water or oxygen. One day there was an accident. And Don Astronaut was cast out into space. Don Astronaut orbited the earth and was very scared. Until he remembered his special suit that kept him alive. But nobody's government came to rescue Don Astronaut because it would cost too much money. (There was a conspiracy, and they said he had died, but he hadn't.) So Don Astronaut orbited the earth again and again, fourteen times each day. And Don Astronaut orbited the earth for months. And Don Astronaut orbited the earth for decades. And Don Astronaut orbited the earth for fifty-three years before he died a very lonely and crazy man—just a shell of a thing with hardly a spark for a soul.

Nothing could be more torturous than existing permanently in such a disconnected state; aware of billions of other people but completely unable to connect with a single one. Sadly, that is a state in which more and more of us find ourselves. We are surrounded in life with colleagues and co-workers. We are surrounded online with "followers" and "friends." Yet we seem unable to connect with all but a very few.

And we'd pay almost any price to gain some intimacy. In Mark Twain's, *The Adventures of Huckleberry Finn*, Miss Watson tries her best to pound religion into Huck.[5] She warns Huck that if he doesn't straighten up, he'll not be going to heaven. Instead, hell will be his eternal home. Huck asks Miss Watson if his friend Tom Sawyer will be going to heaven. "Not by a considerable sight," she replied. Tom will wind up in the same fire-and-brimstone cell as Huck. Surprisingly, Huck is relieved. He reports, "I was glad about that, because I wanted him and me to be together." There's something so rare and so valuable about a good friendship that at least some of us would be willing to sell our soul for one. Heaven can wait. But real friendship can't.

Such connection is, in fact, what we were created for. John Ortberg points out that the only thing in all creation called "not good" is a human being alone.[6] It's not just that Adam, this "male," is alone and needs a "female." It's that Adam, this "human," is alone and needs another human. There's not another human on the planet. There are lots of animals. There is God. But there's something that no animal and not even God can fulfill in Adam. Though he has perfect intimacy with God, it is still "not good" that Adam is alone—isolated from humans. Ortberg writes

> Sometimes in church circles when people feel lonely, we will tell them not to expect too much from human relationships, that there is inside every human being a God-shaped void that no other person can fill. That is true. But apparently, according to the writer of Genesis, God creates inside this man a kind of "human-shaped void" that God himself will not fill. No substitute will fill this need in you for human relationships: Not money; Not achievement; Not busyness; Not books; Not even God himself.

Sadly, we are missing the very thing for which we were made. We are disconnected. We have few strong ties with other people. We lack the experience of intimacy. Bonding does not come easily.

Divided

And neither does bridging. In addition to being disconnected, we are also divided. We have few strong ties with different people. We lack the experience of unity.

Former Secretary of State Madeleine Albright revealed a moment she shared with Holocaust survivor and author, Eli Wiesel:[7]

> Not long after September 11, I was on a panel with Eli Wiesel. He asked us to name the unhappiest character in the Bible. Some said Job, because of the trials he endured. Some said Moses, because he was denied entry into the Promised Land. Some said Mary, because she witnessed the crucifixion of her son. Wiesel said he believed the right answer was God, because of the pain he must surely feel in seeing us fight, kill, and abuse each other in the Lord's name.

Wiesel had seen and experienced the marriage of two great tragedies of humanity. First, we fight, kill and abuse each other—especially those who are different from us. Second, we do so in the name of God. We burn bridges and condemn those unlike ourselves because we believe God loves us and hates them.

Our failure to bridge is most easily seen when it comes to race. A recent poll asked whites and blacks how serious a problem they think racial bias is in this country.[8] Forty-nine percent of blacks said it was very serious. When asked if they had ever been the victim of racial discrimination, fifty-one percent of blacks said they had.[9] Racial division is still an embarrassingly strong problem in this country.

And it's not simply one race which is the victim. CNN reporter John Blake writes about a suburban church in California.[10] Shortly after their new preacher was hired, a group of members came to him with a disturbing issue. They were worried about how the racial makeup of the church was changing. They warned their new preacher that the church's newest members would seize control because members of that race were inherently aggressive. They wanted to know what the preacher was going to do if any more of "them" joined this church. It turns out that the nervous members were African-Americans. The new members they wanted out were white.

Few things still divide us like race.

As I write this chapter it is Martin Luther King, Jr. Day. Here in Memphis, you can stand in the actual room at the Lorraine Motel where Martin Luther King, Jr. stayed and near which he was murdered. You can walk through the room across the street from which the shot was fired that ended King's life. Chills run up and down my spine when I visit those spots. I am reminded just how difficult unity still is. If ever a city had reason to experience transformation in this area, it's Memphis. We know too well the cost of division and intolerance. And in some ways, that transformation has taken root. I think of the local church which gained a national spotlight because they offered Memphis Muslims a place to gather when their mosque wasn't completed in time for an Islamic holy day. But in other ways race still divides here. Even today, on MLK day, the people of the Greater Memphis Area are up in arms about our school system. Public debates, newspaper stories, and local news reports are focused on the deep division among county and city leaders, and county and city residents, regarding the structure and funding of our schools. And some on each side are playing the race card—accusing each other of taking a position designed to keep their kids far from kids of "the other" race.

But race is not our only divider. Politics also hinders bridging. Just a few months ago a man named Jared Loughner murdered multiple people who differed from him politically. Finally fed up with what he viewed as the wrong direction some national politicians were taking our country, Loughner decided to do something about it. Early that morning he posted "Goodbye Friends" on his MySpace page. He packed his semiautomatic handgun with an extended magazine containing about thirty bullets, another extended magazine of bullets, two standard magazines, and a knife. He took a cab to a Tuscon Safeway where Rep. Gabrielle Giffords was greeting constituents. Loughner walked to Gifford's table and started firing—killing six people and wounding thirteen, including Rep. Giffords. In the wake of this national tragedy, many reflected on how it was time to tone down political rhetoric before more people started resolving their differences in the same way.

Robert Putnam points out our difficulty with bridging. He writes, "The problem is that bridging social capital is harder to create than bonding social capital—after all, birds of a feather flock together. So the kind of social capital that is most essential for healthy public life in an increasingly diverse society like ours is precisely the kind that is hardest to build."[11]

The kind of relationship "that is most essential" is the kind "that is hardest to build." Whatever challenges we have with bonding, they pale in comparison to our difficulties with bridging. Many of us may indeed be disconnected from those similar to us and lack intimacy. But far more are divided from those unlike us and lack true unity. Some of us have few strong ties to those similar to us. Even more have few strong ties to those dissimilar to us.

A Contrast Community

Imagine, then, what it might be like to stumble onto a world in which the exact opposite was true. Rather than disconnection, it seemed almost every person you interviewed was experiencing intimacy. Each person had a list the length of their arm when asked who they confide in and who they could call at two o'clock in the morning with a problem. Bonding was as vital to their society as breathing is to the body. And rather than division, it appeared almost every person you interviewed was enjoying unity. Each person you polled could name several others of different skin color, country of origin, income, and political persuasion whom they counted as a dear friend. Bridging was as central to their society as blood is to the body.

In their book, *Introducing the Missional Church*, Alan Roxburgh and Scott Boren call this kind of community a "contrast society."[12] They argue that what is most needed in our world today is the church acting as a contrast society. The authors mean that the church must become a living model, a laboratory, in which people see and experience the opposite of what they see and experience in the world. If what people see and experience in the world is brokenness, in the church they should see and experience bonding. If what people see and experience in the world is hostility, in the church they should see and experience bridging.

If the rest of the world knows disconnection (no strong ties with other people), then the contrast community knows intimacy (very strong ties with other people). If the rest of the world experiences division (no strong ties with different people), then the contrast community experiences unity (very strong ties with different people). In one there is little bonding and even less bridging. In the other there is abundant bonding and overflowing bridging.

And it is possible for the church, the community of Jesus' followers, to become this kind of contrast community.

Fred Craddock writes about visiting a small church one Sunday morning.[13] About one hundred twenty people filled the pews. As the service began, Craddock noticed the minister. He was very tall, about 6'4", and very large, about three hundred pounds. He had an awkward lumbering way of walking. As he moved, he appeared to be near falling. His long arms hung loosely at his sides. The minister's head was strangely shaped and his hair was all messed up. Thick glasses hung on his nose. One of his eyes was covered with a milky white film. As he read the Bible aloud, the minister had to hold the pages up to his nose in order to see. He spoke like he had just recently learned to speak—haltingly and roughly.

After the service, Craddock waited to speak to the minister. He overheard a woman say to the minister, "I wish I could know your mother." The minister said, "My mother's name is Grace." Finally, everyone left and Craddock introduced himself to the minister. He said, "That was an unusual response you gave to that woman, 'My mother's name is Grace.'" The minister replied, "When I was born, I was put up for adoption at the Department of Family Services. But no one wanted me. So I went from foster home to foster home until I was about sixteen or seventeen. I saw some people going into a church. I wanted to be with young people, so I went in. That's where I met grace–the grace of God."

What the minister found was a church acting as a contrast community. A group of people who took in the one everyone else kicked out. A group of people who embraced the one everyone else shunned. A group so quick to bond and so eager to bridge that the one experiencing it could only think of one word to describe it: grace.

Imagine if the church was known around the world as this place of grace.

Naturally Impossible

But notice where this once-was-lonely-but-now-is-loved man believed that grace came from: God. The grace was expressed in other humans accepting him, welcoming him, and loving him. But the minister believed those expressions originated in God. "That's where I met grace—the grace of God." When he experienced bridging and bonding for the first time in his life, he was led to believe that it came from God. Only God could make possible the exact opposite of what he had experienced in the world.

In his John 17 prayer, Jesus makes a similar connection:

"I do not ask for these only, but also for those who will believe in me through their word, that they may all be one, just as you, Father, are in me, and I in you, that they also may be in us, *so that the world may believe that you have sent me.* The glory that you have given me I have given to them, that they may be one even as we are one, I in them and you in me, that they may become perfectly one, *so that the world may know that you sent me and loved them even as you loved me*" (John 17:20-23, emphasis added).

If the community of Jesus' followers becomes a group in which people experience the kind of oneness that Jesus and the Father experience, Jesus says outsiders witnessing it will "believe that you have sent me." That is, they will believe that the founder of that community, Jesus, must have come from God. When the world sees this bridging and bonding, they will be led to believe that it comes from God. Only God can make possible the exact opposite of what they experience in the world.

The implication is that a community characterized by unity and intimacy is not naturally possible. It is only supernaturally possible. Human creatures are unlikely to bring it about through their own ordinary effort. But the human Creator can bring it about through his extraordinary effort. As such, the very existence of this community becomes the ultimate apologetic. It becomes the ultimate proof that God exists. Only a god could bring such disconnected people together. Only a god could bring such divided people together. Timothy Jones writes, "The world will be won not through the wisdom of our words but through the witness of our oneness."[14]

In his book, *The Safest Place on Earth*, Larry Crabb describes two contrasting pictures of the church.[15] One picture comes from something he saw in Miami Beach. On an enormous beachside porch, there were at least a hundred chairs arranged in neat rows. In each chair sat an elderly person staring straight ahead. There was no interaction among them. And too often, Crabb says, that's what the church is—a bunch of people all in the same room with no meaningful interaction. By contrast, Crabb envisions the circle in which the Father, Son, and Holy Spirit live. A circle of intimacy. It's the circle Jesus pictures in this prayer. That, Crabb says, is Jesus' vision for the church. Jesus believes the church, and the church alone, has the potential to become the true contrast community. The church can become the one place where humans can experience with humans what Father, Son, and Spirit have experienced for all eternity. The church alone has the capacity to be that place of ultimate grace where all who are lonely are loved, all who are rejected are accepted, and the walls that separate us are demolished.

But such community is only possible through God.

Praying Required

This then, is why Jesus prays

> *"I do not ask for these only, but also for those who will believe in me through their word, that they may all be one, just as you, Father, are in me, and I in you,* that they also may be in us, so that the world may believe that you have sent me. The glory that you have given me I have given to them, *that they may be one even as we are one, I in them and you in me, that they may become perfectly one,* so that the world may know that you sent me and loved them even as you loved me" (John 17:20-23, emphasis added).

In this, his longest prayer ever, Jesus prays for the Father to make possible what remains humanly impossible: true intimacy and true unity. Jesus prays against the qualities that dominate far too many hearts and lives across the globe: disconnection and division. Jesus devotes a third of his John 17 prayer to begging God to transform his followers into a contrast community which experiences the kind of bridging and bonding that will persuade outsiders that God himself is behind it. Jesus understands that such community is not naturally possible. It is only supernaturally possible. Thus he is compelled to pray, plead, and beg for God to make happen what only God can make happen.

In his classic work on friendship called *Spiritual Friendship* the Scottish monk, Aelred wrote in the 1100's, "... scarcely any happiness whatever can exist among mankind without friendship."[16] This is what Jesus prays about. He prays that his community will become the happiest place on earth—the one place where true friendship can happen for all people.

In 1937, researchers at Harvard University began a study on what factors contribute to well-being.[17] The research team selected 268 well-adjusted male Harvard students. They studied these individuals for seventy-two years to determine what affected their levels of health and happiness. The study tracked a number of factors, including physical exercise, cholesterol levels, marital status, use of alcohol, smoking, education levels, and weight. Over the period of seventy two years, several directed the research. For the last four decades, the director was George Vaillant. In 2008 someone asked Dr. Vaillant what he had learned about human health and happiness from these 268 men. Here's what the doctor revealed: "The only thing that really matters in life are your relationships to other people." Relationships to other people—this is what Jesus prays about in John 17. Jesus, the ultimate researcher, knows that besides a relationship with God, the one thing that really matters in life are our relationships to other people. Jesus prays for his followers to become the kind of community where that truth is applied to its ultimate degree.

Tom Rath, head of research at the Gallup Organization, drew on eight million interviews for his book, *Vital Friends*.[18] In a recent interview Rath summarized his findings in this way: "Close relationships and friendships are the single most important human need when it comes to our satisfaction with life."[19] This is what Jesus prays about in John 17. Jesus, the ultimate interviewer, knows what truly lies in the heart of humanity. Besides a close relationship with God, the single most important human need is our need for close relationships with people. Jesus prays that his church will become the contrast community in which this need is fulfilled.

Practicing This Prayer

Jesus' prayer urges us to pray for the same things. We might consider three stages of prayers motivated by this John 17 prayer. In the first stage, we pray about ourselves. Spend time this week praying for God to empower you to truly bond with one or two others who are similar to you. Pray for God to enable you to truly bridge with one or two others who are unlike you. Pray that your own life this week will begin to be a miniature contrast community. Pray for God to lead you deeply into the kind of friendship with one or two people that could only be attributed to him. Pray this week for God to lead you into a few relationships with people who are so different from you, only God could be behind it.

In the second stage, we might pray about people like us who are already in Jesus' community. Pray this week for the people in your congregation. If you don't attend church regularly, then pray for congregations near where you live. Pray that God will enable every person already in that congregation to experience true intimacy with another human and true unity with someone different from themselves. Pray that this week God will begin using your congregation or an other local congregations as a contrast community.

In the third stage, we might pray for those outside Jesus' community. We might pray that God would send them to our congregations so that we might bond and bridge with them in a way that leads them to believe only God could be responsible for what they are experiencing. Mark Buchanan writes about attending a prayer meeting at the Brooklyn Tabernacle, led by Jim Cymbala.[20] He reports

> Afterward, my friend and I went out to dinner with the Cymbalas. In the course of the meal, Jim turned to me and said, "Mark, do you know what the number one sin of the church in America is?" I wasn't sure, and the question was rhetorical anyhow. "It's not the plague of internet pornography that is consuming our men. It's not that the divorce rate in the church is roughly the same as society at large." Jim named two or three other candidates for the worst sin, all of which he dismissed. "The number one sin of the church in America," he said, "is that its pastors and leaders are not on their knees crying out to God, 'Bring us the drug-addicted, bring us the prostitutes, bring us the destitute, bring us the gang leaders, bring us those with AIDS, bring us the people nobody else wants, whom only you can heal, and let us love them in your name until they are whole.'"

That's the stage-three prayer. This week, with passion and conviction, start praying that prayer: "God, bring us the drug-addicted, bring us the prostitutes, bring us the destitute, bring us the gang leaders, bring us those with AIDS, bring us the people nobody else wants, whom only you can heal, and let us love them in your name until they are whole."

---

1. Robert Putnam, *Bowling Alone: the collapse and revival of American community* (Simon and Schuster, 2001), 22-23.
2. Miller McPherson, Lynn Smith-Lovin, and Matthew E. Brashears, "Social isolation in America: Changes in Core Discussion Networks over Two Decades," *American Sociological Review.*
3. Paul Adams, *Social Circles: How offline relationships influence online behavior and what it means for design and marketing* (New Rider Press, 2010).
4. Donald Miller, *Blue Like Jazz: Nonreligious Thoughts on Christian Spirituality* (Thomas Nelson, 2003), 159-171.
5. Mark Twain, *The Adventures of Huckleberry Finn* (Fawcet Columbine, 1996), 5-6.
6. John Ortberg, *Everybody's Normal Till You Get to Know Them* (Zondervan, 2003), 31-32.
7. Madeleine Albright, Yale Divinity School (March 2004).
8. http://www.cnn.com/2006/US/12/12/racism.poll/index.html.
9. Ibid.
10. "Why Many Americans Prefer Their Sunday Segregated," John Blake, Why Many Americans Prefer Their Sunday Segregated *CNN.com* (2008). http://www.cnn.com/2008/LIVING/wayoflife/08/04/segregated.sundays/index.html#cnnSTCText.
11. Robert Putnam, Lewis Feldstein and Donald J. Cohen, *Better Together: Restoring the American community* (Simon & Schuster, 2004), 3.
12. Alan Roxburgh and M. Scott Boren, *Introducing the Missional Church: What It Is, Why It Matters, How to Become One* (Baker Books, 2009).
13. Fred B. Craddock *Craddock Stories* (Chalice Press, 2001), 49-50.
14. Timothy P. Jones, *Praying Like the Jew, Jesus: Recovering the Ancient Roots of New Testament Prayer* (Lederer Books, 2005), 95.
15. Larry Crabb, *The Safest Place on Earth* (Word Publishing, 1999).
16. Aelred of Rievaulx, *Spiritual Friendship* (Cistercian Publications, 1977), 71-72.
17. Joshua Wolf Shenk, "What Makes Us Happy?" *The Atlantic* (June 2009), 36–53.
18. Tom Rath, *Vital Friends: the people you can't afford to live without* (Gallup Press, 2006).
19. Caroline Wilbert, "You Schmooze, You Win" *Fast Company* (July/August 2006), 109.
20. Mark Buchanan, "Messy, Costly, Dirty Ministry," Leadershipjournal.net (5/15/09).

Chapter 13

An Outward Prayer of Compassion:
Forgive Their Faults (Luke 23)

Hurting

Marvin leaned in closely so he could share his story without others hearing. We were talking in a school cafeteria filled with students and staff. "We asked Nancy to make a Christmas wish list," Marvin said. Nancy is his elementary-aged daughter. She had recently started attending a new school. It was a rough start. Not only was Nancy navigating a new building, getting used to new teachers, and walking hallways filled with new faces—she was also being tormented by a bully. A girl named Jacquelyn made it her mission to terrorize and tease Nancy. Nancy came home from school most days with tears in her eyes. Marvin told me that the situation had now found its way onto Nancy's Christmas wish list. "Do you know what Nancy wrote down as the last item on her Christmas list?" he asked me. "She wrote this: 'I pray that God takes Jacquelyn home.'" Simply put, Nancy wanted Jacquelyn dead. That's how deeply she had been hurt.

Sadly, even at a young age we experience what becomes all too common throughout life. People hurt us. Some intentionally. Some unintentionally. The reality of life is that, at times, we will be disappointed and devastated by people around us.

Heather Gemmen Wilson is the author of *Startling Beauty*.[1] When Heather and her husband were penniless college students, the only place they could afford was an inner-city apartment. They planned to leave the apartment as soon as they could afford to move. But they started attending a church which had a vision for community development and racial reconciliation. They were hooked. They decided to live long-term in the inner city. They began to raise a family. For four years they reached out to the neighborhood. They held block parties and community rummage sales. Then one night while her husband was at a meeting at the church building and her two young children were sleeping, Heather woke to find a stranger standing by the side of her bed. Before she could do anything the man attacked her. She survived. Her church rallied around her. She still has a loving family. She writes and speaks publicly about the event. But it was a defining moment in her life. This righteous and godly woman—dedicated to serving the inner city—was not immune from the ugliness of that same inner city.

Even in the midst of serving and saving others, we can be hurt. Deeply. And sometimes those hurts define us for the rest of our lives.

Nowhere is the hurt caused by humans greater than at the cross of Christ. Consider all the people who are there, just to harm Jesus. The people in the government abuse him. The people in the religious leadership reject him. The people in his friendship circle abandon him. The person being executed on the next cross ridicules him. Even the Son of God endures pain from other people.

Like some of those who hurt Jesus, some of the people who hurt us are people who claim to follow God. A preacher who betrays a confidence. A church-going father who rarely ever says, "I'm proud of you." Like some of those who hurt Jesus, some who hurt us have nothing to do with God. An agnostic university professor who won't give us a second chance. An unbelieving mother who ridicules our faith. Like some who hurt Jesus, some who hurt us are those closest to us. A spouse who walks out the door. A friend who steals our boyfriend. And like some who hurt Jesus, some who hurt us are complete strangers. A woman who cuts in front of you in the long line at the grocery store. A customer who complains to the boss about you. There are few seasons in life when we are not forced to deal with an abrasion or two from those around us: the godly, the godless, friends, and strangers.

Help Me and Hurt Them

With these injuries in mind, Jesus prayed. Specifically, he prayed for help. In the Garden of Gethsemane, Jesus prayed for help—that God would make it possible for Jesus to escape the hurt that people were about to cause. On the cross, Jesus prayerfully lamented the pain he was experiencing because of others. The lament was essentially a plea for God to end the pain. And, on the cross, Jesus turned his hurt over to the hands of God. This was a cry for God to receive him now that his life had been severed by painful people. When people hurt Jesus, he prayed "Help me."

Others, in similar circumstances, have prayed "Hurt them." There is a collection of psalms called "imprecatory psalms." They are written by people who have been hurt by others. But these petitioners don't just ask for help. They ask for hurt. For example, in Psalm 69 David writes, "More in number than the hairs of my head are those who hate me without cause; mighty are those who would destroy me, those who attack me with lies" (Psalm. 69:4). David is following God. He is obedient. Yet people are hurting him. So, like Jesus, he prays. Like us, he prays.

But listen to how he prays: "Let their own table before them become a snare; and when they are at peace, let it become a trap. Let their eyes be darkened, so that they cannot see, and make their loins tremble continually. Pour out your indignation upon them, and let your burning anger overtake them. May their camp be a desolation; let no one dwell in their tents. For they persecute him whom you have struck down, and they recount the pain of those you have wounded. Add to them punishment upon punishment; may they have no acquittal from you. Let them be blotted out of the book of the living; let them not be enrolled among the righteous" (Psalm 69:22-28). David doesn't just pray for help. He prays for hurt. He prays for God to hurt those who hurt him.

These are the words we might like to pray about the people who hurt us. Punish them! Make them pay! Blind them! Break their backs! When we are hurt by others, we may be tempted to pray for hurt. At our best we just pray "Help me." At our worst we pray "Hurt them."

Almost every Sunday morning after services at Highland, I hug a young woman whose wedding I conducted. After only a year or so of marriage, she caught her husband sending sexually suggestive text messages to another woman. She confronted her husband. He apologized—then did it again. She feels humiliated and used. How should she pray? Help me? Or Hurt him?

How many of us go to bed at night nursing the wounds caused by a hateful child, a hard-hearted parent, an insensitive spouse, an incompetent doctor, an uncompromising teacher, or a demanding boss? What do we pray? Help me? Or hurt them? Neither seems completely effective in dealing with these difficulties.

Praying Another Way

Once again, a prayer of Jesus provides an alternative. From the cross Jesus prays another way into existence. It is a way that may not even seem possible in our world. Yet it is a way that can truly change everything: "And Jesus said, 'Father, forgive them, for they know not what they do'" (Luke 23:34). Notice what Jesus prays. He doesn't pray "Help me." He doesn't pray, "Hurt them." Instead, he prays, "Forgive them."

Luke literally writes that Jesus "was saying" this prayer. The language suggests ongoing action. It means something like this: They beat him and Jesus was saying, "Father, forgive them, for they know not what they do."

They cursed at him and Jesus was saying, "Father, forgive them, for they know not what they do." They nailed the right hand and Jesus was saying, "Father, forgive them, for they know not what they do." They nailed the left hand and Jesus was saying, "Father, forgive them, for they know not what they do." Again and again Jesus prayed for the forgiveness of those making his life so miserable.

And it's not just that Jesus himself forgave them—that would be assumed by this prayer. It's that he also asked God to forgive them. Jesus actively spoke up on their behalves before God. He testified in the heavenly court—not as a witness for the prosecution, but as a witness for the defense. "Father, forgive them, for they know not what they do."

Notice, next, when this prayer came. It came immediately after the hurt:[2]

> Two others, who were criminals, were led away to be put to death with him. And when they came to the place that is called The Skull, there they crucified him, and the criminals, one on his right and one on his left. And Jesus said, "Father, forgive them, for they know not what they do." And they cast lots to divide his garments. And the people stood by, watching, but the rulers scoffed at him, saying, "He saved others; let him save himself, if he is the Christ of God, his Chosen One!" The soldiers also mocked him, coming up and offering him sour wine and saying, "If you are the King of the Jews, save yourself!" There was also an inscription over him, "This is the King of the Jews" (Luke 23:33-35).

The pain arrives and the prayerful pardon immediately rises. The prayer for forgiveness did not come at the very end of the torment, after Jesus had time to process the hurt; after Jesus had time work up some kind of compassion for these people. Instead, it's the first prayer out of his lips on the cross. It's as if Jesus' gut reaction was to pray for forgiveness. His instinctual response, the one that happens almost without thought, was intercessory forgiveness.

Finally, notice for whom Jesus prayed. Jesus did not simply pray for someone who cut him off in traffic. He did not simply pray for a stranger who flung an unkind word. Jesus prayed this prayer of forgiveness for his worst enemies, for those trying to end his life. Consider this: Jesus' prayer list included his worst enemies. If we could look over his intercession journal we'd find not only the names of his disciples, not only the names of some of the poor and lame and crippled he helped, and not only the names of children. We'd also find the names of the people who hurt him most deeply. And we'd find this prayer by their names: "Father, forgive them, for they know not what they do."

The Other Lord's Prayer

This is the same prayer which Jesus taught us to pray earlier in his ministry. In his Sermon on the Mount, Jesus addresses people who are hurting. In Matthew 5 he implies that some of his listeners are being persecuted, some are the object of verbal abuse at home, some have critics among their religious circles, some have people dragging them to court, some have unfaithful spouses, some have people lying to them, and some have Roman soldiers and others forcing them into labor. What are they to do? Are they to pray for help? Are they to ask for God to hurt their "thorns in the flesh"?

Jesus leads them in none of those directions. Instead, he teaches them a prayer:

> "Pray then like this: Our Father in heaven, hallowed be your name. Your kingdom come, your will be done, on earth as it is in heaven. Give us this day our daily bread, and *forgive* us our debts, as we also have *forgiven* our debtors. And lead us not into temptation, but deliver us from evil. For if you *forgive* others their trespasses, your heavenly Father will also *forgive* you, but if you do not *forgive* others their trespasses, neither will your Father *forgive* your trespasses" (Matthew 6:9-15, emphasis added).

Six times in these seven verses the same word pops up: "forgive." In our world of hurt and injustice, Jesus points to forgiveness. Jesus teaches us to pray for the pardon of those who cause our pain.

The placement of this prayer for forgiveness just after the prayer about daily bread is suggestive—just as daily bread is necessary in a world filled with hunger, so forgiveness is necessary in a world filled with hurt. The world must have both bread and forgiveness in order to function.

To those being hit, sued, and forced to meet unreasonable demands, Jesus says, "Pray this: 'Forgive us our debts, as we also have forgiven our debtors.'" To those promised one thing and given another, Jesus says, "Pray this: 'Forgive us our debts, as we also have forgiven our debtors.'" To victims of emotional and physical adultery, Jesus says, "Pray this: 'Forgive us our debts, as we also have forgiven our debtors.'" To people dragged to court and criticized in church, Jesus says, "Pray this: 'Forgive us our debts, as we also have forgiven our debtors.'" It's the sibling of the prayer Jesus prays from the cross.

Notice that while we want to think about our debtors and people who sin against us, Jesus wants us to think about our debts and those we've sinned against: "Forgive us our debts, as we also have forgiven our debtors." Rather than have us focus on those who victimized us, Jesus has us focus on our victims. We can't pray this prayer, and deal with people who have hurt us, without first admitting that we have hurt others. We have caused pain to others and we need forgiveness from God for that pain. Before we even think about what to do about the pain others have caused us, Jesus makes us first think about the pain we've caused others.

And this pain we've caused others has actually wounded God. Jesus doesn't urge us to first ask forgiveness from the people we've hurt. He urges us to ask forgiveness from the God we've hurt. Jesus shows God to be the ultimate victim of our own intentional and unintentional offenses against others. Just as those who have hurt us have little idea that they've hurt us or how deeply they've hurt us, so we hurt others and God with little idea that we've done so or how deeply we've done so.[3] I am ashamed at how often my wife Kendra has to come to me and say, "What you just did or what you just said really hurt me." She has to say that because I'm totally oblivious. I have no idea that I have hurt her. That very thing happens every day in many relationships. We hurt others without even realizing it. And, we hurt God without even realizing it.

Thus Jesus teaches us a prayer which forces us to realize this problem. Just as you stand before God wrestling with pain and struggling to forgive the person who caused it, someone else is standing before God wrestling with the pain you caused and struggling to forgive you. And God himself wrestles with the thoughtless and insensitive things we've done to him and to others. Today, God will wrestle with six billion people, each of whom will likely wound, offend, or crush him in some way. Six billion times God could say today, "What you just said or did really hurt me." And this view of God puts our pains in perspective. How much easier it becomes to extend forgiveness. Our world is no longer one of victims (us) and victimizers (others). It is one where each of us is a victimizer and God is the ultimate victim.

But Jesus doesn't just show God as the ultimate victim. Jesus shows God as the ultimate forgiver. Jesus fully expects that when we pray, "Forgive us our debts," God will do just that. He teaches us to address God in this prayer as "Our Father." We are not approaching an uncompromising boss, a revenge-driven spouse, or a callous co-worker. We are approaching the Father of Fathers, one with a tender heart toward his children. And though six billion times today humanity may need to say, "Forgive us our debts," six billion times our Father will say, "I forgive."

For those of us who go to bed at night nursing the wounds caused by a hateful child, a hard-hearted parent, an insensitive spouse, or a demanding boss, forgiveness becomes much more possible when we experience forgiveness from God. You simply cannot visit the cross and have your debt erased with Jesus' blood and then not extend forgiveness to that child, parent, spouse, or boss. As we pray Jesus' prayer—"forgive us our debts"—we experience that forgiveness. We come to see God not only as the ultimate victim, but as the ultimate forgiver. And that experience can lead us to forgive others.

Jesus makes explicit this connection between receiving forgiveness and extending forgiveness. In his commentary on the prayer for pardon, Jesus says, "For if you forgive others their trespasses, your heavenly Father will also forgive you, but if you do not forgive others their trespasses, neither will your Father forgive your trespasses."

We tend to create two separate areas related to forgiveness. There's God's forgiveness of me. And there's my forgiveness of others. They are two unrelated file drawers in our hearts. But Jesus shows that they are related. We cannot speak of one without the other. They coexist in the same file. A wife giving forgiveness to her husband for the way he insensitively treated her at a large business party is intimately connected to her receiving forgiveness from God for the way she lied during a recent job interview. A man who seeks forgiveness from God for the way he flew off the handle at his boss is intimately connected to that same man extending forgiveness to his aged parent who always complains that the man doesn't love him. If we forgive others, God will forgive us. If we don't forgive others, God will not forgive us.

Jesus is saying that once received, forgiveness cannot be hoarded. The forgiveness I receive from God today for the selfish way I spent my money cannot be held. It must be released to the driver who cut me off and cursed at me.

It is like a door.[4] When a door is closed, it is not just closed to those on one side of it, but also closed to those on the other side of it. A closed door keeps people from entering a house and from exiting a house. Concerning forgiveness, each of us is a door. When someone hurts us and we slam the door in his or her face, refusing to extend forgiveness, we have also slammed the door in the face of the God who wishes to extend forgiveness to us. The door that prevents our forgiveness from exiting our heart to the one who hurt us also prevents God's forgiveness from entering our heart for the wrongs we've committed. But as long as that door of forgiveness is kept open to every person who wounds us, it is also kept open to the forgiveness God extends for our own wrongs.

It is like a hand.[5] When a hand is closed, it cannot release what it is holding inside. But neither can it receive something else that someone may want to give. If I close my hand and refuse to release forgiveness to someone who has hurt me, I cannot receive forgiveness from God whom I have hurt. I cannot hold a grudge against another and receive forgiveness from God. But as long as my hand is open and releasing forgiveness to others, it is also able to receive the forgiveness God longs to grant.

Thus not only is God the ultimate victim. Not only is God the ultimate forgiver. But here Jesus shows us that God is the ultimate source of all forgiveness. The forgiveness you need to extend to someone who has hurt you comes from God. As he releases forgiveness to you, you receive it, and then release it to others. God is the ultimate source of forgiveness. We can forgive because the forgiveness he's extended to us is now available to be passed along to others.

Father Forgive

This line in the Lord's Prayer leads us back to the ultimate Lord's Prayer: "Father, forgive them, for they know not what they do." This may be the greatest lesson about prayer we learn from Jesus—the call to pray for the forgiveness of those who hurt us. This is the peak of the Mount Everest of prayer. It is the ultimate mark of spiritual maturity. It is the greatest practice toward which we should strive: to pray for the forgiveness of people who hurt us.

Immaculee Ilibagiza is the author of the New York Times bestseller, *Left to Tell*.[6] In 1994 during the Rwandan genocide, Immaculee and seven other women hid from murderous warlords. A local preacher, at risk of his own life, took the eight women in and hid them in a small bathroom in his home. Using large furniture he hid the bathroom from those searching for the women. Immaculee spent ninety-one days huddled silently with the seven others in that small bathroom. On the day she fled for her life into that room she was a one hundred fifteen pound university student with a loving family. On the day she was able to escape, she was only sixty-five pounds. And with the exception of a brother who had been studying outside of the country, her entire family was murdered.

Immaculee credits her ability to survive to prayer. Anger and resentment ate at her day after day in that bathroom. But rather than succumb to the rage, she prayed. Each day she prayed from the moment she awoke to the moment she fell back asleep. It was prayer, she said, that enabled her to deal with her pursuers and her family's murderers.

She later came face to face with the killer of her mother and her brother. She forgave him. In 1998, Immaculee immigrated to the United States. She shared her story with co-workers and friends who were so impacted they urged her to write it down. Immaculee's book, *Left to Tell*, has been translated into fifteen languages worldwide. She has appeared on *Sixty Minutes* and *CNN*, and in *The New York Times* and *USA Today*. She has been featured in Michael Collopy's "Architects of Peace" project, which has honored legendary people like Mother Teresa, Jimmy Carter, Nelson Mandela, and the Dalai Lama. She has been recognized and honored with numerous humanitarian awards. *Left to Tell* has been adopted into the curriculum of high schools and universities, including Villanova University, which made it mandatory reading for six thousand students.

What amazes people around the world about this story? What is it about Immaculee that makes teachers tell six thousand students, "You must read her book"? Why has she been honored time and time again? Because she was able to pray something so few pray. She was able to pray this prayer of Jesus: "Father, forgive them, for they know not what they do."

Warren Larson is an associate professor of Islam in South Carolina.[7] From 1969 through 1991 he was a church planter in Pakistan. He tells of a time in 1979 when a local holy place was run over by insurgents. A rumor was spread that the blasphemy was the work of Americans. When the rumor hit the city where Larson was living, a mob formed and descended upon Larson and his family. The mob burned the family's jeeps, smashed their furniture, burned their literature and threatened to kill the Larsons. A few days later the news revealed that those who had desecrated the holy site had not been Americans, but Saudis. The police and military rescued the Larson's and put some of the mob in jail. Larson visited them and said, "We forgive you. We are not going to lodge a case against you." When Larson's neighbors learned of what he had done, they embraced him. They said, "Mr. Larson, we now know the difference between you and us. We do not forgive our enemies. When there's trouble between us, Sunnis and Shiites, we fight and burn one another's shops. But you have forgiven us." Larson replied, "We're just doing what Jesus taught us to do."

It's what Jesus teaches us all to do: "Father, forgive them, for they know not what they do."

Gladys Staines has become the best-known Christian in India.[8] She and her husband worked for decades among the leprosy victims in India. But several years ago an anti-Christian mob descended on her husband's jeep while he and his two young sons were sleeping in it. The mob doused the jeep with fuel and set it on fire, killing all three. During the trial and conviction of the Hindu activist who led the mob, Staines said she intended to remain in India and continue her work with lepers. And, she said, she forgave her husband's killers. A reporter talked with her about it. "We have to forgive," she said. "Jesus taught us to forgive."

It was taught most powerfully through his prayer: "Father, forgive them, for they know not what they do."

In his book, *No Future Without Forgiveness*, retired Archbishop Desmond Tutu recounts the events of 1994 when South Africa was freed from apartheid.[9] Before that day, South Africans had been tear-gassed, bitten by police dogs, struck with batons, detained, tortured, imprisoned, and murdered. But on April 27, 1994 South Africans elected Nelson Mandela as President. It was a new day. But once the euphoria of the new day passed, a hard question remained: How was South Africa to deal with the injustices perpetrated under apartheid? They followed the path of Christ. Desmond Tutu once summarized their experience in these words:[10]

> I have been overwhelmed by the depth of depravity and evil that has been exposed by the amnesty process of the Truth and Reconciliation Commission appointed to deal with the gross human rights violations that happened in our apartheid past. I am devastated to hear police officers describe how they drugged the coffee of one of their charges, shot him behind the ear, and then set his body on fire...That is the one side. There is also another side—the story of the victims, the survivors who were made to suffer so grievously, yet despite this are ready to forgive...So, what would I have done? I answer by pointing to the fact that the people who have been tortured, whose loved ones were abducted, killed, and buried secretly...can testify to the Commission and say they are ready to forgive the perpetrators. It is happening before our very eyes. But there are others who say that they are not ready to forgive, demonstrating that forgiveness is not facile or cheap. It is a costly business that makes those who are willing to forgive even more extraordinary...Our president, Nelson Mandela, was incarcerated for twenty-seven years and not mollycoddled. His eyesight has been ruined because he had to work in the glare of a quarry; his family was harassed by the state security police. He should by rights be consumed

by bitterness and a lust for revenge. The world watched with awe when he so magnanimously invited his white jailer to his inauguration as South Africa's first democratically elected president. I could tell of others, both black and white and less well known, who if asked, "What would you have done?" would have done the same—they have forgiven amazingly, unbelievably. Many claim to be Christians. They say they follow the Jewish rabbi who, when he was crucified, said, 'Father, forgive them for they know not what they do.' I sit and marvel at it all..."

When we finally and fully learn this ultimate prayer-lesson from Jesus, the entire world will sit and marvel at it all.

Father, forgive them, for they know not what they do.

Practicing this Prayer

First, imagine the person who is praying this prayer because you are the one who has hurt them. Something you said or didn't say, did or didn't do has caused a deep wound. Today that person is praying this prayer for you: Father, forgive them. Each day this week, talk to God about this sin of yours, asking forgiveness for the injury you caused to someone else. Receive God's gracious and abundant forgiveness. Give thanks that someone might pray on your behalf in this way.

Now, bring to mind someone who has hurt you. Each day this week pray this prayer: "Father, forgive _____ , for they know not what they do."

1. Heather Gemmon Wilson, "Calling on the Saints," *Christianity Today* (February, 2008), 50-51.
2. John Indermark, *Traveling the Prayer Paths of Jesus* (Upper Room Books, 2003), 146.
3. R. T. Kendall, "Forgiving the Unrepentant," *Christianity Today*, (March 2005), 78.
4. Jon Stubblefield "Matthew 6:5-15" *Review & Expositor* (1990).
5. David Garland, "The Lord's Prayer in the Gospel of Matthew" *Review & Expositor* (Spring 1992).
6. Immaculee Ilibagiza, *Left to Tell: Discovering God Amidst the Rwandan Holocaust* (Hay House, 2006).
7. Stan Guthrie, "Waging Peace with Islam," *Christianity Today* (June, 2005), 46-47.
8. Tim Stafford, "India Undaunted," *Christianity Today* (May, 2004), 34-35.
9. Desmond Tutu, *No Future Without Forgiveness* (Doubleday, 1999).
10. Simon Wiesenthal, *The Sunflower: On the Possibilities and Limits of Forgiveness* (Schocken Books, 1998), 266-268.

40 Days Following
the Prayer Steps of Jesus

Overview

This resource leads you through most of the references to the prayers and prayer-life of Jesus in the Gospels. These references are covered in chronological order. Days 1-7 are introductory in nature. The chronological references begin on Day 8.

■ Day 1

I often think of prayer as a pathway to two things: resources and relationships. I pray in order to gain the resources which I cannot produce myself. And I pray in order to gain the relationship with God which I cannot deepen any other way. Yet on both of these counts, it would seem that Jesus would not need prayer.

Consider resources. Jesus has the power to create most resources himself. He has the ability to create food—he multiplied fish and loaves. He has the capacity to heal illness—he cured blindness and cleansed leprosy. He can control the weather—he stilled a storm with just a phrase. Why would someone like Jesus even need to pray? What resources would Jesus require that he could not produce himself?

In addition, consider the issue of relationship. Jesus and the Father are one. If one purpose of prayer is to cultivate intimacy with God, it would appear Jesus already has the deepest intimacy possible. He is so intimate with God that the two are one.

In spite of all of this, Jesus still prays. There are about thirty references in the Gospels to the prayers and prayer-life of Jesus. From his baptism in Luke 3:21 to his ascension in Luke 24:51, we find Jesus praying. As Luke explains in Luke 5:16, "But he would withdraw to desolate places and pray." Prayer is a habit. It is something Jesus constantly does. Jesus prays at the feeding of the five thousand (Mark 6:41) and after the feeding of the five thousand (Mark 6:46). He prays for the forgotten (children) (Mark 10:15-16), his fellow workers (John 17), his global family (John 17), and his foes

(Luke 23:34). He prays when healing (Mark 7:32-34) and when hurting (Matthew 27:46).

There were resources needed by Jesus that he could gain in no other way but through prayer. There was a level of relationship with the Father that could be experienced in no other way but through prayer. Because of this, Jesus prayed.

The mere fact that Jesus prays so passionately and consistently is striking. As those who wear the name of Jesus, it seems especially crucial for us to make room in our lives for prayer in the same way Jesus did.

■ Day 2

For about ten years, my family has gathered at the same house on New Year's Eve with (mostly) the same people. We eat finger foods, play board games, and bring in the New Year with toasts, sparklers, and fireworks. It's become a tradition—a meaningful way to mark a significant event.

In fact, it's one of many traditions in our family. For example, at Christmas our kids always open one present on Christmas Eve and the rest on Christmas morning. In addition, on the last Saturday of summer break, we used to always visit *Libertyland*—a local amusement park (until it went bankrupt). Further, each November and December our family donates food and toys to those in need. Finally, when a good report card comes in, we all go out to eat to celebrate.

Not only do we as individuals and families seek out meaningful ways to mark significant events, but we as cities, states, and nations do as well. Few cities mark Martin Luther King, Jr. Day or the anniversary of Elvis Presley's death like Memphis, Tennessee. The United States marks July 4 with enormous fireworks displays. And most nations have some form of New Year's Eve celebration.

Given our tendency to mark significant moments in time, it is interesting to watch how Jesus did the same. At key events in his ministry, Jesus consistently and intentionally marked the moment. Time and time again, Jesus marked it in the same way:

1. After his baptism: "Now when all the people were baptized, and when Jesus also had been baptized and was praying" (Luke 3:21).

2. Prior to the choosing of the Twelve: "In these days he went out to the mountain to pray, and all night he continued in prayer to God. And when day came, he called his disciples and chose from them twelve" (Luke 6:12-13).

3. Prior to Peter's confession: "Now it happened that as he was praying alone, the disciples were with him. And he asked them, 'Who do the crowds say that I am?'" (Luke. 9:18).

4. At the Transfiguration: "And as he was praying, the appearance of his face was altered, and his clothing became dazzling white" (Luke 9:29).

5. At the Lord's Supper: "Now as they were eating, Jesus took bread, and after blessing it broke it and gave it to the disciples, and said, 'Take, eat; this is my body'" (Matthew 26:26).

6. In Gethsemane: "And he withdrew from them about a stone's throw, and knelt down and prayed, saying, 'Father, if you are willing, remove this cup from me'" (Luke 22:41, 42).

7. On the cross:
   1) "And Jesus said, 'Father, forgive them, for they know not what they do'" (Luke 23:34).
   2) "My God, my God, why have you forsaken me?" (Matthew 27:46; Mark 15:34).
   3) "Father, into your hands I commit my spirit" (Luke 23:46).
   4) "After this, Jesus, knowing that all was now finished, said (to fulfill the Scripture), 'I thirst'" (John 19:28).
   5) "When Jesus had received the sour wine, he said, 'It is finished,' and he bowed his head and gave up his spirit" (John 19:30).

Jesus regularly marked the most important moments of his life with prayer. Jesus wanted to experience these events in communion with the Father.

What are the key moments in your life? Your city's life? Your state's life? Your country's life? Your world's life? How might you mark those moments with prayer?

■ Day 3

For whom did Jesus pray? We have about thirty references in the Gospels to Jesus' prayers and prayer-life. Of these references, we have ten actual prayers Jesus prayed. For whom did Jesus pray? If we could look at his prayer list, who would be on it?

While it's almost certain Jesus prayed for many others, we do know he prayed specifically for four groups of people:

We find Jesus praying for children:

"Truly, I say to you, whoever does not receive the kingdom of God like a child shall not enter it." And he took them in his arms and blessed them, laying his hands on them (Mark 10:15-16).

We find Jesus praying for the apostles/disciples:

"I am praying for them. I am not praying for the world but for those whom you have given me, for they are yours... Holy Father, keep them in your name, which you have given me, that they may be one, even as we are one... I do not ask that you take them out of the world, but that you keep them from the evil one. They are not of the world, just as I am not of the world. Sanctify them in the truth; your word is truth. As you sent me into the world, so I have sent them into the world. And for their sake I consecrate myself, that they also may be sanctified in truth" (John 17:9-19).

"Simon, Simon, behold, Satan demanded to have you, that he might sift you like wheat, but I have prayed for you that your faith may not fail" (Luke 22:31-32).

Then he led them out as far as Bethany, and lifting up his hands he blessed them. While he blessed them, he parted from them and was carried up into heaven (Luke 24:50-51).

We find Jesus praying for the church:

"I do not ask for these only, but also for those who will believe in me through their word, that they may all be one, just as you, Father, are in me, and I in you, that they also may be in us, so that the world may believe that you have sent me. The glory that you have given me I have given to them, that they may be one even as we are one, I in them and you in me, that they may become perfectly one, so that the world may know that you sent me and loved them even as you loved me" (John 17:20-23).

And we find Jesus praying for his enemies:

And Jesus said, "Father, forgive them, for they know not what they do' (Luke 23:34).

In other words, we find Jesus praying for those who cannot speak for themselves, those with whom he's engaged in mission and ministry, those who make his life difficult, and those around the world who would follow him. The *forgotten*, his *fellow-laborers*, his *foes*, and his international *family*.

Which of these four show up on your prayer list? Which do not? Why? Why not?

■ Day 4

New Testament scholar, I. Howard Marshall, points out why the Gospel accounts of Jesus' prayers are so important.[1] He notes that the Gospels do not usually record normal life situations like Jesus eating, or Jesus sleeping, or Jesus washing himself. For the most part, the Gospels take for granted that Jesus did such things. But when the Gospels do stop to indicate that Jesus ate, or slept, or washed, they do so because something unusual is taking place (e.g., Jesus is entering a deliberate fast or Jesus is sleeping at an unusual time).

In the same way, Marshall writes, the Gospels take for granted that Jesus prayed. Prayer for Jews was a normal practice of everyday life. They, and Jesus, would have prayed set prayers in the synagogue, said grace before meals, and uttered personal prayers in the morning, afternoon, and evening. When the Gospels do stop to highlight a prayer practice of Jesus, they do so because there is something unusual or out of the ordinary taking place.

For example, we are told that Jesus often prayed in the early hours of the morning. This is mentioned because it is outside of the norm. The average pious Jew would not have engaged in such a practice. In addition, we are told that after feeding the crowd, Jesus spends the late night period in prayer. This also seems to be mentioned because it is outside of the norm. The average pious Jew would not have done such a thing. Marshall's point is that Jesus not only prayed—he prayed above and beyond the religious expectations and norms of his day. Jesus' prayer-life stood above that of other pious Jews.

Too often I am content if I can point to the way in which my prayer-life is keeping up with other people whom I consider pious. As long as my prayer-life is nearly equivalent to prayerful people whom I admire, I am satisfied. When I look to Jesus, however, I am forced to stretch and push and grow. Because he prayed even beyond the norm, I am also compelled to do so.

■ Day 5

In Luke 11 we find Jesus' followers intrigued by Jesus' prayer-life: "Now Jesus was praying in a certain place, and when he finished, one of his disciples said to him, 'Lord, teach us to pray, as John taught his disciples'" (Luke 11:1).

Joachim Jeremias writes that in the Judaism of Jesus' time it was common for individual religious groups to have their own customs and practices regarding prayer.[2] The Pharisees and Essenes had prayer practices unique to their groups. John's disciples did as well. Thus, here, the disciples ask Jesus to give them their unique prayer. They want a prayer that will set them apart from the other religious groups. They literally want a "Jesus Prayer."

But what was the "Jesus Prayer"? What prayer would distinguish followers of Jesus from all others? What would it mean to pray in a distinctly Christ like way? Here is the prayer Jesus gave in response to the request: "Father, hallowed be your name. Your kingdom come. Give us each day our daily bread, and forgive us our sins, for we ourselves forgive everyone who is indebted to us. And lead us not into temptation" (Luke 11:2-4).

Jeremias argues that one particular word makes this prayer distinctly Christian. One specific word sets this prayer, and all of Jesus' prayers, apart from the known prayers of other religious groups of the time: the word "Father." What makes Jesus' prayer distinct is the way he not only addresses God as Father but the way he interacts with God as Father through prayer. Jesus' "Lord's Prayer" gives us one manifestation of this distinctiveness: "Father, hallowed be your name." As we listen to the Son talk to the Father, we learn what it means to be truly "Christian" in our prayers.

■ Day 6

New Testament scholar I. Howard Marshall writes that what made Jesus' prayers distinctive was the way in which they focused on God as "Father."[3] In the Old Testament, which is about 3 times the length of the New Testament, the word "Father" is used over 1,200 times. In the New Testament, the word is used over 400 times. These figures are about what we would expect since the Old Testament is 3 times the length of the New and therefore has about 3 times as many references to Father. But if we count only the number of times that "Father" is used with reference to God, then we find that only 40 (3%) of the occurrences of the word in the Old Testament refer to God. In the New Testament 260 (63%) of the occurrences refer to God. The New Testament takes a giant leap from the Old Testament in speaking about God as "Father". How do we explain this leap? What happened from the Old Testament to the New Testament?

Marshall suggests that what happened is Jesus. Jesus frequently referred to God as Father in his teaching. In addition, Jesus often spoke of God as Father in his prayers. While this was not necessarily novel, Jesus' laser-like focus on God as Father in his teaching and in his prayers led to

Father becoming the dominant way of understanding God in the New Testament.

Every time we pray, "Father, help me…" or "Father, please be with…" or "Our Father in heaven…" we have Jesus to thank.

■ Day 7

> Now when all the people were baptized, and when Jesus also had been baptized and was praying, the heavens were opened, and the Holy Spirit descended on him in bodily form, like a dove; and a voice came from heaven, "You are my beloved Son; with you I am well pleased" (Luke 3:21-22).

All four Gospels mention the baptism of Jesus (Matthew 3:13-17; Mark 1:9-11; John 1:32-34). Only Luke tells us that the descent of the Spirit and the voice from heaven were preceded by the prayer of Jesus (Luke 3:21). The anointing presence of God (the dove/Holy Spirit) and the loving affirmation of God (the voice) came in response to prayer. Jesus' ministry begins here, and as it begins, God speaks to Jesus through prayer: "I am with you; I love you."

Spend a few moments in silence right now. Think of the day, month, or year ahead of you. Ask God to be with you. Listen for God's voice: "I am with you." And, ask God to affirm you. Listen for God's voice: "I love you."

■ Day 8

> That evening at sundown they brought to him all who were sick or oppressed by demons. And the whole city was gathered together at the door. And he healed many who were sick with various diseases, and cast out many demons. And he would not permit the demons to speak, because they knew him. And rising very early in the morning, while it was still dark, he departed and went out to a desolate place, and there he prayed. And Simon and those who were with him searched for him, and they found him and said to him, "Everyone is looking for you." And he said to them, "let us go on to the next towns, that I may preach there also, for that is why I came out." And he went throughout all Galilee, preaching in their synagogues and casting out demons (Mark 1:32-39).

The "whole city" shows up at the door of Peter's home—an endless line of the sick and oppressed. Jesus heals and cleanses them, but apparently not all of them. Because the next morning "everyone is looking" for Jesus.

Yet as they *draw near* to Jesus, *Jesus retreats away from* them. Jesus trades "activity" for "receptivity." He stops giving so that he might start receiving. Jesus prays.

There are times when the spiritual life must be about receptivity, not activity. Prayer makes this possible. There are times when prayer is more about getting rather than giving. How is the balance between receptivity and activity in your spiritual life? Spend a few quiet moments right now to receive something from the Father in prayer.

■ Day 9

> But now even more the report about him went abroad, and great crowds gathered to hear him and to be healed of their infirmities. But he would withdraw to desolate places and pray (Luke 5:15-16).

Success. Busyness. Tyranny of the Urgent. All three hit Jesus.
- *Success*: "even more the report about him went abroad..." Jesus becomes a household word.
- *Busyness*: "great crowds gathered to hear him and to be healed..." Jesus has increasing crowds to tend to and teach.
- *Tyranny of the Urgent*: everywhere Jesus turns there is a life begging to be touched.

Yet what does Jesus do? "But he would withdraw to desolate places and pray." Luke's language indicates this was a habit. Regularly, Jesus would step away from the spotlight, the to-do list, and the legitimate needs of others in order to pray to the Father.

Which is keeping you from prayer: Success? Busyness? Tyranny of the Urgent? Walk away from it today, and every day for the remainder of these forty days. Every day for these forty days spend significant time in prayer. Trust that God will still be at work even when it seems you are not. Believe that your need for prayer is more urgent than anything else today.

■ Day 10

> In these days he went out to the mountain to pray, and all night he continued in prayer to God. And when day came, he called his disciples and chose from them twelve, whom he named apostles: Simon, whom he named Peter, and Andrew his brother, and James and John, and Philip, and Bartholomew, and Matthew, and Thomas, and James the son of Alphaeus, and Simon who was called the Zealot, and Judas the son of James, and Judas Iscariot, who became a traitor (Luke 6:12-16).

This is one of those critical next-chapters in Jesus' story: the selection of a small group to mentor, invest in, and equip so that the story would carry on when Jesus ascended. Isn't choosing someone for an important task always a bit unsettling? You have to choose a new doctor, a new dentist, a new insurance agent, a new baby-sitter, a new preacher, a new secretary, a new teacher, a new investment broker. It is a difficult task because those we choose end up handling very important things for us.

Because of this, Jesus precedes his selection of the Twelve with supplication for the Twelve. Two things characterize this prayer. First, its *place*: "the mountain." Jesus chooses an isolated and quiet place. Second, its *persistence*: "all night he continued in prayer." Jesus prays all night long.

Is there an important decision you need to make or an important task you need to undertake? Find an isolated place. And devote significant time to pray about the issue. The choice you are facing cannot be any greater than the one Jesus' faced. Therefore, your need for prayer cannot be any less than Jesus' need.

■ Day 11

> So Jesus said to them, "Truly, truly, I say to you, the Son can do nothing of his own accord, but only what he sees the Father doing. For whatever the Father does, that the Son does likewise . . . I can do nothing on my own. As I hear, I judge, and my judgment is just, because I seek not my own will but the will of him who sent me" (John 5:19-30).

Jesus describes his ministry as one of imitation—what he *hears* his Father saying, he says; what he *sees* his Father doing, he does. Andrew Lincoln writes, "When did this listening and observing . . . occur? The formulations suggest that these activities . . . were part of his continuing relationship with his Father during his public ministry—a relationship in which he saw visions and heard auditions, and for which prayer would not be an inappropriate description." In other words, prayer is the way in which Jesus hears what the Father is saying and sees what the Father is doing. For Jesus, prayer is not merely a time to talk, but also a time to listen. Prayer is not just closing the eyes, but also opening the eyes. Through prayer Jesus saw God's activity and heard God's guidance.

Sit in silence for the next ten minutes. Ask God to speak to your heart. Ask God to open your eyes. He just may have something to say or show.

■ Day 12

And taking the five loaves and the two fish he looked up to heaven and said a blessing and broke the loaves and gave them to the disciples to set before the people. And he divided the two fish among them all. And they all ate and were satisfied. And they took up twelve baskets full of broken pieces and of the fish. And those who ate the loaves were five thousand men (Mark 6:41-44).

This is one of several occasions on which Jesus "blesses." Here, Jesus blesses the loaves and fish. A blessing could be either a petition for God to bless someone/something or a praise to God for someone/something. Here, it seems to be the latter. In this prayer, Jesus thanks God for the loaves and fish. Before consuming, Jesus communes. Before Jesus eats, he exalts. Before he passes the plate, he praises the Father. It is just dried fish and plain bread. Not steak and lobster. Not prime rib and cheesecake. Still, for this basic provision, Jesus praises.

Think of something basic and routine in your life. Something you take for granted. Your health? Your office? The lunch you packed? The shoes on your feet? Now, say a blessing. Thank God for it. Over these forty days, regularly thank God for the plain and ordinary things in your life.

■ Day 13

Immediately he made his disciples get into the boat and go before him to the other side, to Bethsaida, while he dismissed the crowd. And after he had taken leave of them, he went up on the mountain to pray. And when evening came, the boat was out on the sea, and he was alone on the land (Mark 6:45-47).

Jesus dismisses the crowd whom he's fed. He requests that the disciples leave. He seeks out a place far from distraction—the mountain. And he prays. Jesus was unwilling for his prayer life to be dictated by circumstances. Too often we pray only when the right situation finds us. We blame our surroundings, our position, our season in life, or our schedule for our lack of prayer. Yet Jesus was different. Circumstances did not dictate his prayer life. His prayer life dictated his circumstances. He didn't wait for the right situation to find him. He created the right situation.

What keeps you from prayer? How might you take control of that barrier today?

■ Day 14

> Then he returned from the region of Tyre and went through Sidon to the Sea of Galilee, in the region of the Decapolis. And they brought to him a man who was deaf and had a speech impediment, and they begged him to lay his hand on him. And taking him aside from the crowd privately, he put his fingers into his ears, and after spitting touched his tongue. And looking up to heaven, he sighed and said to him, "Ephphatha," that is, "Be opened." And his ears were opened, his tongue was released, and he spoke plainly (Mark 7:31-35).

Jesus looked at a man needing help. Then Jesus looked to heaven. Jesus saw this person. Then he prayed. He observed an individual. Then he interceded.

What do you do when you see someone in need? Look down? Look away? Look within? The next time you find yourself in front of a person in need, let your first look be to heaven. Open your eyes today, and every day left in these forty days. Each time you observe an individual requiring help, look to heaven and intercede for that person.

■ Day 15

> Now it happened that as he was praying alone, the disciples were with him. And he asked them, "Who do the crowds say that I am?" And they answered, "John the Baptist. But others say, Elijah, and others, that one of the prophets of old has risen." Then he said to them, "But who do you say that I am?" And Peter answered, "The Christ of God" (Luke 9:18-20).

This is the first of two occasions in Luke 9 on which *perception* is preceded by *prayer*. Here, Peter's perception that Jesus is truly the promised Christ/Messiah (rather than a resurrected prophet) is preceded by Jesus "praying alone." Luke would not have gone to the trouble to show us Jesus praying alone prior to Peter's confession if there was only a coincidental link between the two. Could it be that Jesus' prayers (here and elsewhere) allowed Peter to see something of Jesus' heart and that this contributed significantly to Peter believing that Jesus was the Christ? Perhaps this prayer which Peter either observed or overheard became a tipping point that led Peter to finally understand who Jesus really was.

How about you? What conclusions do you tend to draw when you watch or listen to someone praying? What conclusions would someone draw about *you* if they could watch or listen to you pray for the next seven days? What does your prayer-life reveal about you?

■ Day 16

Now about eight days after these sayings he took with him Peter and John and James and went up on the mountain to pray. And as he was praying, the appearance of his face was altered, and his clothing became dazzling white. And behold, two men were talking with him, Moses and Elijah, who appeared in glory and spoke of his departure, which he was about to accomplish at Jerusalem. Now Peter and those who were with him were heavy with sleep, but when they became fully awake they saw his glory and the two men who stood with him. And as the men were parting from him, Peter said to Jesus, "Master, it is good that we are here. Let us make three tents, one for you and one for Moses and one for Elijah"—not knowing what he said. As he was saying these things, a cloud came and overshadowed them, and they were afraid as they entered the cloud. And a voice came out of the cloud, saying, "This is my Son, my Chosen One; listen to him!" (Luke 9:28-35).

This is the second time in Luke 9 where *perception* follows *prayer*. Jesus prays and is literally transformed before Peter, John, and James. A veil is lifted and the three are permitted to see Jesus' glory and hear the divine affirmation: "This is my Son." Jesus' prayer leads to them seeing and hearing what they had never heard nor seen before.

I often lament that God does not audibly speak today as he did during the days of the events of the Bible. I often complain that God does not visibly appear today as he did during the days of the events of the Bible. But could it be that God *is* speaking—I am just not listening? Could it be that God *is* appearing—I am just not watching? Could it be that through a deeper practice of prayer, I too might see and hear what I have never heard nor seen before?

Pray throughout this day this simple prayer: "Open the eyes of my heart, Lord. I want to see you."

■ Day 17

And when Jesus saw that a crowd came running together, he rebuked the unclean spirit, saying to it, "You mute and deaf spirit, I command you, come out of him and never enter him again." And after crying out and convulsing him terribly, it came out, and the boy was like a corpse, so that most of them said, "He is dead." But Jesus took him by the hand and lifted him up, and he arose. And when he had entered the house, his disciples asked him privately, "Why could we not cast it out?" And he said to them, "This kind cannot be driven out by anything but prayer" (Mark 9:25-29).

This incident is preceded by the Transfiguration—a moment at which Jesus' deity is clearly revealed. Never has Jesus appeared stronger. Never has he seemed mightier. Yet here we find Jesus dependent and needful: "This kind cannot be driven out by anything but prayer." The statement describes why the disciples *could not* drive out the boy's demon. They relied on their own power. They did not ask for help from above. Yet it also appears to describe why Jesus *could* drive out the boy's demon. Though not explicitly stated here, it seems Jesus did not rely on his own power. He asked for help from above. At some point "in between the lines" of this text, Jesus prayed. Not even the Transfigured Messiah could do this alone.

"This...cannot be [accomplished] by anything but prayer." Are you willing to believe that there are some things that cannot be accomplished except through prayer? If you took that line seriously, how would it impact your life? What is something you've been trying to do on your own power? In what area of your life are you more like the disciples (I can do this) and less like Jesus (God can do this)? Pray today as if nothing will happen unless you pray.

■ Day 18

> "I thank you, Father, Lord of heaven and earth, that you have hidden these things from the wise and understanding and revealed them to little children; yes, Father, for such was your gracious will" (Matt. 11:25-26).

Matthew 11 finds Jesus in what could be one of the most discouraging seasons of his life. First, John the Baptist, one of Jesus' most trusted partners, appears to *doubt*: "Are you the one who is to come, or shall we look for another?" (Matthew 11:4). Second, the crowds, who have been so enthusiastic, now appear *disappointed* with Jesus: "We played the flute for you, and you did not dance; we sang a dirge, and you did not mourn" (Matthew 11:17). Third, entire cities in which Jesus has done "most of his mighty works" still appear to be places of spiritual *desolation* (Matthew 11:20).

It seems that God is no longer in charge. It seems that God is no longer at work. It seems God no longer rules. I would have responded to this with complaint. Jesus responds with confidence. Through prayer, Jesus remembers *who* God is. God is still "Lord of heaven and earth." God is still in charge, in spite of recent events. And through prayer, Jesus remembers *what* God is doing. God is "hiding" and "revealing." That is, God is still at work, in spite of recent events. Even in a difficult time, Jesus prayerfully remembers that God still rules—he's still in charge and he's still at work.

Take a moment to think of a circumstance in your life which has filled you with disappointment. Things haven't worked out as you wished. Now pray to God as "Lord of heaven and earth" and confess that He's still in charge of that circumstance. And, confess in prayer that God's still working in that situation, despite all appearances.

■ Day 19

> Now Jesus was praying in a certain place, and when he finished, one of his disciples said to him, "Lord, teach us to pray, as John taught his disciples." And he said to them, "When you pray, say: 'Father, hallowed be your name. Your kingdom come. Give us each day our daily bread, and forgive us our sins, for we ourselves forgive everyone who is indebted to us. And lead us not into temptation'" (Luke 11:1-4).

Jesus' disciples ask Jesus to tutor them in prayer. In response to the request, Jesus urges them to learn to pray a simple prayer that begins with "Father." What is the significance to you of the fact that we pray to "Father," and not just "God" or "LORD"? Take a few moments and write on a sheet of paper ten qualities of an ideal father. Now, pray to God, thanking him for being each of those qualities.

■ Day 20

> The man answered, "Why, this is an amazing thing! You do not know where he comes from, and yet he opened my eyes. We know that God does not listen to sinners, but if anyone is a worshiper of God and does his will, God listens to him. Never since the world began has it been heard that anyone opened the eyes of a man born blind. If this man were not from God, he could do nothing" (John 9:30-33).

Jesus heals a man born blind. The Pharisees attack the veracity of the miracle and the character of the Messiah (he performed this deed on the Sabbath). They demand to know from the once-blind man how such a thing could have happened, if indeed it happened at all.

Notice how the man replies: "We know that God does not *listen* to sinners, but if anyone is a worshiper of God and does his will, God *listens* to him." Though John never explicitly describes such a scene, this man's comments suggest that the healing was in response to a prayer which Jesus prayed and to which God *listened*.

Even when it appears Jesus was dancing solo, he was pairs dancing. An observer would have only noticed Jesus healing a blind man. But the blind man knew it was Jesus, through prayer, acting in partnership with God. Prayer had become so habitual and natural to Jesus that it was as if he was always in prayer.

How about you? Are you dancing solo most of the day and only occasionally pausing to prayerfully partner with God? Or is prayer as much a part of your minute-by-minute life that it's like breathing?

■ Day 21

And they were bringing children to him that he might touch them, and the disciples rebuked them. But when Jesus saw it, he was indignant and said to them, "Let the children come to me; do not hinder them, for to such belongs the kingdom of God. Truly, I say to you, whoever does not receive the kingdom of God like a child shall not enter it." And he took them in his arms and blessed them, laying his hands on them (Mark 10:13-16).

To "bless" someone in Jesus' day was a form of prayer. It was a way of asking God to look favorably upon an individual. Here, Jesus blesses or prayerfully intercedes for children. And it's no cold and stately blessing. He takes them in his arms, lays his hands on them, and blesses them. Can you imagine what it must have felt like for a child, having just been dismissed by Jesus' disciples, to have Jesus pick you up, hold you, and bless you?

Look for opportunities today to pray prayers of blessings over people, especially over people who, like these children, may be forgotten or dismissed by others. Bless your children, a friend, your spouse, your boss, your waitress, the janitor, your teacher, your parents, your neighbor, your mail carrier, or the man with the cardboard sign asking for money. Utilize the following biblical blessings out loud or silently as you pray over people today:

- The LORD bless you and keep you; the LORD make his face to shine upon you and be gracious to you; the LORD lift up his countenance upon you and give you peace (Numbers 6:24-26).
- May the LORD give strength to you! May the LORD bless you with peace! (based on Psalm 29:11).
- May God be gracious to you and bless you and make his face to shine

upon you, that His way may be known on earth, His saving power among all nations (based on Psalm 67:1-2).

- May you be blessed by the LORD, who made heaven and earth! (Psalm 115:15).
- The LORD bless you! May you see the prosperity of his work all the days of your life! May you live a long life! Peace be upon you! (based on Psalm 128:5-6).
- May the LORD bless you, he who made heaven and earth! (based on Psalm 134:3).

■ Day 22

Now when Jesus came, he found that Lazarus had already been in the tomb four days. Bethany was near Jerusalem, about two miles off, and many of the Jews had come to Martha and Mary to console them concerning their brother. So when Martha heard that Jesus was coming, she went and met him, but Mary remained seated in the house. Martha said to Jesus, "Lord, if you had been here, my brother would not have died. But even now I know that whatever you ask from God, God will give you' (John 11:17-22).

Jesus' reputation as a person of powerful prayer precedes his arrival at Bethany. Martha has witnessed enough of Jesus' prayers or heard enough about Jesus' prayers that she has no doubt—if this man prays for her brother to rise from the dead, then her brother will rise from the dead! Martha has a prayer request that tops all prayer-requests: rescue Lazarus from death. And who does she bring the prayer request to? She brings it to Jesus. She believes that "whatever" Jesus asks "from God, God will give" to him.

Are you known by others as a person of powerful prayer? If someone in your circle of influence had a unusually challenging prayer request, would they bring it to you? Why? Why not?

■ Day 23

When Jesus saw her weeping, and the Jews who had come with her also weeping, he was deeply moved in his spirit and greatly troubled. And he said, "Where have you laid him?" They said to him, "Lord, come and see." Jesus wept. So the Jews said, "See how he loved him!" But some of them said, "Could not he who opened the eyes of the blind man also have kept this man from dying?" Then Jesus, deeply moved again, came to the tomb. It was a cave, and a stone lay against it. Jesus said,

"Take away the stone." Martha, the sister of the dead man, said to him, "Lord, by this time there will be an odor, for he has been dead four days." Jesus said to her, "Did I not tell you that if you believed you would see the glory of God?" So they took away the stone. And Jesus lifted up his eyes and said, "Father, I thank you that you have heard me. I knew that you always hear me, but I said this on account of the people standing around, that they may believe that you sent me" (John 11:33-42).

Timothy Jones points out that Jesus does not speak this prayer of thanksgiving after Lazarus has been raised from the dead.[4] Jesus speaks this prayer of thanksgiving while Lazarus is still decomposing in a tomb. Jesus is not thanking God because he is certain God will raise Lazarus. He thanks God simply because God hears him.

And what does God hear? Jones argues that God hears Jesus' tears: "When [Jesus] found himself in the shadow of his friend's tomb, he couldn't put his prayers into words, so he put them into tears instead. And his Father heard his cries." Jones concludes: "Perhaps it's because at the heart of all our prayers, what we really want is not an answer but an assurance—an assurance that our Father is listening."

Jesus thanks God simply because God hears. Even in the midst of a painful time, Jesus believes that God hears. And here, that's all Jesus needs.

Is it enough for you to know that God hears? Why? Why not? Take a few moments and just thank God for his open ears, for the way his door is always open, for how God is always willing to listen.

■ Day 24

"Now is my soul troubled. And what shall I say? 'Father, save me from this hour'? But for this purpose I have come to this hour. Father, glorify your name.' Then a voice came from heaven: 'I have glorified it, and I will glorify it again'" (John 12:27-28).

As with all of the prayers for which we have Jesus' actual words, this one is prayed in the shadow of the cross. Here, Jesus lays out the two options we have when faced with pain and suffering: "Father, save me" or "Father, use me." The prayer, "Father, glorify your name," is a plea for God to use the cross and Jesus' suffering for His purposes, to reveal something about Himself.

Save me. Use me.

Take a few moments right now to identify a circumstance in your life that brings you pain or suffering. Rather than asking God to save you from that circumstance, ask Him right now to use you in the midst of that circumstance.

■ Day 25

> When it was evening, he reclined at table with the twelve. And as they were eating, he said, "Truly, I say to you, one of you will betray me." And they were very sorrowful and began to say to him one after another, "Is it I, Lord?" He answered, "He who has dipped his hand in the dish with me will betray me. The Son of Man goes as it is written of him, but woe to that man by whom the Son of Man is betrayed! It would have been better for that man if he had not been born." Judas, who would betray him, answered, "Is it I, Rabbi?" He said to him, "You have said so." Now as they were eating, Jesus took bread, and after blessing it broke it and gave it to the disciples, and said, "Take, eat; this is my body." And he took a cup, and when he had given thanks he gave it to them, saying, "Drink of it, all of you, for this is my blood of the covenant, which is poured out for many for the forgiveness of sins. I tell you I will not drink again of this fruit of the vine until that day when I drink it new with you in my Father's kingdom" (Matthew 26:20-29)

What a stunning contrast—Jesus reveals his betrayer but then blesses the bread and gives thanks for the cup! Here is another example of Jesus blessing—in this case, giving thanks. Jesus has every reason to complain, to groan, and to grieve. Yet, he blesses the bread and gives thank for the cup.

Jesus was following the prescribed routine associated with the Passover meal. By custom, he was supposed to bless the bread and give thanks for the cup. Yet this scene demonstrates how habits and traditions like "saying grace" or "saying the blessing" can be critical. Especially in difficult times, the simple habit of still "thanking God for this meal" can be formative.

Do you "say grace" at every meal? Why? Why not? How could you be more intentional about this practice so that it cultivates a more thankful spirit within you? When you do "say grace," what do you say? What other words or phrases might make this habitual prayer more formative?

■ Day 26

> "Simon, Simon, behold, Satan demanded to have you, that he might sift you like wheat, but I have prayed for you that your faith may not fail. And when you have turned again, strengthen your brothers." Peter said to him, "Lord, I am ready to go with you both to prison and to death."v

Jesus said, "I tell you, Peter, the rooster will not crow this day, until you deny three times that you know me" (Luke 22:31-34).

One of Jesus' three closest friends is about to stab him in the back. Still, Jesus prays for him. Jesus prays that Peter's "faith may not fail." Jesus spends some of his last moments praying for the faith of one who won't even have the courage to admit that he is a follower of Jesus.

Whether you keep a mental or written prayer list, how many people like Peter are on it? My tendency is to remove from my prayer list the people who make my life painful. Jesus' tendency is to add them to his list. Who are the challenging, difficult, irritating, disappointing, and aggravating people in your life? Add them to your prayer list and start praying!

◼ Day 27

When Jesus had spoken these words, he lifted up his eyes to heaven, and said, "Father, the hour has come; glorify your Son that the Son may glorify you, since you have given him authority over all flesh, to give eternal life to all whom you have given him. And this is eternal life, that they know you the only true God, and Jesus Christ whom you have sent. I glorified you on earth, having accomplished the work that you gave me to do. And now, Father, glorify me in your own presence with the glory that I had with you before the world existed. I have manifested your name to the people whom you gave me out of the world. Yours they were, and you gave them to me, and they have kept your word. Now they know that everything that you have given me is from you. For I have given them the words that you gave me, and they have received them and have come to know in truth that I came from you; and they have believed that you sent me" (John 17:1-8).

Here, Jesus prays, "The hour has come." In other words, "It's time to die." It is the darkest moment of Jesus' life. "It's time to die." Yet rather than pray a lament or complaint, which would be well-deserved, Jesus offers a prayer of confidence: "Glorify me with glory."

"Glory" and "glorify" are important words in John. They are found fourteen times in the first eleven chapters and nineteen more times in the Gospel's concluding chapters. They are used ten times in this prayer. Here, the words carry two possibilities. First, Jesus may be praying for God to exalt him. Just as his death on the cross will be inglorious, so he prays for God to follow that death with a glorious resurrection. He prays for God to exalt him. Second, Jesus may be praying for God to reveal himself through the death. In the Old Testament, God's glory is his visible manifestation (e.g., Exodus 16:7-10). Jesus may be praying that through the crucifixion and resurrection, God will reveal himself.

Both possibilities point in the same direction: Jesus prays that through this painful time, God will bring the best from the bad; God will bring triumph from tragedy; God will let the story end spectacularly.

The word "glory" carried then as it does now the hint of light. Something that is glorious is something that is full of light. Jesus prays that out of this darkness, God will bring light.

Consider a painful time in your life. Pray for God to bring triumph where you see only tragedy. Pray for God to bring the best from the bad. Pray for the story to end spectacularly. Pray for God to bring light from the darkness.

■ Day 28

> "I am praying for them. I am not praying for the world but for those whom you have given me, for they are yours. All mine are yours, and yours are mine, and I am glorified in them. And I am no longer in the world, but they are in the world, and I am coming to you. Holy Father, keep them in your name, which you have given me, that they may be one, even as we are one. While I was with them, I kept them in your name, which you have given me. I have guarded them, and not one of them has been lost except the son of destruction, that the Scripture might be fulfilled" (John 17:9-12).

These lines are part one of a three-part prayer which Jesus lifts on behalf of his disciples. Here, what he has been doing ("I have kept them in your name"), he now asks the Father to do ("keep them in your name"). As the disciples have prepared for their mission, Jesus has kept them, guarded them, and protected them. Now, as the disciples pursue their mission, Jesus asks the Father to keep them, guard them, and protect them. Jesus places them in the protective custody of the Father so they may engage fully in ministry.

Think of the names of people or organizations who are involved heavily in ministry, Christian charity, or Christian education. Spend this day in constant prayer for them, asking the Father to keep them, protect them, and guard them.

■ Day 29

"I do not ask that you take them out of the world, but that you keep them from the evil one" (John 17:15).

This is part two of a three-part prayer Jesus offers on behalf of his disciples. Even though Jesus has every right to only pray about himself in these final hours, he finds the compassion to pray for others. Here, Jesus prays that God might keep the disciples from the evil one.

Andrew Lincoln notes that in part one of this prayer, Jesus prays for the disciples to be kept in the Father's name. In part two, Jesus prays for the disciples to be kept from the evil one. Thus, Jesus demonstrates "the two antithetical spheres of power operative in the world." Positively, Jesus prays that the disciples would be guarded by the Father's power. Negatively, Jesus prays that the disciples would be protected from Satan's power.

Satan is real. He is active. And prayer is one of the primary ways in which we combat his reality and his activity. Not by our own power. But by the Father's power.

Consider the list of people for whom you regularly pray. How might your prayers for them change if you believed that the evil one could be targeting them, attacking them, or endangering them? Consider the things you generally pray for yourself. How might those prayers change if you believed the evil one could be targeting you, attacking you, or endangering you? Do you pray as if the evil one is real? Why? Why not?

■ Day 30

"Sanctify them in the truth; your word is truth. As you sent me into the world, so I have sent them into the world. And for their sake I consecrate myself, that they also may be sanctified in truth" (John 17:17-19).

To be "sanctified" is to be set apart. Set apart for what? In this prayer—part three of a three-part prayer for his disciples—Jesus links being "sanctified" with being "sent." Just as Jesus was set apart for the purpose of being sent into the world, so now he prays for the disciples to be set apart for the purpose of being sent into the world. Jesus prays about their mission. He begs the Father to set these men apart for the holy task of continuing Jesus' mission. He prays that they might fulfill their true purpose in life.

Consider the people in your life: friends, family members, fellow believers, church/organizational/governmental leaders, etc. Pray for each today, that God would set him/her apart for His mission to the world. Pray that each would fulfill his/her true purpose in life.

■ Day 31

"I do not ask for these only, but also for those who will believe in me through their word, that they may all be one, just as you, Father, are in me, and I in you, that they also may be in us, so that the world may believe that you have sent me" (John 17:20-21).

Jesus now turns his prayer thoughts from his immediate disciples to us—to all those who will believe in him through the word of the disciples. Jesus prays for our unity. Andreas Kostenberger writes that Jesus is praying for us to have a "common mind and common purpose."[5] Jesus is praying for our "togetherness in mission."

I'd put it this way: Community and Cause. Cause: "that the world may believe…" Community: "that they may all be one…" Community is not an end in itself. It is a means to an end—the Cause. As we engage in our Cause, we do so in Community. Jesus prays that we will not pursue our Cause as individuals, but as a family.

Yet not only do we pursue Cause in Community, Community actually fulfills the Cause. When the world sees true Community which overcomes what humans cannot—racism, sexism, ageism—the world will conclude that this Community is divine—it must come from God. Community fulfills the Cause.

If you attend a congregation regularly, do you pray regularly for that congregation? If not, why not? If you do, how often do you pray about that congregation's Community and Cause and the link between the two? Why? Why not?

■ Day 32

"Father, I desire that they also, whom you have given me, may be with me where I am, to see my glory that you have given me because you loved me before the foundation of the world" (John 17:24).

Whereas much of John 17 has focused on the near-future, this final part of Jesus' prayer seems to focus on the distant-future. Jesus prays for our heavenly reunion—that we who follow him might be with him in the place where he has spent an eternity being loved.

"Father, bring them safely home." "Father, lead them back to me." "Father, let them live in this place of love."

Jesus is rooting for me to make it to heaven. He's not hoping I'll slip up. He's not holding his breath, just waiting to see me fail. He's not shaking his head every time I fall, saying, "He's never going to make it." No, Jesus is spending some of his final breath praying for me and you to make it to heaven. Jesus is pulling for us. "Father, whatever you do, please make sure they wind up right here with me."

Do you tend to imagine Jesus praying for you or against you? Why? Close your eyes and imagine Jesus praying (put your name in the blank): "Father, I'm rooting for _____. I'm pulling for _____. I want nothing more than for _____ to be with me. Please make sure _____ makes it to heaven."

■ Day 33

> Then Jesus went with them to a place called Gethsemane, and he said to his disciples, "Sit here, while I go over there and pray." And taking with him Peter and the two sons of Zebedee, he began to be sorrowful and troubled. Then he said to them, "My soul is very sorrowful, even to death; remain here, and watch with me." And going a little farther he fell on his face and prayed, saying, "My Father, if it be possible, let this cup pass from me; nevertheless, not as I will, but as you will." And he came to the disciples and found them sleeping. And he said to Peter, "So, could you not watch with me one hour? Watch and pray that you may not enter into temptation. The spirit indeed is willing, but the flesh is weak." Again, for the second time, he went away and prayed, "My Father, if this cannot pass unless I drink it, your will be done." And again he came and found them sleeping, for their eyes were heavy. So, leaving them again, he went away and prayed for the third time, saying the same words again. Then he came to the disciples and said to them, "Sleep and take your rest later on. See, the hour is at hand, and the Son of Man is betrayed into the hands of sinners. Rise, let us be going; see, my betrayer is at hand" (Matthew 26:36-46).

Notice the first part of this prayer: "My Father, if it be possible, let this cup pass from me…" These words flow from a heart that is "sorrowful and troubled" and a soul that is "very sorrowful, even to death." Three times, Luke tells us, this sorrowful and troubled Jesus prayed "the same words."

"My Father, if it be possible, let this cup pass from me…"

"My Father, if it be possible, let this cup pass from me…"

"My Father, if it be possible, let this cup pass from me…"

This is a lament. A complaint. Jesus is despondent. He deeply dislikes his circumstances and desperately begs God to change them. Jesus does not keep his "happy face" on. He does not piously pretend nothing is wrong. Instead, he is honest with the Father about his feelings and frustrations. He puts the sorrow and trouble into words and groans them out to the Father.

What frustrations have you been holding back? What despair has gone unspoken to God? Take some time today and be honest and transparent with God. Put your own sorrow and trouble into words and pray them out loud.

■ Day 34

> Then Jesus went with them to a place called Gethsemane, and he said to his disciples, "Sit here, while I go over there and pray." And taking with him Peter and the two sons of Zebedee, he began to be sorrowful and troubled. Then he said to them, "My soul is very sorrowful, even to death; remain here, and watch with me." And going a little farther he fell on his face and prayed, saying, "My Father, if it be possible, let this cup pass from me; nevertheless, not as I will, but as you will." And he came to the disciples and found them sleeping. And he said to Peter, "So, could you not watch with me one hour? Watch and pray that you may not enter into temptation. The spirit indeed is willing, but the flesh is weak." Again, for the second time, he went away and prayed, "My Father, if this cannot pass unless I drink it, your will be done." And again he came and found them sleeping, for their eyes were heavy. So, leaving them again, he went away and prayed for the third time, saying the same words again. Then he came to the disciples and said to them, "Sleep and take your rest later on. See, the hour is at hand, and the Son of Man is betrayed into the hands of sinners. Rise, let us be going; see, my betrayer is at hand" (Matthew 26:36-46).

Because Jesus is fully divine, it may be surprising to hear him praying, "Let this cup pass from me.... Let this cup pass from me.... Let this cup pass from me." But because Jesus is also fully human, it may also be surprising to hear him praying, "Nevertheless, your will be done.... Nevertheless, your will be done.... Nevertheless, your will be done."

In one prayer, Jesus says things we often won't say because we fear offending the Father ("Let this cup pass from me... "), and he says things we often can't say because we fear surrendering to the Father ("Nevertheless, your will be done..."). Our spirit longs for us to submit our will to God's, but the flesh is so often weak. Our flesh longs for us to be honest and transparent with God, but the spirit so often refuses.

Think right now of a circumstance in your life or in the life of someone else which is discouraging. For a few moments, praying nothing but "Let this cup pass.... Let this cup pass.... Let this cup pass..." After some silence, begin praying again. This time, however, pray nothing but "Nevertheless, your will be done.... Nevertheless, your will be done.... Nevertheless, your will be done."

■ Day 35

Two others, who were criminals, were led away to be put to death with him. And when they came to the place that is called The Skull, there they crucified him, and the criminals, one on his right and one on his left. And Jesus said, "Father, forgive them, for they know not what they do" (Luke 23:32-34).

This intercessory prayer represents the height of prayer. There is no other prayer in Scripture that demonstrates the level of maturity and compassion found here. If prayer is a ladder, this one is the top rung. If prayer is a building, this is the top floor. If prayer is a mountain, this is the peak.

When despair and darkness hit, the *natural* reaction is to pray about ourselves and our pain. Jesus has elsewhere demonstrated how to do this. The *non-natural* reaction in times of pain is to pray about others, those whom we love. Jesus has also demonstrated how to do this—praying earlier for his disciples even as he faces death. Yet the *supernatural* reaction is to pray for the very people responsible for our pain. That is what Jesus does here. He takes prayer to its greatest height. There is no greater sign of spiritual maturity than to intercede for people who have injured us.

Bring to your mind someone who has hurt you, disappointed you, or caused you some pain. Now, repeat after Jesus: "Father, forgive them, for they know not what they do."

■ Day 36

And when the sixth hour had come, there was darkness over the whole land until the ninth hour. And at the ninth hour Jesus cried with a loud voice, "Eloi, Eloi, lema sabachthani?" which means, "My God, my God, why have you forsaken me?" And some of the bystanders hearing it said, "Behold, he is calling Elijah." And someone ran and filled a sponge with sour wine, put it on a reed and gave it to him to drink, saying, "Wait, let us see whether Elijah will come to take him down." And Jesus uttered a loud cry and breathed his last (Mark 15:33-37).

Forsaken. This is a strange word coming out of the mouth of the Son. After all, Jesus is the One-in-Three. Just as you and I have never known life without skin or oxygen or a heartbeat, Jesus has never known life without Trinitarian community.

"Remembered." That's the word that should be coming out of the mouth of the Son. That's the word that describes what has been as characteristic to Jesus' life as breathing is to ours. Yet here Jesus is, forsaken.

Note what Jesus does: he prays. He prays to the very one whom he feels has abandoned him. Jesus prays hard words. He prays raw words. But the important thing is that Jesus prays. He keeps communicating. He does not hang up just because he feels the Father has.

Therein lays the most important aspect of lament or complaint. When we are wounded and upset, what matters most is not the kind or quality of our words, but the presence of our words. Keep communicating. Keep talking. Keep praying.

Is there something in your life about which you've just stopped talking to God? Is there a pain, an injury, or a wound that you no longer share with God? Take time today and this week to restart the communication with God in that area. Even if you have to use hard and raw words, just start talking to God again.

■ Day 37

> After this, Jesus, knowing that all was now finished, said (to fulfill the Scripture), "I thirst." A jar full of sour wine stood there, so they put a sponge full of the sour wine on a hyssop branch and held it to his mouth (John 19:28-29).

There was once a time when Jesus proclaimed, "I quench." For example, in John 4, Jesus tells an outcast woman that he is the source of "living water." Later, in John 8, Jesus tells a curious crowd, "If anyone thirsts, let him come to me and drink. Whoever believes in me, as the Scripture has said, 'Out of his heart will flow rivers of living water.'" There was a time when Jesus said, "I quench."

But now Jesus can only pray, "I thirst." Here Jesus hangs, without the ability to satisfy his own deprivation. The one who once provided for all that others needed is now destitute of all that he needs. So in humility, Jesus petitions. He asks the Father to supply that basic requirement which he cannot secure himself. Jesus asks for a drink.

On the list of things the Son of God might pray for, this may seem miniscule, hardly worthy of a prayer. We could imagine Jesus praying for world peace, for an end to all violent regimes, or for the kingdom to come. Today, however, he prays for a drink. Jesus taught us to pray for bread for the day. Now, he prays for water for the moment.

And God answers. Those tending the cross lift a sponge drenched in sour wine. And for a moment, Jesus' cracked lips are moistened and his dry throat is soothed.

Do you have needs that are important to you but which you think may not be important to God? Pray about them. Is your prayer list filled with things you fear may be too small and petty to mention? Keep them on the list. No matter how miniscule, if it is one of your greatest needs, it is one of your Father's greatest concerns. Even if it's just a drink of water.

■ Day 38

> It was now about the sixth hour, and there was darkness over the whole land until the ninth hour, while the sun's light failed. And the curtain of the temple was torn in two. Then Jesus, calling out with a loud voice, said, "Father, into your hands I commit my spirit!" And having said this he breathed his last (Luke 23:44-46).

John Ortberg tells of being at a hotel swimming pool with his two daughters who were three and five years old.[6] Before getting into the water, Ortberg gave his daughters a stern lecture about the danger of drowning. Then, while his five year old jumped into Ortberg's waiting arms in the water, the three year old accidently slipped from the pool's edge into the water. Within a second Ortberg grabbed the three year old and lifted her out of the water. The three year old starting bawling: "I drowned, Daddy. I drowned." "No you didn't, honey," Ortberg replied. "You didn't drown. You were only underwater for a second." The brief submersion was terrifying to her, but Ortberg knew she was always within reach of her father's arms.

Jesus knows this truth. Though submerged in a deep and dark pool of suffering, he knows that he remains within reach of his Father's hands. Jesus understands that though the circumstances may suggest that the Father's hands have slipped, those hands actually still hold. Jesus is able to entrust himself into those reliable and ready hands.

Sometimes there is nothing we can do but trust that those hands still hold. We may not be able to change a thing about our situation. We may have no control over the source of our suffering. We may not be able to pause the pain. But one thing we can do: fall into the Father's hands.

Is there something in your life which now seems endangered? A dream? A plan? A relationship? A desire? Picture it in your mind and then pray: "Into your hands, I commit my _____."

■ Day 39

When Jesus had received the sour wine, he said, "It is finished," and he bowed his head and gave up his spirit (John 19:30).

It seems that pain is a necessary part of God's plan. It appears that God's story does not turn its pages without requiring suffering. But it is always a temporary pain. It is never a forever pain. Never is that clearer than here on the cross. Jesus is able to confidently pray to the Father, "It is finished." Through prayer, Jesus is able to assert that his own pain is temporary and that the Father has completed what he needed through that pain.

The challenging truth is that God uses pain and suffering. There are some things that God must do in us or through us that will not happen without discomfort. The comforting truth, however, is that God stops pain and suffering. Whenever we enter into a season of despair, we can confidently believe that the moment will come when we can say with Jesus, "It is finished."

Are you in the midst of a time of darkness? Pray to God: "Father, I trust that at the proper time, when you've done all you've needed, this darkness will be finished." Have you recently come through a time of hurt? Pray to God: "Father, I thank you that all you needed from that time has been finished." Do you know someone who is overcome by pain? Intercede for him or her today: "Father, let my friend know that this pain will come to an end."

■ Day 40

Then he led them out as far as Bethany, and lifting up his hands he blessed them. While he blessed them, he parted from them and was carried up into heaven (Luke 24:50-51).

This is the last appearance of Jesus in the timeline covered by the Gospels. We'll hear from Jesus again in Acts, Luke's second volume. But as far as the story told by the four Gospels, this is the final word and prayer from Jesus. As he has done several times before, Jesus does again—he blesses. Jesus ascends to the right hand of the Father and prays for the Father to bless those who remain behind.

Imagine the scene. Before your very eyes Jesus is ascending. You are standing beneath him. He looks at you. Then he lifts his eyes to heaven and he prays for you. What does he pray? Does he pray, "Father, help _____ to get straightened out!" "Father, help _____ to be worthy of the sacrifice I've just made." "Father, don't you have anyone else but _____ to carry on the mission?" I fear that for many of us, as we imagine this scene, the prayer we hear from Jesus' lips is not a positive prayer.

But here is the truth: Jesus' last prayer for you in the Gospels is a prayer of blessing. His last action was to pray for the Father to bless you. Not to curse you. Not to put up with you. Not to make due with you. But to bless you.

As Jesus ascends to the Father, a reunion he has ached for, Jesus has every reason to only be thinking of himself, the Father, and the Spirit. Yet his heart is still oriented toward us. As much as he anticipates his own homecoming, he longs even more for blessings upon us.

Take some time today to thank God for the way he has answered Jesus' final prayer. Thank the Father for each blessing he has bestowed upon you.

---

1. I. Howard Marshall, "Jesus—Example and Teacher of Prayer in the Synoptic Gospels," *Into God's Presence: Prayer in the New Testament* (W.B. Eerdmans Publishing, 2002).

2. Joachim Jeremias, *The Prayers of Jesus* (Fortress Press, 1978), 63

3. Marshall.

4. Timothy P. Jones, *Praying Like the Jew, Jesus: Recovering the Ancient Roots of New Testament Prayer* (Lederer Books, 2005), 71.

5. Crossway Bibles. 5. *The ESV Study Bible.* (Crossway Bibles, 2008)

6. John Ortberg, *The Me I Want to Be: becoming God's best version of you* (Zondervan, 2010), 114.

Bible Class
and Small Group Guides

Overview

Below you will find Scriptures, readings from this book, and questions which are designed to facilitate a thirteen session Bible class/workshop on the prayers of Jesus and a seven session small group experience regarding the prayers of Jesus. There is a "*" next to the chapters intended for the small group sessions (chapters 1, 3, 5, 8, 9, 11, 13).

* Chapter 1 / **Prayers from the Pit:**
  Discovering the Importance of the Prayers of Jesus

1. Chris suggests that we cannot understand Jesus without understanding his prayers. Do you agree/disagree? How can listening to someone's prayers help us better understand a person?

2. Chris asks: "How do you pray in the midst of pain? How do you talk to God when God seems absent? What kind of supplication fits suffering?" What's your answer to these questions? What do you find most difficult about praying when in pain?

3. Read Luke 9:51. Each of the ten prayers of Jesus explored in this book come after Jesus sets his face toward Jerusalem in Luke 9:51. Of the ten prayers of Jesus for which we have his spoken words, two take place during the final journey toward Jerusalem. The other eight take place within Jerusalem during Passion Week. What significance do you find in the fact that the Gospel authors gave us only the prayers Jesus prayed in light of the cross?

4. Read Psalm 13. Chris writes this: "Psalms of disorientation are prayers gasped and groaned when life is at its worst. In them, God does not seem dependable or desirable. Those who are praying lament their situation in life and beg God for a change in their circumstances. These are the most disturbing prayers in the Old Testament. They include Psalm 13,

51, and 69.... Prayers of the pit are those psalms in which life is hard and horrible and we give voice to our harshest feelings. They are the prayers which are colored primarily by challenge and suffering in life. What the prayers from the pit in the Psalms are to the Old Testament, the prayers of Jesus in the Gospels are to the New Testament.... And just as the prayers from the pit in the Psalms are intended to guide us in praying through our pain, so Jesus' prayers from the pit in the Gospels are similarly intended. There is no greater assistance in knowing how to pray and what to pray in darkness and despair than that found in the ten prayers of Jesus from the pit." What makes Jesus a suitable guide for praying in the midst of pain? Who else in your life has modeled how to pray in times of pain? What lessons have you learned about praying in times of pain?

5. We find three types of prayers from Jesus' lips. One type helps us know how to complain to God when in pain. Another type helps us know how to trust in God when in pain. A third type helps us focus on others even when we are in pain. Which type do you think you'd most benefit from in times of pain?

6. Read the closing story in Chapter 1 under the headline "Your True Possession." The story suggests that the prayers of Jesus may be our most valuable spiritual possession. Do you agree/disagree? Why?

7. Close with this prayer practice: This session has covered all ten of Jesus' prayers. Thus the practice will focus on all ten prayers as well. This week pray through all ten of Jesus' prayers each day. Become familiar with their language. Get used to their content. Strive to feel what Jesus felt as he prayed them. As much as possible, use Jesus' own words. Where necessary, paraphrase using your own words. Resource 1 will provide you easy access to all ten prayers for this practice.

Chapter 2 / **An Inward Prayer of Complaint:**
I Am Despondent (Matthew 26)

1. Chris writes: "When we face frustrations and disappointments we keep silent. We don't voice those dark feelings to the Father. Why? Because we fear that God doesn't want to hear them. We suspect God will respond, with 'Stop being so dramatic!' or 'If you don't have anything good to say, don't say anything at all.' Sometimes we envision a Father who might snap back 'If you want something to complain about, I'll give you something to complain about!' Thus, Rather than say something

bad in prayer, we just don't say anything at all." Does this describe you? What might keep some of us from voicing our complaints or laments to God when we are in pain?

2. Chris writes, "Some of us operate with a 'polar model' of prayer in which 'faith' is one end of a continuum and 'lament' is the opposite end of the continuum. As lament and complaint in our prayers increase, we move farther and farther away from faith and trust in God. But as faith and trust in God increases in our prayers, we move farther and farther away from lament and complaint. Only the spiritually immature and those of puny faith groan or moan in prayer." What is the connection between spiritual maturity and lament/complaint in prayer?

3. Of the ten prayers saved for us by Matthew, Mark, Luke, and John three are laments or complaints. Almost one-third of Jesus' prayers are acts of unfaith—if we use a model in which "faith" and "lament" are opposite ends of a continuum. Why do you think the Gospel authors recorded these laments from Jesus? What do you learn about the appropriateness of complaining or lamenting based on the fact that it was so prevalent in Jesus' prayers?

4. Read Matthew 26:36-46. How do you imagine Jesus feels as he prays?

5. Chris writes: "Notice the descriptions from Matthew: Jesus is 'sorrowful and troubled' (Matthew 26:37); Jesus confesses being 'very sorrowful, even to death' (Matthew 26:38); Jesus falls on his face (Matthew 26:39); Jesus prays not once, but three times for the cup to pass (Matthew 26:44). It's the only prayer we know of that Jesus repeated multiple times.... Rather than counterfeiting a smile, cleaning up his emotions, or cloaking his anxiety, Jesus lifts it all up messily to God in prayer. Not once, but three times." Is Jesus faith-full or faith-less because he complains like this in prayer? Chris writes, "These loud cries and tears were not the result of a lack of faith. They were the fruit of deep faith. Jesus' appeal for altered circumstances flows not from the fact that he is unspiritual or unhealthy. Just the opposite—it flows from the fact that he has never been more spiritual or more healthy." In what ways is lament a sign of spiritual health?

6. Chris writes, "Jesus gives us permission to say to God, 'Let this cup pass. Let this cup pass. Let this cup pass.'" Is this difficult or easy for you to accept? Why?

7. What gave Jesus the courage to pray in this way? Chris writes, "What made such honesty possible in prayer?... George Martin argues that

Jesus' view of God as 'Abba, Father' gives him the ability to lament in this way. The Gethsemane prayer is the only prayer in which Jesus addresses God as 'Abba'—a term of endearment. This intimacy gaves rise to Gethsemane's honesty." How does viewing God as "Abba" provide courage to lament?

8. Close with this prayer exercise: This week practice a "no holds barred" type of prayer. Practice a prayer characterized by brutal honesty. Let God have it. When you are faced with situations that disturb you, get vocal in prayer about them. Put your deepest and darkest feelings into words. As you do, remember that the one to whom you speak is not just Creator or Lord, but Father. He welcomes your lament because of the intimacy you share together as child and Father. If it helps, use this formula with all circumstances that trouble you this week: "Father, let _____ pass." In addition, consider praying Psalm 13—a brief but passionate lament prayer—once a day during the week. It may provide the words for those feelings you cannot quite put into words yourself.

* Chapter 3 / **An Inward Prayer of Complaint:**
   I Am Deserted (Mark 15)

1. Chris tells of a time when he was young and he fell into a hole in the hay in a large barn. He was afraid he'd be stuck there forever. Can you share a time when you felt alone, isolated, or forgotten as a child?

2. Read Mark 15:33-39.

3. Chris writes: "Jesus is deserted by his greatly esteemed pals.... James, we must assume, has fled. Peter, we know for certain, has rejected his master no less than three times. John remains (John 19:26).... Craig S. Keener, author of a dozen books and professor of New Testament at Palmer Seminar, says the whole world abandoned Jesus at the cross. In Jesus' day the whole world was comprised of two people-groups: Jews and Gentiles. At the cross, we see Roman soldiers—that is, Gentiles— mocking and rejecting Jesus...Jewish rulers condemn Jesus. Jewish crowds ridicule Jesus. Both groups of people reject him.... But it gets worse. Because not only has every human deserted Jesus—so has every deity. The absence of the other two members of the Holy Trinity to which Jesus belongs pains Jesus more than the abandonment of Peter, James, and John." Jesus feels abandoned by the Father. Had you been in such a situation, would you have prayed? If so, what would you have said?

4. Chris suggests that when faced with a situation that persuades us that God has abandoned us, we tend to pray in one of two ways. First, some of us pray irregularly—our prayers lessen and we only rarely pray to God. Second, some of us pray dishonestly—we pretend nothing is wrong and don't even bring the issue up to God. Do either of those types of prayer describe the way you respond to times when it seems God has abandoned you?

5. Read Psalm 22:1-2. What significance do you find in the fact that this prayer gave Jesus the words to pray as he hung on the cross?

6. What does Jesus' simple prayer—My God, my God, why have you forsaken me?—teach us about praying at times when we feel abandoned?

7. Chris writes: "First,... Jesus is teaching us to pray honestly. As I noted earlier, lament psalms like the one Jesus leans on here are an 'act of bold faith about reality.' They insist that we experience the world as it really is, not as we might wish it to be. They insist that nothing is out of bounds when it comes to prayer. God is big enough to handle your harshest words and your darkest emotions.... Second Jesus teaches us to pray hopefully. The lament psalms—including the one Jesus groans— don't leave us in the dark. They ultimately point us to God who is still there and who still cares. Psalm 22 begins with a direct statement about God being absent. But near its conclusion it includes a hope-filled statement about God being present: 'For he has not despised or abhorred the affliction of the afflicted, and he has not hidden his face from him, but has heard, when he cried to him' (Psalm 22:24) Jesus gives us permission to speak the unspeakable. But he also gives us courage to consider the unimaginable. God does not desert. God does not abandon.... Third, and most importantly, Jesus is teaching us to pray—simply to pray. The darh holes of life should not suppress prayer. They should unleash prayer." When faced with a circumstance that persuades you that God has abandoned you, which lesson from Jesus' prayer here do you find most helpful?

8. Close with this prayer exercise: Have you fallen in a hole and as a result just stopped talking to God? Is there a pain, an injury, or a wound that you no longer even bring up with God because you don't even think he's listening? Jump-start your communication with God—even if you have to use hard and raw words. Just start talking again. Make a commitment to pray at least one time every day. Even if it's a short prayer, commit to praying something to God every day. Specifically, this week commit to

praying honestly and hopefully. Close each day this week with a two-fold prayer. First, at day's end share with God as honestly as possible one way in which he seemed painfully absent to you that day. Second, share with God one way in which he seemed refreshingly present to you that day.

Chapter 4 / **An Inward Prayer of Complaint:**
I Am Deprived (John 19)

1. Read John 4:1-26. What thirst was the woman fulfilling? What thirst did Jesus offer to fulfill?

2. Chris writes, "But while abandoning herself to her craving for men, she's avoided her true inner thirst. She's overlooked what she most needs. Perhaps she's rarely, if ever, prayed about that which she desperately requires—that which Jesus envisions when he invites her to ask for 'living water.' She's a woman obsessed with quenching the wrong thirst in the wrong way. He's a Savior longing to fill her right thirst in the right way. If she'd only ask. If she'd only pray." What do you think kept her from recognizing the nature of her thirst?

3. Read Mark 15:21-23. Chris writes, "This liquid is a kind of sedative. Offered by compassionate women from Jerusalem, it is designed to take the sharpest edge off of the pain the condemned men are about to endure. A stiff drink before leaping into the boxing ring. A prescription painkiller before grueling physical therapy. A heavy dose of anesthesia before the surgery. As men sentenced to crucifixion anticipate the agony and slow death ahead of them, they yearn for some assistance with their anxiety. They thirst for some distraction from their despair. And caring women quench this thirst with the wine mixed with myrrh. Jesus, however, will not consume it." Why do you think Jesus refused to fulfill this thirst?

4. Read John 19:23-29. Chris writes, "Jesus is deeply and painfully thirsty. He's not craving drugs or elixir. He's already walked away from that thirst. Now he's craving a simple soothing for his dry throat. He just wants the equivalent of a sip of water. D. A. Carson, a New Testament scholar and author of over fifty books, reports that, '...a man scourged, bleeding, and hanging on a cross under the Near-Eastern sun would be so desperately dehydrated that thirst would be part of the torture.' Jesus is experiencing a deep and primal thirst. He groans for this refreshment just as he gasps for air. It's not going to dull the searing pain or end the

excruciating agony. It will merely relieve his parched lips and refresh his dusty mouth for a few seconds." Why do you think Jesus seeks for this thirst to be fulfilled?

5. To whom was Jesus' cry "I thirst" directed?

6. Read Psalm 22:1-15. Chris writes, "Whereas the first thirst was rejected and not even deemed worthy of attention, this thirst is elevated so high that it makes Jesus' prayer list. How do we know 'I thirst' is a prayer and not just a cry from a desperate man? When John tells us that Jesus says, 'I thirst' in order 'to fulfill Scripture,' John is telling us that Jesus allowed Scripture to guide him regarding this need. Faced with a legitimate thirst he is helpless to fill, Jesus turns to Scripture for direction. And according to Scripture, in that circumstance, one would lift the thirst up to God in prayer. Jesus' prayer of 'I thirst,' fulfills Scripture because that is how others in Scripture addressed similar needs. They lifted their thirst to God.... What Scripture then does 'I thirst' fulfill? Where in Scripture do we find people praying about their thirst? Jesus probably has in mind a Psalm, specifically Psalm 22. Psalm 22 has just been quoted by John as he describes the way the soldiers divvied up Jesus' garments (John 19:24; Psalm 22:18). In addition, we've heard another of Jesus' prayers which originated from Psalm 22: 'My God, My God, why have you forsaken me?' (Matthew 27:46; Psalm 22:1). Psalm 22 is filling Jesus' mind in these final moments. It is the text which carries him through this terror. And now, as Jesus experiences dehydration, he is perhaps reflecting on Psalm 22:15: 'my strength is dried up like a potsherd, and my tongue sticks to my jaws; you lay me in the dust of death.' Here the psalmist's tongue sticks to his mouth from desperate thirst. And what does the psalmist do? He talks to God about it."

7. Why would Jesus pray about something so seemingly "small" as a drink? What does this teach you about prayer—what is or is not appropriate to pray about?

8. Chris writes, "But like Jesus on the cross, there are times when we become aware of a deep and legitimate thirst. There are moments when we do indeed need the very thing we believe we need. It may be a small thing in the eyes of others. A simple thing. A less than 'spiritual' thing. But it is something we can hardly do without. And what do we do in those moments? What do we do with a craving which we believe is genuine yet which we are helpless to fill? We lift it to God in prayer." Are there things that you sometimes hesitate to pray about because, at least in the eyes of others, they may appear small or trivial?

9. Chris writes, "We are quick to pray about the magnificent things we want. Yet we are slow to pray about miniscule things we actually need. We are ready to petition God for the rousing things of heaven. Yet we are reluctant to lobby God for the routine things of earth. Jesus' prayer 'I thirst' remedies this." How do you feel about approaching God concerning "little" concerns?

10. Read Matthew 6:9-15. Try to divide the content of this prayer into "rousing things of heaven" and "routine things of earth." What would you put in each category? Why does Jesus' model prayer include "routine things of earth?"

11. Close with this prayer exercise: This week bring your prayers down to earth. Do not pray for a single magnificent or heavenly thing. Instead, pray every day this week only for mundane and earthly things. Pray for clean water to drink and hot food to eat. Pray for physical health and emotional stability. Pray for an upcoming test. Pray about that trip you'll be taking in a couple of weeks. For one week only, eliminate all praying that focuses on the "big" and "spiritual" things of life. Instead, fill your days with prayers about the "small" and "earthly" things of life. One way to do this is to begin every day this week by finishing this statement: "I am…" Perhaps hungry is what you are. Discouraged is what you are. In need of help on a project at work is what you are. Answer that statement each day, and then allow that answer to form the focus of your prayer for that day.

* Chapter 5 / **An Upward Prayer of Confidence:**
  You Still Rule (Matthew 11)

1. Have you ever started a new job, new semester, new relationship, or new season in life strongly, only to stumble and falter later? Explain.

2. Read Matthew 11:2-6. After a strong start in his ministry, recorded in Matthew. 1-10, Jesus hits three obstacles. The first is doubt. Chris writes, "But make no mistake—John doubts. John had predicted that Jesus was coming to 'clear his threshing floor and gather his wheat into the barn, but the chaff he will burn with unquenchable fire' (Matthew 3:12). John predicted that Jesus would come with flames of judgment. Jesus would burn up all this chaff in the religious and political world. But now, John's been tossed in prison by the same political establishment he expected Jesus to blaze away. Jesus hasn't unseated or punished anyone in political power or religious power…. John doubts." Do you think John's doubts had an effect on Jesus? Why/why not?

3. Read Matthew 11:16-19. A second obstacle Jesus hits is disappointment. Chris writes, "Earlier in Matthew 5-7 the crowds were astonished at Jesus. But in Matthew 11, they demonstrate a different reaction.... Jesus pictures groups of children sitting in the marketplace. They are complaining because one group won't do what the other group wants. They are frustrated because each group disappoints the expectations of the other. The crowds' recent reactions to Jesus and to John the Baptist remind Jesus of these children. 'We played the flute for you, and you did not dance.' Some wanted a joyful spiritual leader but found John the Baptist too stern and serious—why, he wouldn't even eat or drink! 'We sang a dirge, and you did not mourn.' Some wanted a serious and stern religious leader but found Jesus too joyful—why, all he does is eat and drink! At one time the crowds were astonished at Jesus' teaching. Now, they complain because Jesus doesn't meet their expectations. The once devoted crowds are now disappointed." Do you think the disappointment of the crowds affected Jesus? Why/why not?

4. Read Matthew 11:20-24. A third obstacle Jesus hits is desolation. Chris writes, "On the positive side, Jesus' ministry has held major campaigns in three Jewish cities: Chorazin, Bethsaida, and Capernaum. We're told in verse 11 that 'most of his mighty works' had been performed in these places. The best miracles. The best healing. The best preaching. These cities should now be bearing abundant spiritual fruit.... But here's the harsh reality: the cities are dry deserts of spiritual desolation. Jesus preached his finest sermons and conducted his most powerful miracles but these cities remained as unjust, corrupt, and dark as Sodom.... Jesus didn't simply find indifference in these cities. He found outright rejection. These people treated Jesus and his volunteers so badly Jesus says those Jewish cities will be worse off on judgment day than three pagan cities: Tyre, Sidon, and Sodom." Do you think the desolation of these cities affected Jesus? Why/why not?

5. Had you been in Jesus' place, how would you have reacted after experiencing the doubts of John, the disappointment of the crowds, and the desolation of the cities where you had done your best work?

6. Read Matthew 11:25-26. Within the context of these three obstacles, Jesus thanks God: "I thank you, Father." Would your prayer in a similar situation have started in the same way?

7. What gave Jesus the ability to be thankful in such a difficult situation? Jesus recognized two things: God was still in charge and God was still

at work. These two conclusions allowed Jesus to be thankful even in a difficult time. Chris writes, "What makes it possible for Jesus to pray with thanks on such a thankless day? Two things. First, notice how Jesus addresses God: 'Lord of heaven and earth.' Jesus envisions the one to whom he prays as the CEO, President, King, and Lord of everything in heaven and on earth. Prayer is what enables Jesus to remember that the Father is in control. External circumstances like John wondering, crowds being childish, and cities not responding may seem like evidence that God is not in control. But prayer is how Jesus grounded himself in this fundamental fact—God is still in charge. God is still Lord of heaven and earth." In what ways does it help, in tough times, to remember through prayer that God is still in charge?

8. There is a second thing which enables Jesus to be thankful in this tough time. Chris writes, "Jesus praises God not simply for who God is but also for what God is doing. Not only does Jesus realize through prayer that God is still in charge. He also realizes that God is still at work. Based on the events of the day, it may seem that God is doing nothing. How could God be active when allies are dropping like flies, the crowds are becoming wishy-washy, and perfect ministry brings pathetic results? Surely God has taken a break. Yet in this prayer, Jesus recognizes that God is still at work: 'I thank you, Father, Lord of heaven and earth, that you have hidden these things from the wise and understanding and revealed them to little children; yes, Father, for such was your gracious will.'... Through prayer, Jesus remembers that God generally doesn't work in a way that is high profile or with methods that persuade the sophisticated and the elite. Instead, Jesus remembers that God works in humble ways, in unseen ways, and in ways that impact the lowly and unsophisticated. Jesus may not be able to see much fruit being borne among the notable and noteworthy. But God's doing a great work through Jesus among the nobodies. Jesus is able to recognize that God is still at work. God still rules over all things which seem to challenge his mission and ministry." In what ways does "you have hidden these things from the wise and understanding and revealed them to little children" indicate that God is at work—but in hidden and unexpected ways? How does it help, in tough times, to remember through prayer that God is indeed still at work?

9. Close with this prayer exercise: This week, carry a three-fold prayer with you into every situation: "You are still in charge. You are still at work. You are still worthy of praise." Especially as you encounter challenges or

trials, every day this week pray this prayer, "You are still in charge. You are still at work. You are still worthy of praise." As you stumble upon doubt, disappointment, or desolation, pray this three-fold prayer.

Chapter 6 / **An Upward Prayer of Confidence:**
You Still Listen (John 11)

1. When going through difficult times, sometimes all we really need is to know someone is listening—to know we are heard. Who do you call or meet with when you just need someone to listen?

2. Read John 11:1-40. Describe the emotions and feelings of each of the following people/groups: The disciples. Martha. Mary. Jesus.

3. Read John 11:41,42. Jesus thanks God for hearing. What has God heard that leads Jesus to pray with thanksgiving? Chris writes, "Perhaps this is a thanksgiving of anticipation—an acknowledgement that God will hear his request to raise Lazarus.. A sort of 'Thank you for hearing the prayer I'm about to pray.' Jesus is so close to the Father that perhaps he gives thanks now because he knows, in just a moment, that God will hear his request to raise Lazarus." Do you think Jesus is thanking God for the fact that God is about to hear his request to raise Lazarus? Why? Why not?

4. Chris writes, "But Jesus does not pray, 'Father, I thank you that you will hear me.'. . . He prays, 'Father, I thank you that you have heard me.' Jesus praises God because he is certain God has heard him." What do you think God has already heard which now leads Jesus to pray with thanksgiving?

5. Chris writes, "In his examination of the Jewish roots of the prayers of Jesus, Timothy Jones argues that what God heard was Jesus' weeping: 'When [Jesus] found himself in the shadow of his friend's tomb, he couldn't put his prayers into words, so he put them into tears instead. And his Father heard his cries.' In other words, what catches God's ears is the sound of Jesus' tears. Jesus thanks God because the Father has heard his heart breaking. Such an interpretation of Jesus' prayer becomes more and more likely when we read the prayers of others who also thanked God simply because God heard their cry: 'LORD, you hear the desire of the afflicted' (Psalm10:17); 'From his temple he heard my voice, and my cry to him reached his ears' (Psalm 18:6); 'For he has not despised or abhorred the affliction of the afflicted, and he

has not hidden his face from him, but has heard' (Psalm 22:24); 'This poor man cried, and the LORD heard him' (Psalm 34:6); 'I cry aloud to God, aloud to God, and he will hear me' (Psalm 77:1).

6. Read Psalm 6. Chris writes, "Jesus' circumstance and prayer closely mirror the circumstance and prayer of David in Psalm 6.: Jesus is portrayed as 'deeply moved in his spirit and greatly troubled.' David pictures himself as 'greatly troubled.' We are told that 'Jesus wept.' David writes 'I drench my couch with my weeping.' Jesus praises, 'Father, I thank you that you have heard me.' David remarks, 'For the LORD has heard the sound of my weeping.' Could it be that as Jesus faces this trial, he is reminded of one of the similar trials his forefather David faced? Could it be as Jesus searches for the words to pray, he remembers the words David prayed? Could it be that just as David was grateful simply for the way God heard his grief, so now Jesus rejoices in the fact that his Father has heard his grief? 'Father, I thank you that you have heard the sound of my weeping.' When people in pain go to God, what they almost always thank God for is the simple fact that he hears their pain. The sound that thunders most loudly through God's hallowed halls is the sound of a sob." In what ways do you find it helpful simply to know that God hears your cries, that God listens to your tears?

7. Chris writes, "Jesus' prayer at the tomb of Lazarus draws us back to one of those basic elements of prayer. Timothy Jones writes, 'at the heart of all our prayers, what we really want is not an answer but an assurance—an assurance that our Father is listening.'... Sometimes all I need to know is that I am heard." What do you need most from God when in pain: an answer to your prayer or an assurance that he hears your prayer? Why?

8. Why do you think Jesus prays this prayer out loud so that others hear his gratitude toward God?

9. Close with this prayer exercise: Each day this week bring to mind an issue you believe God has ignored. You feel like he's not engaged in this issue. You wonder if he's even paying attention to this issue. Now picture God speaking to you: "I am listening. I have heard. Nothing you've said or felt about this issue has escaped my notice." Then, give thanks to God, praising him for listening to your plea. In addition, each day this week intercede for others using this prayer. There are others who feel God is ignoring them or not hearing them. For them, each day this week, pray something like this: "Father, I thank you that you hear them. I know

that you always hear them. But help them to know that. Help them to believe what I believe—that you are truly the God who hears."

Chapter 7 / **An Upward Prayer of Confidence:**
You Still Reveal (John 12, 17)

1. When you know you've got something unpleasant that you have to do on a given day, how do you handle the anxiety?

2. Read John 7:28-30; 8:20; 12:20-23; 13:1; 12:27; 17:1. Jesus knows "the hour" is approaching—the hour of his trial and painful crucifixion. He is about to pray with this hour in mind. What would characterize your prayer if you knew a similar "hour" was at hand?

3. Chris writes, "Jesus shows there are two possible ways of praying. The first prayer sounds like this: 'Now is my soul troubled. And what shall I say? 'Father, save me from this hour?' (John 12:27) One way to pray when passing through a painful time is to say, 'Save me from this hour.' Rescue me. Deliver Me." When would it be permissible or appropriate to pray this prayer when facing some difficult situation? When would it be inappropriate?

4. Chris writes, "But there is a second possibility. One that is rarely taken. One demanding deep faith. Yet one that can change everything about our experience in moments of misery. This is the path Jesus takes as he prays about his hour: 'Now is my soul troubled. And what shall I say? 'Father, save me from this hour'? But for this purpose I have come to this hour. Father, glorify your name' (John 12:27-28) . . . 'When Jesus had spoken these words, he lifted up his eyes to heaven, and said, 'Father, the hour has come; glorify your Son that the Son may glorify you' (John 17:1)." What does this prayer mean: Glorify your name? How is this different from "Save me from this hour"?

5. Read John 1:14, 18; 2:11; 11:4, 40. What is the glory of God?

6. Chris writes, "As Jesus awaits his agony, he prays for God to be glorified. He asks that the darkness of the hour provide the perfect setting for God to be illuminated. Jesus requests that God publicize something about his person through the misery of this moment. Rather than, 'Save me so that I will be safe,' Jesus prays 'Show yourself so that you will be seen.' Jesus embraces his hour because he knows that others will see God in a way they would not have seen without this hour. . . . This trial will become a viewfinder through which others will more clearly picture

the heart of God." In what ways have you seen God more clearly when you or someone you know faced a time of difficulty?

7. Close with this prayer exercise: You may be facing an hour or two this week. Take some time to make a short list of all the challenges, obstacles, or difficulties waiting for you at school, home, or work this week. Each day this week, pray this prayer over that list: "God reveal yourself through this painful time. Let people see something about you they never would have seen had I never entered this challenging moment." Perhaps this week finds you free from such hours. If so, spend time each day this week praying this prayer on behalf of others. Make a short list of people whom you know are facing an hour: a disease, a death in the family, job instability, family concerns, emotional difficulties, or health issues. Each day pray this week for them: "God reveal yourself through their painful time. Let people see something about you they never would have seen had these never entered this challenging moment."

* Chapter 8 / **An Upward Prayer of Confidence:**
You Still Matter (Matthew 26)

1. Can you think of some times in the Bible when God did not answer a prayer or plea in the way the person expected?

2. Read Deuteronomy 3:26-37; 1 Chronicles 28:1-3; 1 Kings 19:4-5; Jonah 4:3-4; 2 Corinthians 12:8-9. Why did God say "No" to these prayers?

3. Can you share a prayer in which God answered you with a "No"?

4. Read John 17:20-21; Luke 22:31-32; Luke 22:54-57; Matthew 26:39, 42, 44. In what ways do these represent prayers that were not answered with a "Yes"?

5. What do you do when a prayer is answered with "No"?

6. Chris writes, "One extreme is this: I seek my wish. Jesus indeed seeks his wish. He boldly prays, 'Let this cup pass.' His heartfelt wish is for the cup to pass. But his prayer-life does not exist solely at this edge. Another extreme is added to his prayer. Another perspective modifies this perspective. However, too often our prayers perch only on this end of the continuum. Too frequently, this is the only ingredient in our petitions. Our sole focus becomes this: I seek my wish. What matters most to us is our need. Prayer is generally about getting God to grant our wish." Have there been times when your prayer-life revolved around this one agenda: I seek my wish? What was the result?

7. When this is our primary approach to prayer, what happens to us when that wish is denied, when God says "No"? Chris writes, "When God says no we are devastated. When prayer is only me seeking my wish, a wish denied leads to discouragement with prayer and disillusionment with God. If our heart is devoted only to our wish, when God says no, our heart gets broken. This type of prayer is unable to cope with the reality for prayers answered in the negative." Have you ever been broken-hearted by God's "No"?

8. Chris writes, "Thankfully, Jesus prayer in Gethsemane displays a second extreme. Jesus does seek his wish. But he also seeks God's will. He prays, 'Let this cup pass.' But he also prays, 'Your will be: 'Let this cup pass' and 'Your will be done.' For Jesus prayer is not merely I seek my wish. It is also I seek your will.' But for some of us, prayer can move too far in this other direction. Surrender becomes the only ingredient in our petitions. We cease confessing our wishes and only seek God's will." In what ways would it be unhealthy to never tell God what we actually wish and only seek his will through our prayers?

9. Chris writes, "Neither of these two extremes deals effectively with unanswered prayers. The first—'I seek my wish'—can't handle it when God says no. The second—'I seek your will'—doesn't even give God a chance to say no." Why would it be important for us to share with God what we really want, even if we know he may deny that wish?

10. Chris writes, "There is a third way . . . ."; it should be "On the one hand, Jesus seeks his wish: 'let this cup pass from me.' But Jesus also seeks God's will: 'nevertheless, not as I will, but as you will.' For Jesus prayer is not either 'I seek my wish' or 'I seek your will.' It is both. Jesus finds a way of praying which permits him to ask for exactly what he wants yet also enables him to honestly leave the final decision up to God." Why is it important to pray in such a way that we communicate both what our true desire is and a willingness to submit to whatever God's true desire is?

11. Chris writes, "Ultimately, the Gethsemane prayer is about learning to say yes to God. Even though God may occasionally say no to us, prayer is always an opportunity for us to say yes to God. Every time we combine 'I seek your will' and 'I seek my wish,' we are telling God that he matters more to us than anything else. We are communicating through him that our answer to him will always be yes regardless of his answer to us." Why is it important to learn to say yes to God through prayer?

12. Close with this prayer exercise: Each day this week bring to your mind a discouraging circumstance in your life or in the life of someone you care about. For a few moments, pray nothing but "Let this cup pass...Let this cup pass.... Let this cup pass..." After some silence, begin praying again. This time, however, pray nothing but "Nevertheless, your will be done.... Nevertheless, your will be done.... Nevertheless, your will be done."

* Chapter 9 / **An Upward Prayer of Confidence:**
   You Still Hold (Luke 23)

1. Share something you have had to place in the hands of others, trusting them to take care of it, follow through with it, protect it, or preserve it.

2. Is handing something valuable over to others easy for you? Why? Why not?

3. Chris writes, "We all know this is a trust issue. Specifically, it's a trust issue regarding competency and character. Can I trust the competency of the one whose hands now hold my treasures? Are those hands strong enough? Are they skilled enough? Can those hands do any better than mine?... We also wonder about character. Can I trust the character of the one whose hands now hold the things most precious to me? Maybe they have strong muscles and fine skills. But do they also have strong ethics and fine morals?" Do these two issues lie behind your struggle with handing things over? Can you share a time when you trusted in the competency or character of someone and thus were able to hand something over to that person?

4. Read Luke 23:44-46. Do you think it was easy for Jesus to hand himself over to the Father's hands? Why? Why not?

5. Read 1 Samuel 5:11; Exodus 32:11; Deuteronomy 3:24; 4:34; 5:15; 7:19; 9:26; 11:12; Joshua 4:24. What do you hear in these passages regarding the competency of God's hands? Chris writes, "The trust is rooted in Jesus' deep and intimate knowledge of the competency and character of God's hands. First, the prayer focuses on competency: 'into your hands I commit my spirit! In the Bible, the human hand is an expression of power and control.... The same is true regarding God's hands.... In the Bible, the hands of God are synonymous with the greatness and might of God. Jesus has witnessed God's hands for an eternity past. He knows beyond any doubt that these hands are the most skilled and

most powerful hands that exist. He knows these hands are greater than the hands which placed him on the cross. He believes these hands are superior to the nails which pierced his hands. Jesus trusts completely in the competency of God's hands."

6. What persuades you to believe in the competency of God's hands?

7. Read Psalm 10:12; 95:7; 123:2; 31:5. What do these verses point to regarding the character of God's hands? Chris writes, "But Jesus not only points to the competence of God's hands in his prayer, he also points to the character of those hands.... Scripture not only speaks of God's hands as mighty and magnificent. It also speaks of God's hands as caring and compassionate.... It's not hard to imagine that Jesus has these images in mind when he prays his prayer. After all, his prayer is a quote from the Psalms. Jesus knows how the psalmists celebrate the kindness and mercy of the hands of God."

8. What persuades you to believe in the character of God's hands?

9. Read Ps. 31:5 again. Chris writes, "In the original, David prays, 'Into your hands I commit my spirit' (Psalm 31:5). In Jesus' version we hear this important addition, 'Father, into your hands I commit my spirit!' Jesus envisions not merely the grand hands of God or the controlling hands of the Creator. Jesus envisions the loving, caring, and adoring hands of the Father. These are the hands that have applauded, hugged, and held Jesus. Jesus knows the character of these hands as only the Son can know the hands of the Father." When you think of God's hands as the hands of the ultimate father, what images come to mind?

10. Chris writes, "And because of this trust, rooted in his conviction about the competency and character of God's hands, Jesus is able to place something priceless in those hands. Jesus prays, 'Father, into your hands I commit my spirit!' The word 'spirit' refers to the innermost part of Jesus. . . . This is Jesus core. This is the most fragile and vulnerable piece of himself. Jesus entrusts into God's hands not just something important or someone important. Jesus entrusts his spirit—the most fundamental part of himself. When we genuinely understand the competency and character of God's hands, we are able to entrust those hands with what is most important." What might be something analogous in your life to "spirit"—that is, what are some of the most important, valuable, and precious things in your life? In what ways does knowing the character and competency of God's hands make it easier for you to hand over those valuable things to God?

11. Close with this prayer practice: Jesus' prayer is a powerful one to utilize on those occasions when something precious seems endangered. Consider your life this week. Is something threatened—a dream?—a plan?—a relationship?—a desire?—an important person? Every day this week picture that endangered person or possession in your mind and then pray: "Father, into your hands, I commit my _____." This prayer is also beneficial for praying over all the things which are important to us—whether or not they seem endangered. Prayed daily, this petition becomes a habitual way of surrendering everything and every person in our life to God. Make a list of the most important people in your life, the most important possessions in your life, and the most important plans you have for life. Each day this week, one by one, day by day, pray: "Father, into your hands, I commit _____."

Chapter 10 / **An Upward Prayer of Confidence:** *You Still Stop* (John 19:30)

1. Share a time when an important project, season, or accomplishment was finally finished or completed.

2. Chris writes of his high school graduation: "When I think back to that day, I struggle to find one word that captures the rich experience. But I recently stumbled upon a Greek word that fits the need nicely. The word is 'tetelestai.' It means 'It is finished' or simply 'Finished.' It's the perfect word for using when tossing a graduation cap into the air. *Tetelestai!* It is finished!" Have you had seasons in your life that were marked by a definite "finish"? How did finishing make you feel?

3. Read John 19:28-30. Chris writes, "Three times John uses a form of the word 'tetelestai': twice in vs. 28 (translated once as 'fulfilled,' and once in vs. 30. John literally writes that Jesus knew everything was 'finished:' and so that Scripture would be 'finished'; and then Jesus said, 'finished' John wants there to be no mistake. Jesus' death on the cross was the finish. Up there on the cross tetelestai is found three times." What does the cross finish or complete?

4. Chris writes, "But what did Jesus' death finish? An important clue is found in one detail revealed only by John. As the other Gospel authors do, John notes that someone takes a sponge, soaks it with wine, and lifts it up for Jesus to drink. This is the second time a drink has been offered to Jesus. At the beginning of the crucifixion, wine is offered to Jesus but he refuses it. This first offering involves a strong wine that would have

been used as a sedative to dull the pain of the cross. Jesus refuses that drink. He will not enter this crucial moment with his mind clouded by drugs. But later, as John recounts, another drink is offered to Jesus. This one is a cheaper wine used merely for quenching thirst. And John is the only author to indicate that this drink was lifted to Jesus on a hyssop plant: 'A jar full of sour wine stood there, so they put a sponge full of the sour wine on a hyssop branch and held it to his mouth' (John 19:29). Only John includes the small detail that this drink was lifted to Jesus on a hyssop plant. Why did John think this was significant? Without a doubt, the most noteworthy biblical reference to hyssop comes at the place where God commands that the hyssop plant be used to spread the blood of the Passover lamb on the doorposts of the Israelite homes (Exodus 12). Perhaps John is struck by the appearance of the hyssop plant at the cross because of its appearance at the Passover. The same hyssop that was used to spread the Passover lamb's blood is now used to lift up a drink to Jesus.... By means of that blood God brought an end to the slavery and oppression of the Hebrews. Similarly, through Jesus' blood God is now bringing an end to the slavery and oppression of all humanity. And that's why Jesus shouts 'Tetelestai!' Our enslavement, our captivity to sin and its power is now finished. Our Passover has come. Our deliverance has come. Tetelestai! It is finished!" Share how you've experienced this end to sin-slavery in your own life.

5. We often think of how the cross was a finish or completion for us. But in what ways was the cross the finish or completion of something for Jesus? Read John 17:4. The word "accomplished" (ESV) is the same word "finished" in John 19:28-30. What did the cross accomplish or complete for Jesus?

6. Chris writes, "Prayed in John 17, 'Finished!' is a prayer of expectation. Even before the final note sounds, Jesus has such expectant trust and hope in God that he knows without a doubt that God will bring this long and hard salvation work to completion. That's why he can pray 'Finished!' before the cross begins. Here, his prayer has this sense: 'I know that this work is as good as done, because I know that you will ensure its completion.' It is a prayer of expectation." How was Jesus able to look to the cross before it was finished and pray expectantly and with trust that it would indeed be finished? What does that prayer teach us about times when we face a daunting task which God has given us? In what ways can we pray expectantly, trusting that what God has given us, he will enable us to finish?

7. Chris writes, "Prayed in John 19, 'Finished!' is a prayer of exultation. This work is truly over. Jesus expresses his gratitude to the Father. He praises. He shouts. He rejoices. Here, his prayer has this sense: 'I thank you for bringing this work to a conclusion. I praise you for seeing it through with me to the very end.' It is a prayer of exultation." Do you often pray to God with thanks when a major accomplishment is finished? How?

8. Close with this prayer exercise: Consider something you are just beginning, or maybe already in the middle of. Some work God has called you to. Some effort you are being required to make. You know there is no way to remain loyal to God and to whom he's called you to be without embracing this work. You cannot go around, over, or under it. Following Jesus requires you to go right through it. Perhaps it is something pleasant like the start of a degree program or the early stages of a new relationship. Perhaps it is daunting like the first steps into a challenging project at work or a decision about seeing your marriage through despite the difficulties. Pray every day this week about that issue. Pray with expectation that what God is beginning, he will also bring to an end. Pray with anticipation that the God who's called you to this work will indeed walk with you through it. Pray with conviction that he will see it to the end. Pray the *tetelestai* prayer of expectation every day this week. Now consider some small or significant task you've recently completed or a matter in which you've experienced resolution. Perhaps you just completed your first year at a job. Maybe you've just ended a season of particularly exhausting parenting problems at home. Perhaps you've just buried a dear friend or family member for whom you provided encouragement and care in the final days. Pray every day this week about that matter. Pray with exultation for the way God brought fulfillment to that task. Pray with thanksgiving and praise for the way that season of winter is now over and spring is becoming visible. Pray with gratitude that God has brought completion to the work. Pray the *tetelestai* prayer of exultation each day this week.

* Chapter 11 / **An Outward Prayer of Compassion:**
   Mind Their Mission (John 17)

1. What's the most dangerous situation you've ever found yourself in?

2. Read John 17:11-19. What dangers does Jesus identify in this prayer? Does it surprise you that in facing this danger, Jesus does not pray for his own safety—instead Jesus prays for the safety of his followers?

3. Chris writes, "Specifically, Jesus prays three things: 'keep them in your name' (John 17:11b); 'keep them from the evil one' (John 17:15); and 'Sanctify them' (John 17:17)." What do these three requests mean? How would you put them into your own words?

4. Chris writes, "First, Jesus prays they will be kept in the Father's presence: 'keep them in your name' (17:11b). The Father's name is an important part of this prayer. Jesus reminds God, 'I have manifested your name to the people whom you gave me out of the world' (17:6). He states 'I kept them in your name' (17:12), and that 'I made known to them your name' (17:26).... To know a name was to know the essence of the person named. In addition, a person's name could carry the same authority as the personal presence of that individual. To come 'in the name' of a ruler or a king was to come with the same authority as if that ruler or king were present himself. Jesus earlier stated that he came in the Father's name (John 5:43; 10:25)—that is, he came with the authority of the Father, as if the Father himself were present. Here, Jesus rehearses in prayer how he manifested God's name or made known God's name—that is, Jesus made God's identity known.... Thus when Jesus asks God to 'keep them in your name' he is praying for God to keep Jesus' followers under his care, under his authority, and by his power; to be present to them and with them; and to keep them close by him. In a word, Jesus prays for God to keep them in his 'presence.'" What do you find meaningful about this request that God keep Jesus' followers in his presence?

5. Chris writes, "He also prays 'keep them from the evil one' (John 17:15). Jesus not only asks that his followers will be kept in the Father's presence. He begs that they also be kept from the devil's power. Jesus' prayer is guided by a kind of magnetic worldview. On the one hand, he believes in a Father to whom all should be drawn and in whom all should be kept. On the other hand, Jesus believes in a devil from whom all should be repelled and from whom all should be kept. Jesus' prayer has a push and a pull. He asks that those he deeply loves will be pushed closer to the Father and pulled farther from the devil. Jesus believes in real evil which emanates from a real devil. And his concern now is that his servants be protected from that dark power." Do you live as if you believed in a dangerous devil? How should a belief in a dangerous devil affect our prayers?

6. Chris writes, "Finally, Jesus prays, 'Sanctify them' (John 17:17). Upon

first hearing, this petition seems out of place. There appears to be no line to draw between this dot and the two prior to it.... The linkage becomes clearer however when we listen to the full prayer: 'Sanctify them in the truth; your word is truth. As you sent me into the world, so I have sent them into the world. And for their sake I consecrate myself, that they also may be sanctified in truth.' Jesus is reflecting upon his mission and theirs. He's pondering how he's been sent into the world to accomplish a greater purpose and how his followers are similarly being sent into the world. In John 17 "sanctify" and "sent" are almost synonymous.... When applied to people and things, "holy" refers to them being reserved for God and his use. Jesus has been sanctified. He's been reserved for God and his use. He's been sent into the world for God's purposes. Now Jesus prays the same for his followers.... He prays that they might fulfill their purpose in life." How significant do you find it that Jesus did not just pray for his followers to be safe, but more importantly that they would accomplish their mission?

7. One of the things this prayer urges us to imitate is Jesus' devotion to intercessory prayer. What are some of the ways in which you pray for others (e.g., who do you pray for, when, how, etc.?).

8. Close with this prayer practice: Make a list of friends, family members, fellow believers, those involved in Christian ministry/para-church organizations, those serving in Christian charities, and those who are involved with Christian education. Pray three times over this list. On your first intercessory pass, pray for these men and women to be kept in the Father's presence. Pray for them to remain under the Father's powerful and passionate care. On your second intercessory pass through the list, pray for these people to be kept from the devil's power. Pray that none will give in to temptation. Pray that none will fall prey to demonic tricks and traps. On your final intercessory pass, pray for these men and women to be kept for their global purpose. Pray that neither distraction, nor disillusionment nor discouragement will keep them from their kingdom calling and purpose.

Chapter 12 / **An Outward Prayer of Compassion:**
Concentrate Their Community (John 17)

1. Chris writes, "A few years ago the *American Sociological Review* reported that friendships are on the decline in the United States. Over a period of two decades, researchers found an increasing number of Americans

saying they do not discuss important matters with anyone. For those Americans who do discuss important matters with someone, the number of confidants was decreasing. Those who say they have no one to discuss important matters doubled during the study: one out of four. In addition, the number of close confidents Americans said they had in their lives dropped from three to two. Increasingly, we seem disconnected." Do you feel that people are more disconnected today than ten or twenty years ago? What keeps people from having deeper friendships and connections? How about you—are you more or less connected than you were ten or twenty years ago?

2. Chris writes, "In his widely acclaimed book, *Bowling Alone*, Robert Putnam…argues that there are two kinds of relationships critical in society: bridging and bonding. Bonding refers to relationships that are built between people who are similar to each other…. Bridging refers to relationships that are built between people who are dissimilar to one another…." In another work Putnam writes, "The problem is that bridging social capital is harder to create than bonding social capital— after all, birds of a feather flock together. So the kind of social capital that is most essential for healthy public life in an increasingly diverse society like ours is precisely the kind that is hardest to build.' The kind of relationship 'that is most essential' is the kind 'that is hardest to build." Bonding is harder and harder to find. We are disconnected and lacking the experience of intimacy. We have fewer strong ties to other people. But bridging is ever more difficult to discover. We are divided and lacking the experience of true unity. We have fewer strong ties to different people. Why do we struggle so much with bridging—building true community with people different than us?

3. Chris writes, "Imagine, then, what it might be like to stumble onto a world in which the exact opposite was true. Rather than disconnection, it seemed almost every person you interviewed was experiencing intimacy. Each person had a list the length of their arm when asked who they confide in and who they could call at two o'clock in the morning with a problem. Bonding was as vital to their society as breathing is to the body. And rather than division, it appeared almost every person you interviewed was enjoying unity. Each person you polled could name several others of different skin color, country of origin, income, and political persuasion whom they counted as a dear friend. Bridging was as central to their society as blood is to the body. In their book, *Introducing the Missional Church*, Alan Roxburgh and Scott Boren call

this kind of community a 'contrast society.'" Have you ever been part of a group or family in which intimacy and unity were far more prevalent than disconnection and division? Where bridging and bonding were extremely common? Explain.

4. Read John 17:20-23. What is Jesus praying about here in terms of disconnection, intimacy, or bonding? What is Jesus praying about here in terms of division, unity, or bridging?

5. Chris writes, "In this, his longest prayer ever, Jesus prays for the Father to make possible what remains humanly impossible: true intimacy and true unity. Jesus prays against the qualities that dominate far too many hearts and lives across the globe: disconnection and division. Jesus devotes a third of his John 17 prayer to begging God to transform his followers into a contrast community which experiences the kind of bridging and bonding that will persuade outsiders that God himself must be behind it. Jesus understands that such community is not naturally possible. It is only supernaturally possible. Thus he is compelled to pray, plead, and beg for God to make happen what only God can make happen." Of all Jesus could have prayed for, why do you think he prayed about this?

6. Close with this prayer exercise: Consider three stages of prayers motivated by this John 17 prayer. In the first stage, we pray about ourselves. Spend time right now praying for God to empower you to truly bond with one or two others who are similar to you. Pray for God to enable you to truly bridge with one or two others who are unlike you. In the second stage, we might pray about people like us who are already in Jesus' community. Pray right now for the people in your congregation or small group. Pray that God will enable every person already in that congregation or group to experience true intimacy with another human and true unity with someone different from them. In the third stage, we might pray for those outside the Jesus' community. We might pray that God would send them to our congregations so that we might bond and bridge with them in a way that leads them to believe only God could be responsible for what they are experiencing.

* Chapter 13 / **An Outward Prayer of Compassion:**
  Forgive Their Faults (Luke 23)

1. Chris writes: "Sadly, even at a young age we experience what becomes all too common throughout life. People hurt us. Some intentionally. Some unintentionally. The reality of life is that, at times, we will be

disappointed and devastated by people around us." How has this been true in your life?

2. Chris writes: "Nowhere is the hurt caused by humans greater than at the cross of Christ. Consider all the people who are there, just to harm Jesus. The people in the government abuse him. The people in the religious leadership reject him. The people in his friendship circle abandon him. The person being executed on the next cross ridicules him. Even the Son of God endures pain from other people." What examples stick out in your mind of the way in which Jesus was hurt by people?

3. Chris writes, "With these injuries in mind, Jesus prayed. Specifically, he prayed for help. In the Garden of Gethsemane, Jesus prayed for help—that God would make it possible for Jesus to escape the hurt that people were about to cause." Is it appropriate to pray "Help me" when facing painful people? Why? Why not?

4. Read Psalm 69:1-4, 22-28. Chris writes, "David doesn't just pray for help. He prays for hurt. He prays for God to hurt those who hurt him." Is it appropriate to pray "Hurt them" when facing painful people? Why? Why not?

5. Read Luke 23:34. How is Jesus' prayer different than our prayers when facing difficult people?

6. Chris writes: "Notice what Jesus prays. He doesn't pray 'Help me.' He doesn't pray 'Hurt them.' Instead, he prays, 'Forgive them.'... Notice, next, when this prayer came. It came immediately after the hurt.... The prayer for forgiveness did not come at the very end of the torment, after Jesus has time to process the hurt; after Jesus has time work up some kind of compassion for these people. Instead, it's the first prayer out of his lips on the cross.... Finally, notice for whom Jesus prayed. Jesus did not simply pray for someone who cut him off in traffic. He did not simply pray for a stranger who flung an unkind word. Jesus prayed this prayer of forgiveness for his worst enemies, for those trying to end his life." What do you find most challenging: the what, when, or whom of this prayer?

7. Read Matthew 6:9-15. What is the connection between extending forgiveness and receiving forgiveness?

6. Close with this prayer exercise: First, imagine the person who is praying this prayer because you are the one who has hurt them. Something you said or didn't say, did or didn't do has caused a deep wound. Today

that person is praying this prayer for you: Father, forgive them. Each day this week, talk to God about this sin of yours, asking forgiveness for the injury you caused to someone else. Receive God's gracious and abundant forgiveness. Give thanks that someone might pray on your behalf in this way. Now, bring to mind someone who has hurt you. Each day this week pray this prayer: "Father, forgive _____ , for they know not what they do."

Works Cited

Adams, Paul. *Social Circles: How offline relationships influence online behavior and what it means for design and marketing.* Berkley, CA: New Rider Press, 2010. Print.

Albright, Madeleine. Yale Divinity School. Mar. 2004. Talk.

Beck, Richard. "The Psychology of Christianity: Part 5," Experimental Theology. blogspot.com. 12 July 2010. Web. 12 July 2010.

Bergman, Ronen. "Killing the Killers." *Newsweek* 20 Dec. 2010. Print.

Blake, John. "Why Many Americans Prefer Their Sunday Segregated." *CNN.com.* Cable News Network, 2008. Web.

Braveheart. Dir. Mel Gibson. Icon Productions, 1995. DVD

Brueggeman, Walter. *The Message of the Psalms.* Minneapolis, MN: Augsburg Publishing House, 1984. Print.

Brueggeman, Walter. *Spirituality of the Psalms.* Minneapolis, MN: Fortress Press, 2002. Print.

Bruner, Frederick Dale. *Matthew: a commentary.* Dallas: Word, 1987. Print.

Buchanan, Mark. "Messy, Costly, Dirty Ministry." Leadershipjournal.net Web. 15 May 2009.

Caron, D. A. *The Gospel According to John.* Downers Gove, IL: Intervarsity Press, 1991. Print.

Crabb, Larry. *The Safest Place on Earth.* Nashville, TN: Word Publishing, 1999. Print.

Craddock, Fred B. *Craddock Stories.* Ed. Mike Graves and Richard Ward. St. Louis, MO: Chalice Press, 2001. Print.

Dean, Kenda. *Almost Christian: what the faith of our teenagers is telling the American church*. Oxford: Oxford University Press, 2010. Kindle ed.

Easton, M. *Easton's Bible Dictionary*. Logos Research Systems, Inc., 1996. Elec. ed.

ESV Study Bible, The. Wheaton, IL.: Crossway Bibles, 2008. Elec. ed.

Foster, Richard J. *Prayer: Finding the Heart's True Home*. San Francisco: Harper San Francisco, 1992. Print.

Galli, Mark. "The Impossibility of Thanksgiving." *Christianity Today*. Christianity Today. 25 Nov. 2009. Web. 25 Nov. 2009.

Garland, David. "The Lord's Prayer in the Gospel Matthew." *Review & Expositor* 89.2 (Spring 1992). Print.

"Gethsemane" Ed. D. R. W. Wood and I. H. Marshall. *New Bible Dictionary*. 3rd ed. Downers Grove, IL: Intervarsity Press, 1996. Elec. ed.

Gilbert, Greg. Wh*at Is the Gospel*? Wheaton, IL: Crossway, 2010. Print.

Guthrie, Stan. "Waging Peace with Islam" *Christianity Today* May 2004. Print.

Hosseini, Khaled. *A Thousand Splendid Suns*. New York: Riverhead Books, 2007. Audio ed.

Ilibagiza, Immaculee. *Left to Tell: Discovering God Amidst the Rwandan Holocaust*. Carlsbad, CA: Hay House, 2006. Print.

Indermark, John. *Traveling the Prayer Paths of Jesus*. Nashville: Upper Room Books, 2003. Print.

Jeremias, Joachim. *The Prayers of Jesus*. Philadelphia: Fortress Press, 1978. Print.

Jones, Timothy P. *Prayers Jesus Prayed: Experiencing the Father through the Prayers of His Son*. Ann Arbor, MI: Vine Books, 2002. Print.

Jones, Timothy P. *Praying Like the Jew, Jesus: Recovering the Ancient Roots of New Testament Prayer*. Clarksville, MD: Lederer Books, 2005. Print.

Keener, Craig S. *A Commentary on the Gospel of Matthew*. Grand Rapids, MI: W. B. Eerdmans Publishing, 1999. Print.

Kendall, R. T. "Forgiving the Unrepentant" *Christianity Today* Mar. 2005. Print.

Langewiesche, William. *Sahara Unveiled: a Journy Across the Desert.* New York: Pantheon Books, 1996. Print.

Longenecker, Richard N. Introduction. *Into God's Presence: Prayer in the New Testament.* Ed. Richard N. Longenecker. Grand Rapids, MI: W. B. Eerdmans Publishing, 2002. Kindle ed.

Marshall, I. Howard. "Jesus—Example and Teacher of Prayer in the Synoptic Gospels." *Into God's Presence: Prayer in the New Testament.* Ed. Richard N. Longenecker. Grand Rapids, MI: W. B. Eerdmans Publishing, 2002. Print.

Martin, George. *Praying with Jesus: what the Gospels Tell Us About How to Pray.* Chicago: Loyola Press, 2000. Print.

McCullough, David. *Mornings on Horseback.* New York: Simon and Schuster, 1982. Audio ed.

McPherson, Miller, Lynn Smith-Loven, and Matthew E. Brashears. "Social Isolation in America: Changes in Core Discussion Networds over Two Decades." *American Sociological Review.* 71.3 (June 2006). Web.

Miller, Donald. *Blue Like Jazz: Nonreligious Thoughts on Christian Spirituality.* Nashville:Thomas Nelson, 2003. Print.

Moore, Linda A. "Mother, 2 babies, perish in blaze." *The Commercial Appeal.* 9 Jan. 2011. Print.

Morris, Leon. *The Gospel According to Matthew.* Grand Rapids, MI: W. B. Eerdmans Publishing, 1992.

Neff, David. " 'Father, Into Your Hands I Commit My Spirit': Jesus's important addition to David's cry." *Christianity Today.* Christianity Today. Web.

Nouwen, Henri J. *Our Greatest Gift: a meditation on dying and caring.* San Francisco: Harper San Francisco, 1994. Print.

Nouwen, Henri J., *Reaching Out: the Three Movements of the Spiritual Life.* Garden City, NY: Doubleday & Company, 1975. Print.

Ortberg, John. *Everybody's Normal Till You Get to Know Them.* Grand Rapids, MI: Zondervan, 2003. Print.

Ortberg, John. *If You Want to Walk on Water, You've Got to Get Out of the Boat.* Grand Rapids, MI: Zondervan Publishing House, 2001. Print.

Ortberg, John. *The Me I Want to Be: becoming God's best version of you.* Grand Rapids, MI: Zondervan, 2010. Print.

"Perspectives 2010" *Newsweek* 27 Dec. 2010-3 Jan. 2011. Print.

Peterson, Eugene. *Tell It Slant: A Conversation on the Language of Jesus in His Stories and Prayers.* Grand Rapids, MI: William B. Eerdmans Publishing Co., 2008. Elec. Ed.

Putnam, Robert. *Bowling Alone: the collapse and revival of American community.* Touchstone ed. New York: Simon & Schuster, 2001. Print.

Putnam, Robert, Lewis Feldstein and Donald J. Cohen. *Better Together: restoring the American community.* New York: Simon & Schuster, 2004. Print.

Quoist, Michel. *Prayers.* Trans. Agnes M. Forsyth and Anne Marie de Commaille. New York: Sheed and Ward, 1963. Print.

Rath, Tom. *Vital Friends: the people you can't afford to live without.* New York: Gallup Press, 2006.

Ravitch, Diane. "The Language Police." *The Atlantic Monthly* March 2003. Print.

Rievaulx, Aelred of. *Spiritual Friendship.* Kalamazoo, MI: Cistercian Publications, 1977. Print.

Roberts, Mark D. *No Holds Barred: wrestling with God in prayer.* Colorado Springs, CO: Waterbrook Press, 2005. Print.

Roxburgh, Alan, M. Scott Boren, and Mark Priddy. *Introducing the Missional Church: What It Is, Why It Matters, How to Become One.* Grand Rapids, MI: Baker Books, 2009. Elec ed. Allelon Missional Series.

Shenk, Joshua Wolf. "What Makes Us Happy?" *The Atlantic* June 2009. Print.

Stafford, Tim. "India Undaunted" *Christianity Today* May 2004. Print.

Statistics. Obesity Education Intiative. *National Heart, Lung and Blood Institute.* (2010). Web.

Strong, J. *The exhaustive concordance of the Bible: Showing every word of the text of the common English version of the canonical books, and every occurrence of each word in regular order.* Ontario:Woodside Bible Fellowship, 1996. Elec. ed.

Stubblefield, Jon. "Matthew 6:5-15" *Review & Expositor* (1990). Print.

Thomas, Gary. *Sacred Marriage: what if God designed marriage to make us holy more than to make us happy?* Grand Rapids, MI: Zondervan Publishing House, 2000. Print.

Tutu, Desmond. *No Future Without Forgiveness.* New York: Doubleday, 1999. Print.

Twain, Mark. *The Adventures of Huckleberry Finn.* New York: Fawcet Columbine, 1996. Print.

White, William. *Stories for the Journey: a sourcebook for Christian storytellers.* Minneapolis, MN: Augsburg Publishing House, 1988. Print.

Wiesenthal, Simon. *The Sunflower: On the Possibilities and Limits of Forgiveness.* New York: Schocken Books, 1998. Print.

Wilbert, Caroline. "You Schmoose, You Win." *Fast Company* (July-August 2006). Print.

Wilson, Heather Gemmon. "Calling on the Saints." *Christianity Today* February 2008. Print.

Wright, N. T. *The Challenge of Easter.* Downer's Grove, IL: IVP Books, 2009. Print.

Yancey, Philip. *Prayer: Does It Make Any Difference?* Grand Rapids, MI: Zondervan, 2010.

Yancey, Philip. "The Word on the Street: What the homeless taught me about prayer." *Christianitytoday.com.* Christianity Today. 20 July 2010. Web. 20 July 2010.

Zuck, R.B. *A Biblical Theology of the New Testament.* Chicago: Moody, 1994. Elec. ed.

CPSIA information can be obtained at www.ICGtesting.com
Printed in the USA
235896LV00003B/1/P